Design Patterns using Go

First Edition

By Hemant Jain

Design Patterns using Go

Hemant Jain

ACKNOWLEDGMENT

The author is very grateful to GOD ALMIGHTY for his grace and blessing.

I would like to express profound gratitude to my family and friends for their invaluable encouragement, supervision and useful suggestions throughout this book writing work. Their support and continuous guidance enable me to complete my work successfully.

Hemant Jain

Table of Contents

INTRODUCTION TO DESIGN PATTERNS

What are Design Patterns?

Software development is a complex and demanding process that requires a high level of skill and expertise. As projects grow larger and more intricate, managing them effectively becomes increasingly challenging. One approach to address these challenges is by using design patterns.

Design patterns are reusable solutions to common software development problems. These patterns aren't ready-made code that can be directly copied into a program; instead, they offer general solutions that can be adapted to a wide range of specific problems in various contexts.

By providing a shared language and structure for discussing and documenting software designs, design patterns facilitate better communication and collaboration among developers. They help ensure that software designs are modular, maintainable, and extensible.

The Importance of Design Patterns

Design patterns play a critical role in software development for several reasons:

1. **Reusability**: Design patterns offer proven solutions to common development problems. By leveraging these patterns, developers can save time and effort, avoiding the need to reinvent the wheel each time a familiar problem arises.

2. **Maintainability**: As software projects grow, they can become increasingly complex and difficult to maintain. Design patterns promote modular designs that separate concerns, making it easier to manage and update different parts of a system without introducing errors.

3. **Extensibility**: Software often needs to evolve over time, requiring new features or modifications. Design patterns support extensibility by making it easier to add new functionality without disrupting existing components.

4. **Communication**: Design patterns provide a common vocabulary and structure for discussing and documenting software designs. This shared language simplifies communication and collaboration, especially on large teams or among developers with diverse backgrounds.

5. **Quality**: By encouraging best practices and applying tested solutions, design patterns can lead to higher-quality software that is more robust, reliable, and scalable.

Elements of Design Patterns

A design pattern typically consists of three key elements:

1. **Problem**: Design patterns address specific recurring problems in software design. They describe a problem that occurs repeatedly in a particular context, along with the core of the solution.

2. **Solution**: The solution element of a design pattern provides a general, reusable approach to solving a common problem in software design. This solution can be adapted to different situations and contexts.

3. **Consequences**: A design pattern also outlines the consequences and trade-offs of using the pattern. These can be both positive and negative, and understanding them is crucial before applying the pattern to a specific problem.

Categories of Design Patterns

There are five main categories of design patterns:

1. **Creational Patterns**: Creational patterns deal with object creation mechanisms, providing ways to create objects while hiding the creation logic. They allow for flexibility in how objects are created and which objects are instantiated. Examples include the Singleton, Factory Method, Abstract Factory, Builder, and Prototype patterns.

2. **Structural Patterns**: Structural patterns focus on object composition and simplify system structures by defining relationships between objects. They help in forming larger structures from individual classes and objects. Examples include the Adapter, Bridge, Composite, Decorator, and Facade patterns.

3. **Behavioural Patterns**: Behavioural patterns are concerned with the interaction and responsibility between objects. They define how objects communicate and work together to accomplish tasks. Examples include the Command, Iterator, Observer, State, and Strategy patterns.

4. **Concurrency Patterns**: Concurrency patterns address the design and implementation of concurrent and parallel programs. They help manage the complexity of systems that involve multiple threads or processes. Examples include the Active Object, Barrier, and Double checking singleton patterns.

5. **Architectural Patterns**: Architectural patterns deal with the overall structure of a software system, defining the relationships between components and providing a framework for organizing large-scale systems. Examples include the Model-View-Controller (MVC), Model-View-Presenter (MVP), Model-View-ViewModel (MVVM), and Layered patterns.

Design Principles

Design principles are guidelines for creating well-structured and maintainable software. They provide high-level concepts and best practices that can be applied during the design phase. This section explores fundamental design principles, with a focus on the SOLID principles.

Fundamental Design Principles:

1. **Encapsulation**: Encapsulation involves bundling data and methods into a single unit, typically a class. It promotes data hiding and provides a clear interface for interacting with objects, helping to protect the internal state of an object from unintended interference.

2. **Abstraction**: Abstraction focuses on identifying the essential features and behaviours of a system while hiding unnecessary details. This simplification reduces complexity and enhances the clarity and maintainability of the system.

3. **Modularity**: Modularity encourages dividing a system into smaller, self-contained modules, each with a well-defined responsibility. Modules should interact through clear interfaces, promoting easier maintenance and scalability.

4. **High Cohesion**: High cohesion refers to the degree to which the elements within a module are related and contribute to a single, well-defined purpose. High cohesion ensures that each module has a focused responsibility, making the system easier to understand and maintain.

5. **Low Coupling**: Low coupling aims to minimize dependencies between modules, promoting loose coupling. This allows modules to be modified or replaced independently without affecting other parts of the system, enhancing flexibility and maintainability.

SOLID Principles

The SOLID principles are a set of five foundational guidelines that help developers design object-oriented software that is easy to understand, maintain, and extend. The acronym SOLID stands for:

1. S - Single Responsibility Principle

2. O - Open-Closed Principle

3. L - Liskov Substitution Principle

4. I - Interface Segregation Principle

5. D - Dependency Inversion Principle

Overview of SOLID Principles

1. **Single Responsibility Principle (SRP)**: A class should have only one reason to change, meaning it should be responsible for a single task or functionality. This principle ensures that a class is focused on a specific responsibility, reducing complexity and making maintenance easier.

2. **Open-Closed Principle (OCP)**: Software entities (such as classes, modules, functions) should be open for extension but closed for modification. This means that you should be able to add new functionality to a system without altering its existing code, minimizing the risk of introducing bugs.

3. **Liskov Substitution Principle (LSP)**: Objects of a subclass should be able to replace objects of the superclass without affecting the correctness of the program. This principle ensures that a subclass can be substituted for its superclass without causing errors or altering the expected behavior.

4. **Interface Segregation Principle (ISP)**: Clients should not be forced to depend on interfaces they do not use. This principle encourages the creation of smaller, more specific interfaces rather than a large, all-encompassing one, reducing dependencies and making the system more modular.

5. **Dependency Inversion Principle (DIP)**: High-level modules should not depend on low-level modules but on abstractions. This principle advocates for relying on abstract classes or interfaces rather than concrete implementations, enhancing flexibility and ease of maintenance.

Single Responsibility Principle (SRP)

The **Single Responsibility Principle (SRP)** states that a class should have only one reason to change, meaning it should be responsible for only one task or aspect of the system. By adhering to SRP, classes become easier to understand, test, and maintain, as each class is focused on a specific function.

For instance, imagine a class that handles both file input/output operations and data manipulation. This class violates the SRP because it has two responsibilities: managing file operations and processing data. To comply with SRP, you could split this class into two distinct classes—one dedicated to file input/output and the other to data manipulation.

Adhering to SRP results in code that is easier to maintain and extend because each class has a clear and focused purpose.

Example:

```go
type Animal struct {
    name string
}

func (a *Animal) eat() {
    fmt.Printf("%s is eating.\n", a.name)
}

func (a *Animal) sleep() {
    fmt.Printf("%s is sleeping.\n", a.name)
}

func (a *Animal) makeSound() {
    fmt.Printf("%s is making a sound.\n", a.name)
}

type Mammal struct {
    Animal
}

func (m *Mammal) giveBirth() {
    fmt.Printf("%s is giving birth to live young.\n", m.name)
}

type Reptile struct {
```

```go
        Animal
}

func (r *Reptile) layEggs() {
    fmt.Printf("%s is laying eggs.\n", r.name)
}

type Bird struct {
    Animal
}

func (b *Bird) fly() {
    fmt.Printf("%s is flying.\n", b.name)
}

func (b *Bird) layEggs() {
    fmt.Printf("%s is laying eggs.\n", b.name)
}

// Client code
func main() {
    animal1 := Mammal{Animal{"Cat"}}
    animal1.giveBirth()
    animal1.makeSound()
    animal2 := Reptile{Animal{"Snake"}}
    animal2.layEggs()
    animal2.eat()
    animal3 := Bird{Animal{"Eagle"}}
    animal3.layEggs()
    animal3.fly()
}
```

Explanation:

1. **Single Responsibility at the Class Level:**

   - **Animal**: Encapsulates basic behaviours common to all animals, such as eating, sleeping, and making sounds.

   - **Mammal**: Specializes in behaviours unique to mammals, like giving birth to live young.

   - **Reptile**: Focuses on behaviours specific to reptiles, such as laying eggs.

   - **Bird**: Contains behaviours specific to birds, such as flying and laying eggs.

2. This separation of responsibilities ensures that each class has a single, well-defined purpose, making the code easier to understand, modify, and maintain.

3. Single Responsibility at the Method Level:

   o Each method in the classes also adheres to the SRP. For instance, the fly() method in the Bird class is solely responsible for representing the behavior of flying, while the eat() method in the Animal class is responsible for representing the behavior of eating.

   o This adherence to SRP at both the class and method levels enhances the overall maintainability, clarity, and readability of the code.

Open-Closed Principle (OCP)

The Open-Closed Principle (OCP) is a fundamental design principle that states that software entities (such as classes, modules, or functions) should be **open for extension but closed for modification**. This means that you should be able to add new functionality to a system without altering its existing code, which minimizes the risk of introducing new bugs.

The key idea behind OCP is to create software that is both flexible and maintainable. By ensuring that components are open to extension, new features can be incorporated without changing the underlying code, which helps maintain the stability and integrity of the codebase over time.

To adhere to OCP, you can employ techniques like **abstraction** and **encapsulation**:

- **Abstraction** allows you to define general behaviors or properties that can be implemented by different classes or modules.

- **Encapsulation** hides the implementation details, enabling changes without affecting the rest of the system.

Example of OCP Violation

Consider the following code where the Bird class extends the Animal class and includes a fly() method. The fly() method checks the bird's name to determine its flying capability:

```go
type Animal struct {
```

```go
    name string
}

type Bird struct {
    Animal
}

func (b *Bird) fly() {
    switch b.name {
    case "Dodo":
        fmt.Println("The dodo is extinct and cannot fly.")
    case "Penguin":
        fmt.Println("The penguin cannot fly.")
    case "Eagle":
        fmt.Println("The eagle is soaring through the sky!")
    case "Sparrow":
        fmt.Println("The sparrow is fluttering its wings!")
    }
}

// Client code.
func main() {
    bird1 := &Bird{Animal{"Eagle"}}
    bird1.fly()
    bird2 := &Bird{Animal{"Dodo"}}
    bird2.fly()
}
```

While this code works, it violates the Open-Closed Principle. The **fly()** method must be modified whenever a new bird species is introduced, which contradicts the idea of being "closed for modification."

Example of OCP Adherence

Here's an improved version of the code that follows the Open-Closed Principle by using subclassing:

```go
type Bird struct {
    Animal
}

func (b *Bird) fly() {
    // To be overridden by subclasses
}

type Dodo struct {
    Bird
```

```go
}

func (d *Dodo) fly() {
    fmt.Println("The dodo is extinct and cannot fly.")
}

type Penguin struct {
    Bird
}

func (p *Penguin) fly() {
    fmt.Println("The penguin cannot fly.")
}

func (p *Penguin) slide() {
    fmt.Println("The penguin is sliding on its belly!")
}

func (p *Penguin) swim() {
    fmt.Println("The penguin is swimming in the water!")
}

type Eagle struct {
    Bird
}

func (e *Eagle) fly() {
    fmt.Println("The eagle is soaring through the sky!")
}

type Sparrow struct {
    Bird
}

func (s *Sparrow) fly() {
    fmt.Println("The sparrow is fluttering its wings!")
}

// Client code.
func main() {
    bird1 := &Eagle{Bird{Animal{"Eagle"}}}
    bird1.fly()
    bird2 := &Dodo{Bird{Animal{"Dodo"}}}
    bird2.fly()
}
```

Output:

```
The eagle is soaring through the sky!
The dodo is extinct and cannot fly.
```

Explanation:

1. This implementation adheres to the **Open-Closed Principle** by allowing the creation of new bird species as subclasses of **Bird**, without modifying existing code.

2. Each bird species is represented by a subclass that inherits from **Bird** and overrides the **fly()** method with its specific behavior.

3. When new bird types are introduced, they are simply added as new subclasses, preserving the existing code's integrity.

Further Extension Example

If you want to add a new bird species, such as a pigeon, you can easily extend the Bird class:

```go
type Pigeon struct {
    Bird
}

func (s *Pigeon) fly() {
    fmt.Println("The pigeon is fluttering its wings!")
}

func (s *Pigeon) makeCooingSound() {
    fmt.Println("The pigeon is making a cooing sound.")
}
```

Explanation:

1. In this implementation, the Pigeon subclass extends the Bird class and adds a specific behavior, makeCooingSound(), without modifying the Bird class.

2. This demonstrates how following OCP allows for the seamless extension of functionality by creating new subclasses, keeping the codebase both flexible and stable.

Liskov Substitution Principle (LSP)

The **Liskov Substitution Principle (LSP)** is a key concept in object-oriented design, stating that objects of a superclass should be replaceable with objects of its subclasses without altering the correctness of the program. In simpler terms, a subclass should be able to stand in for its superclass without causing any unexpected behavior.

Adhering to LSP ensures that code is modular, extensible, and maintainable. It allows the creation of class hierarchies that can be reused and extended without breaking existing code or introducing bugs. The LSP is closely connected to other principles like the Single Responsibility Principle (SRP), the Open-Closed Principle (OCP), and the Interface Segregation Principle (ISP), all of which together form the SOLID principles of object-oriented design.

By following the LSP, we can write more flexible and reusable code, allowing instances of subclasses to be used interchangeably with instances of their superclass wherever needed.

Example of Adhering to LSP: Consider a superclass **Animal** with a method **makeSound()**, and a subclass **Dog** that inherits from **Animal**. The **Dog** subclass should implement the **makeSound()** method in a way that is consistent with the expectations of the Animal class. This ensures that substituting a **Dog** for an **Animal** will not break the program's logic.

```go
// Animal interface
type AnimalInterface interface {
    MakeSound()
    Name() string // Method to get the name of the animal
}

// Animal struct
type Animal struct {
    name string
}

// NewAnimal constructor
func NewAnimal(name string) *Animal {
    return &Animal{name: name}
}

// Name method for Animal
func (a *Animal) Name() string {
    return a.name
}
```

```go
// MakeSound method for Animal
func (a *Animal) MakeSound() {
    fmt.Println("Animal sound")
}

// Dog struct
type Dog struct {
    *Animal
}

// NewDog constructor
func NewDog(name string) *Dog {
    return &Dog{
        Animal: NewAnimal(name),
    }
}

// MakeSound method for Dog
func (d *Dog) MakeSound() {
    fmt.Println("woof woof!")
}

// Cat struct
type Cat struct {
    *Animal
}

// NewCat constructor
func NewCat(name string) *Cat {
    return &Cat{
        Animal: NewAnimal(name),
    }
}

// MakeSound method for Cat
func (c *Cat) MakeSound() {
    fmt.Println("meow!")
}
```

Example of Violating LSP: Rectangle and Square

Consider the classic example of a **Square** and **Rectangle**. A **Square** should not inherit from a **Rectangle** because it introduces constraints that do not apply to a rectangle. Specifically, in a square, all sides must be equal, while a rectangle can have sides of different lengths. If a **Square** is used where a **Rectangle** is expected, it can lead to unintended behavior.

```go
type Rectangle struct {
    height int
    width  int
}

func NewRectangle(l, w int) *Rectangle {
    return &Rectangle{height: l, width: w}
}

func (r *Rectangle) SetWidth(w int) {
    r.width = w
}

func (r *Rectangle) SetHeight(h int) {
    r.height = h
}

func (r *Rectangle) GetWidth() int {
    return r.width
}

func (r *Rectangle) GetHeight() int {
    return r.height
}

type Square struct {
    *Rectangle
}

func NewSquare(l int) *Square {
    return &Square{Rectangle: NewRectangle(l, l)}
}

func (s *Square) SetWidth(w int) {
    s.width = w
    s.height = w
}

func (s *Square) SetHeight(h int) {
    s.width = h
    s.height = h
```

```go
}

func TestRect(rect *Rectangle) {
    if 10*20 == rect.GetHeight()*rect.GetWidth() {
        fmt.Println("Pass")
    } else {
        fmt.Println("Failed")
    }
}

// Client code
func main() {
    r := NewRectangle(10, 10)
    r.SetWidth(20)
    TestRect(r)
    s := NewSquare(10)
    s.SetWidth(20)
    TestRect(s.Rectangle)
}
```

Explanation:

1. **LSP Violation**: The **Square** class inherits from the **Rectangle** class, but it overrides the **setWidth()** and **setHeight()** methods in a way that breaks the expected behavior of a **Rectangle**. In a rectangle, **setWidth()** and **setHeight()** should be independent, but in a square, they are coupled, leading to unexpected behavior when the **TestRect()** function is called with a **Square** object.

2. **Expected Behavior**: The **TestRect()** function expects that changing the width of a rectangle does not affect its height. This expectation is violated by the **Square** subclass, which causes the function to fail, highlighting the LSP violation.

Another Example of Violating LSP: Birds and Penguins

Consider the case of a Bird class and its subclass Penguin. While a penguin is a type of bird in the real world, in programming, a Penguin may have different behaviors (e.g., it cannot fly) that make it incompatible with code expecting a general Bird object.

```go
type Bird struct {
    name          string
    flightHeight int
}

func NewBird(name string) *Bird {
    return &Bird{name: name, flightHeight: 0}
}

type Sparrow struct {
    *Bird
}

func NewSparrow(name string) *Sparrow {
    return &Sparrow{Bird: NewBird(name)}
}

func (s *Sparrow) Fly() {
    fmt.Println("The sparrow is fluttering its wings.")
    s.flightHeight = 100
}

type Penguin struct {
    *Bird
}

func NewPenguin(name string) *Penguin {
    return &Penguin{Bird: NewBird(name)}
}

func (p *Penguin) Fly() {
    fmt.Println("The penguin cannot fly.")
}

func (p *Penguin) Slide() {
    fmt.Println("The penguin is sliding on its belly!")
}

func (p *Penguin) Swim() {
    fmt.Println("The penguin is swimming in the water!")
}

type Dodo struct {
    *Bird
}
```

```go
func NewDodo(name string) *Dodo {
    return &Dodo{Bird: NewBird(name)}
}

func (d *Dodo) Fly() {
    fmt.Println("The dodo is extinct and cannot fly.")
}

func Test(bird *Bird) {
    if bird.flightHeight > 0 {
        fmt.Println("Bird is flying at a positive height.")
    } else {
        fmt.Println("Error: Fly() method called; flight height is
still zero.")
    }
}

// Client code
func main() {
    sparrow := NewSparrow("Sparrow")
    sparrow.Fly()
    Test(sparrow.Bird)
    penguin := NewPenguin("Penguin")
    penguin.Fly()
    Test(penguin.Bird)
    dodo := NewDodo("Dodo")
    dodo.Fly()
    Test(dodo.Bird)
}
```

Output:

```
The sparrow is fluttering its wings.
Bird is flying at a positive height.
The penguin cannot fly.
Error: fly() method called; flight height is still zero.
The dodo is extinct and cannot fly.
Error: fly() method called; flight height is still zero.
```

Explanation:

1. **LSP Violation**: The **Penguin** subclass violates the LSP because it does not behave as expected in the context of the **Bird** class. Specifically, the **Penguin** class does not modify the **flightHeight** attribute in the **Fly()** method, leading to unexpected behavior when tested with the **Test()** function, which assumes all birds will have a positive **flightHeight** if they can fly.

2. **Behavioural Consistency**: According to the LSP, subclasses should behave in a way that is consistent with the expectations set by the superclass. The **Penguin** and **Dodo** classes violate this principle, as their **Fly()** methods do not align with the behavior expected from a general **Bird** object.

Interface Segregation Principle (ISP)

The **Interface Segregation Principle (ISP)** is one of the SOLID principles of object-oriented design. It states that a client should not be forced to depend on methods it does not use. In other words, interfaces should be broken down into smaller, more specific ones, allowing classes to implement only the functionality they require without being burdened by unnecessary methods.

This principle emphasizes that a class should not be required to implement interfaces that include methods irrelevant to its purpose. Instead, multiple smaller interfaces should be created, each containing only the methods that are directly related to a specific behavior or role that the class fulfils.

The importance of the ISP lies in its ability to reduce coupling between classes, which in turn minimizes the impact of changes in one part of the system on other parts. This approach also enhances code maintainability, testing, and refactoring.

Example: Consider an interface named **Printer** that defines the methods **Print()**, **Scan()**, and **Fax()**. While some printers might support all three functionalities, others might only support one or two. For instance, a basic inkjet printer might only be capable of printing, whereas a high-end office printer might support all three functions.

Here's how the **Printer** interface might initially look:

```go
type Printer interface {
    Print(document string)
    Scan()
    Fax(document string)
}
```

If a basic inkjet printer were to implement the **Printer** interface, it would need to include empty or meaningless implementations of the **Scan()** and **Fax()** methods, which it doesn't actually support. This violates the Interface Segregation Principle (ISP) because the class is forced to depend on methods that it will never use.

To adhere to the ISP, this interface should be divided into smaller, more specific interfaces such as Printable, Scannable, and Faxable. This allows classes to implement only the interfaces they need.

Here's an example of how the ISP is followed:

```go
// Printable interface
type Printable interface {
    Print(document string)
}

// Scannable interface
type Scannable interface {
    Scan()
}

// Faxable interface
type Faxable interface {
    Fax(document string)
}
```

Now, classes can implement only the interfaces that are relevant to their functionality. For example, a **BasicInkjetPrinter** class can implement just the **Printable** interface:

```go
// BasicInkjetPrinter struct
type BasicInkjetPrinter struct{}

// Print method for BasicInkjetPrinter
func (bip BasicInkjetPrinter) Print(document string) {
    fmt.Printf("Printing %s using basic inkjet printer\n",
document)
}
```

Similarly, a **HighEndOfficePrinter** class can implement all three interfaces:

```go
// HighEndOfficePrinter struct
type HighEndOfficePrinter struct{}

// Print method for HighEndOfficePrinter
func (heop HighEndOfficePrinter) Print(document string) {
    fmt.Printf("Printing %s using high end office printer\n",
document)
}

// Scan method for HighEndOfficePrinter
func (heop HighEndOfficePrinter) Scan() {
    fmt.Println("Scanning using high end office printer")
```

```
}

// Fax method for HighEndOfficePrinter
func (heop HighEndOfficePrinter) Fax(document string) {
    fmt.Printf("Faxing %s using high end office printer\n",
document)
}
```

By splitting the original **Printer** interface into smaller, more cohesive interfaces, the code becomes more flexible and easier to maintain. Classes now implement only the interfaces they need, avoiding the need to include unnecessary methods.

Dependency Inversion Principle (DIP)

The Dependency Inversion Principle (DIP) is a core principle of object-oriented design that dictates that high-level modules should not depend directly on low-level modules. Instead, both should depend on abstractions, such as interfaces or abstract classes, which define the expected behavior. This approach enhances decoupling and flexibility within the system.

Example: Consider a simple email-sending application. We have two modules: a high-level **EmailSender** module and a low-level **SmtpServer** module. The **SmtpServer** module is responsible for sending emails using the Simple Mail Transfer Protocol (SMTP).

Without adhering to the DIP, the **EmailSender** module would be directly dependent on the **SmtpServer** module, leading to tight coupling. This means that any changes to the **SmtpServer** module would ripple through and potentially break the **EmailSender** module, reducing the system's flexibility and making it harder to maintain.

By following the DIP, both the **EmailSender** and **SmtpServer** modules rely on an abstraction, such as an interface named **IMailSender**. The **EmailSender** module interacts with the **IMailSender** interface, which specifies the behavior expected from any mail-sending component.

The **SmtpServer** module then implements this interface, enabling the **EmailSender** module to use it without being directly tied to the **SmtpServer** implementation. This approach decouples the modules, increasing system flexibility and maintainability.

Example implementation:

```go
// IMailSender interface
type IMailSender interface {
    SendMail(toAddress, fromAddress, subject, body string)
}

// SmtpServer struct
type SmtpServer struct{}

// SendMail method for SmtpServer
func (s SmtpServer) SendMail(toAddress, fromAddress, subject,
body string) {
    fmt.Printf("Send mail: subject: %s from: %s to: %s body: %s\
n", subject, fromAddress, toAddress, body)
}

// EmailSender struct
type EmailSender struct {
    MailSender IMailSender
}

// SendEmail method for EmailSender
func (e EmailSender) SendEmail(toAddress, fromAddress, subject,
body string) {
    e.MailSender.SendMail(toAddress, fromAddress, subject, body)
}

// Client code
func main() {
    // Create an instance of the SmtpServer class
    smtpServer := SmtpServer{}

    // Create an instance of the EmailSender class and pass in
the SmtpServer instance
    emailSender := EmailSender{MailSender: smtpServer}

    // Send an email using the EmailSender instance
    emailSender.SendEmail(
        "recipient@example.com",
        "sender@example.com",
        "mail subject.",
        "This is a test email body.",
    )
}
```

Explanation:

1. The **IMailSender** interface defines the contract for mail-sending behavior. The **SmtpServer** class implements this interface, providing an SMTP-based email-sending capability.

2. The **EmailSender** class accepts an **IMailSender** object, allowing it to send emails through any implementation of **IMailSender**. This decouples **EmailSender** from the specific details of the email-sending mechanism, making it more flexible and easier to maintain.

3. In the example, an instance of **SmtpServer** is created to serve as the mail-sending implementation. This instance is then injected into the **EmailSender** class.

4. Finally, the **SendEmail()** method of the **EmailSender** instance is used to send an email. The **EmailSender** delegates the actual sending task to the **SmtpServer** instance, which performs the email transmission via SMTP.

Summary

Design patterns are proven solutions to recurring software development challenges. This chapter explores the advantages of utilizing design patterns, including enhanced reusability, maintainability, extensibility, communication, and overall code quality.

The chapter also discusses the SOLID principles—five fundamental design principles that guide developers in creating more robust, maintainable, and scalable software. These principles include:

1. Single Responsibility Principle (SRP)
2. Open/Closed Principle (OCP)
3. Liskov Substitution Principle (LSP)
4. Interface Segregation Principle (ISP)
5. Dependency Inversion Principle (DIP)

In addition, design patterns are categorized into five groups: Creational, Structural, Behavioural, Concurrency, and Architectural. Each category offers a collection of patterns designed to address specific types of problems in software development. By understanding and applying both the SOLID principles and these design patterns, developers can achieve more modular, maintainable, and extensible software designs.

CREATIONAL PATTERNS

In this chapter, we explore the first category of design patterns: Creational Patterns. These patterns focus on the mechanisms of object creation, offering flexibility in how and which objects are created, while hiding the creation logic. This allows for more adaptable and maintainable code.

We begin with the **Singleton pattern**, one of the most widely used Creational patterns. It ensures that a class has only one instance throughout the system and provides a global access point to that instance.

Next, we cover the **Factory Method pattern**, which defines an interface for creating objects in a superclass, while allowing subclasses to specify the type of objects created. This pattern is particularly useful when you want to decouple object creation from the rest of the application logic.

Following that, we discuss the **Abstract Factory pattern**, which is similar to the Factory Method, but it provides an interface for creating families of related or dependent objects without specifying their concrete classes. This is ideal when related objects need to be created together.

We then move on to the **Builder pattern**, which separates the construction of a complex object from its representation, allowing for different representations using the same construction process. This is beneficial when creating objects step-by-step, especially when multiple representations of the same object are required.

Finally, we examine the **Prototype pattern**, which involves creating new objects by cloning existing ones. This pattern is useful when object creation is resource-intensive, and cloning an existing object provides a more efficient solution.

Singleton Pattern

The Singleton design pattern is a Creational pattern that ensures a class has only one instance and provides a global access point to that instance. It is commonly used in scenarios where multiple instances of a class would cause issues, such as global configurations, logging systems, database connections, or thread pools.

Problem: The main issue that the Singleton pattern addresses is controlling the number of instances created for a class. In certain cases, you need to ensure that only one instance of a class exists throughout the application's lifecycle.

Solution: The Singleton pattern ensures that a class has only one instance and provides global access to it. The general approach involves making the class itself responsible for creating and managing its single instance.

Key steps in the classic implementation:

- **Private constructor**: The class's constructor is made private, preventing instantiation from outside the class.

- **Static method or variable**: A static method or variable controls access to the instance, creating it if it doesn't exist and returning it if it does.

- **Lazy initialization**: The instance is created only when it's first requested, ensuring it's only created when necessary.

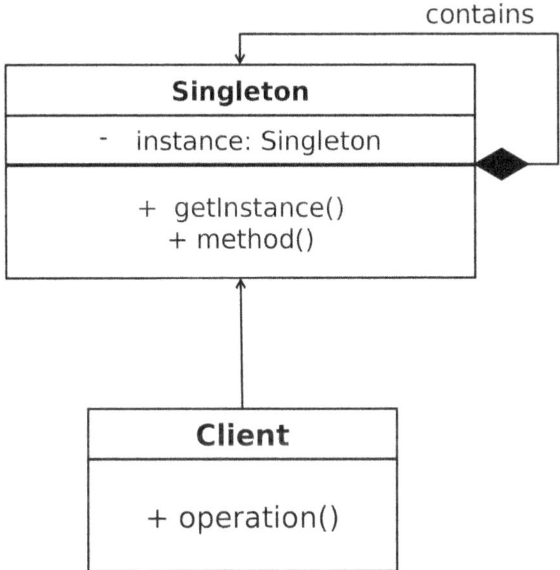

Example Implementation:

```go
type Database struct {
    data string
}

var (
    instance *Database
    once      sync.Once
)
```

```go
func GetInstance() *Database {
    once.Do(func() {
        instance = &Database{}
        fmt.Println("Database created")
    })
    return instance
}

func (db *Database) AddData(dt string) {
    db.data = dt
    fmt.Println("Data added:", db.data)
}

// Client code
func main() {
    s1 := GetInstance()
    s2 := GetInstance()

    s2.AddData("Hello, world!")
    fmt.Println(s1)
    fmt.Println(s2)
}
```

Output:

```
Database created
Data added: Hello, world!
&{Hello, world!}
&{Hello, world!}
```

Explanation:

1. The **Database** class is a Singleton. Its constructor is private, and access to the single instance is controlled through the **GetInstance()** method.

2. The Singleton ensures that both **s1** and **s2** refer to the same instance.

3. When data is added through **s2**, it affects the same instance shared with **s1**, demonstrating the Singleton behavior..

Problem : Implementing Singleton Pattern for SQLite, we need to implement a Singleton pattern for a SQLite database connection to ensure only one instance of the database is created throughout the application's lifecycle.

Solution: The code ensures that only one instance of the Database class is created. If an instance doesn't exist, it is created, and the SQLite database connection is established. Any subsequent calls return the same instance.

Example implementation with SQLite:

```go
package main

import (
    "database/sql"
    "fmt"
    "log"
    "os"
    _ "github.com/mattn/go-sqlite3"
)

type Database struct {
    connection *sql.DB
    cursorobj  *sql.Stmt
}

var instance *Database

func NewDatabase() *Database {
    if instance == nil {
        instance = &Database{}
        fmt.Println("Database created")
        var err error
        instance.connection, err = sql.Open("sqlite3",
"db.sqlite3")
        if err != nil {
            log.Fatal(err)
            os.Exit(1)
        }
    }
    return instance
}

func (db *Database) createTable() {
    _, err := db.connection.Exec("CREATE TABLE IF NOT EXISTS
students (id INTEGER, name TEXT);")
    if err != nil {
        log.Fatal(err)
        os.Exit(1)
    }
}
```

```go
func (db *Database) addData(id int, name string) {
    query := fmt.Sprintf("INSERT INTO students (id, name) VALUES
(%d, '%s');", id, name)
    _, err := db.connection.Exec(query)
    if err != nil {
        log.Fatal(err)
        os.Exit(1)
    }
}

func (db *Database) display() {
    rows, err := db.connection.Query("SELECT * FROM students;")
    if err != nil {
        log.Fatal(err)
        os.Exit(1)
    }

    defer rows.Close()

    for rows.Next() {
        var id int
        var name string
        err := rows.Scan(&id, &name)
        if err != nil {
            log.Fatal(err)
            os.Exit(1)
        }
        fmt.Println(id, name)
    }
}

// Client code
func main() {
    db1 := NewDatabase()
    db2 := NewDatabase()

    fmt.Println("Database Objects DB1", db1)
    fmt.Println("Database Objects DB2", db2)

    db1.createTable()
    db1.addData(1, "john")
    db2.addData(2, "smith")
    db1.display()
}
```

Explanation:

1. The **Database** class implements the **Singleton pattern**. If no instance exists, it creates one and opens a connection to an SQLite database.

2. The **createTable()** method creates a **students** table if it doesn't exist, and **addData()** inserts data into it.

3. Even though two **Database** instances (**db1** and **db2**) appear to be created, they both refer to the same object. Any data added through either instance affects the same database.

Uses of Singleton Pattern

The Singleton pattern is commonly used in situations where only one instance of a class should exist throughout an application's lifecycle. Here are some examples:

1. **Database Connections:** In multi-threaded applications, creating multiple database connections can be expensive and lead to issues like locking and deadlocks. A Singleton can ensure that only one database connection exists, which is shared across all threads.

2. **Configuration Settings:** In large applications, a centralized configuration store is often needed. A Singleton can manage configuration settings, allowing all parts of the application to access a single, consistent configuration object.

3. **Logging:** Applications often require logging of messages to a file or database. A Singleton logging object ensures that all log entries are written to the same destination, preventing duplication and managing log access across the application.

4. **Caching:** Caching improves performance by storing data in memory. A Singleton cache object provides a centralized cache that can be accessed and managed across different parts of the application.

5. **Session Management:** In web applications, managing user sessions is crucial. A Singleton session manager can handle all user sessions centrally, ensuring consistency and avoiding conflicts.

Consequences

While the Singleton pattern offers a solution for controlling the number of instances and providing global access, it comes with some potential drawbacks that need to be considered:

1. **Global State:** Since a Singleton is globally accessible, it can lead to shared global state. This can make the code more difficult to test, maintain, and reason about, as changes to the Singleton affect the entire application.

2. **Thread Safety:** Basic lazy initialization is not thread-safe. In a multi-threaded environment, multiple threads might simultaneously try to create instances, leading to more than one instance. To ensure thread safety, synchronization or double-checked locking mechanisms can be used, though they can introduce performance overhead.

3. **Testing Challenges**: Testing Singleton instances can be difficult because they are tightly coupled with their static instance retrieval method. This makes it hard to replace the Singleton with mock objects during testing, complicating unit testing.

4. **Hidden Dependencies**: The Singleton pattern can lead to hidden dependencies, as it is often accessed directly through its static method. This reduces modularity and can make the code harder to refactor or extend in the future.

Factory Method Pattern

The **Factory Method pattern** is a Creational design pattern that defines an interface for creating objects in a superclass, but allows subclasses to modify the type of objects that will be created. It abstracts the object creation process and delegates it to the subclasses. This pattern is useful when you want to decouple the instantiation of objects from the code that uses them, or when you need to provide a common interface for creating related objects with varying customizations.

Problem: Imagine a scenario where a class needs to create objects, but the exact type of objects isn't known until runtime. Instantiating objects directly in this class would result in tight coupling to the concrete classes, making it difficult to extend and maintain the code. Additionally, introducing new types of objects in the future would require modifying the existing class, violating the Open-Closed Principle (part of the SOLID principles).

Solution: The Factory Method pattern recommends defining an interface or abstract class that declares the method (the factory method) responsible for object creation. The superclass uses this factory method to create objects, but it is not concerned with the actual instantiation process. Instead, subclasses implement the factory method, allowing them to decide which specific type of object to create.

Key Elements of the Factory Method Pattern:

1. **Creator**: An abstract class or interface that defines a factory method for creating objects. This method returns an instance of a Product, but the specific class of Product to be created is determined by the concrete Creator subclasses.

2. **Concrete Creator**: A subclass of Creator that implements the factory method to create a specific type of Product.

3. **Product**: The object that the factory method creates, typically defined as an abstract class or interface that outlines the structure for the objects produced.

4. **Concrete Product**: A subclass of Product that implements the interface defined by Product.

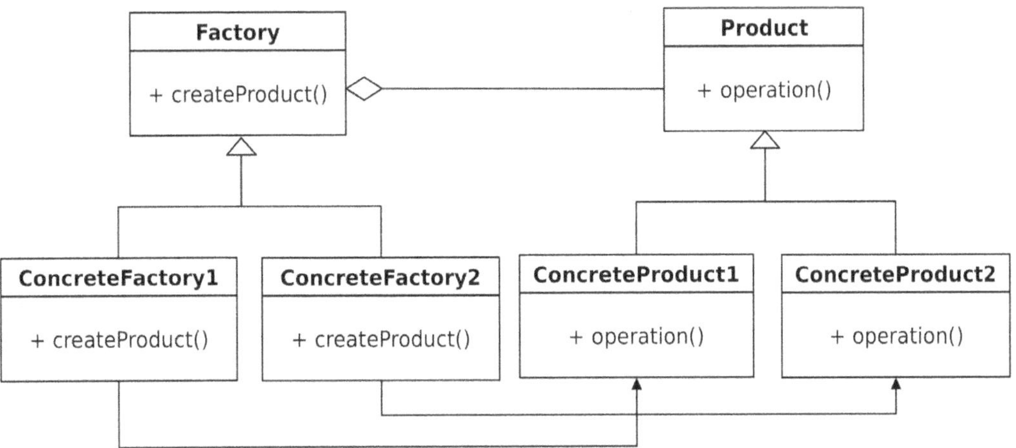

Example implementation:

```go
// Product interface
type Product interface {
    Operation()
}
```

```go
type ConcreteProduct1 struct{}
func (cp1 *ConcreteProduct1) Operation() {
    fmt.Println("Concrete Product1 Operation!")
}

type ConcreteProduct2 struct{}

func (cp2 *ConcreteProduct2) Operation() {
    fmt.Println("Concrete Product2 Operation!")
}

// Creator abstract class
type Factory interface {
    CreateProduct() Product
}

type ConcreteFactory1 struct{}
func (cf1 *ConcreteFactory1) CreateProduct() Product {
    return &ConcreteProduct1{}
}

type ConcreteFactory2 struct{}
func (cf2 *ConcreteFactory2) CreateProduct() Product {
    return &ConcreteProduct2{}
}

// Client code
func main() {
    f1 := &ConcreteFactory1{}
    p1 := f1.CreateProduct()
    p1.Operation()
    f2 := &ConcreteFactory2{}
    p2 := f2.CreateProduct()
    p2.Operation()
}
```

Output:

```
Concrete Product1 Operation!
Concrete Product2 Operation!
```

Explanation:

1. The **Product** interface is subclassed by two concrete products, **ConcreteProduct1** and **ConcreteProduct2**, each defining its own implementation of the **Operation()** method.

2. The **Factory** interface defines a **CreateProduct()** method, which is implemented by **ConcreteFactory1** and **ConcreteFactory2** to create instances of **ConcreteProduct1** and **ConcreteProduct2**, respectively.

3. The client code uses these concrete factory classes to create instances of **ConcreteProduct1** and **ConcreteProduct2** and calls their **Operation()** method.

Problem: Design a system using the Factory Method pattern to abstract the creation of different types of animals (such as Dogs and Cats). The goal is to enable the client code to interact with the animals via an abstract interface without directly instantiating the concrete animal classes.

Solution:

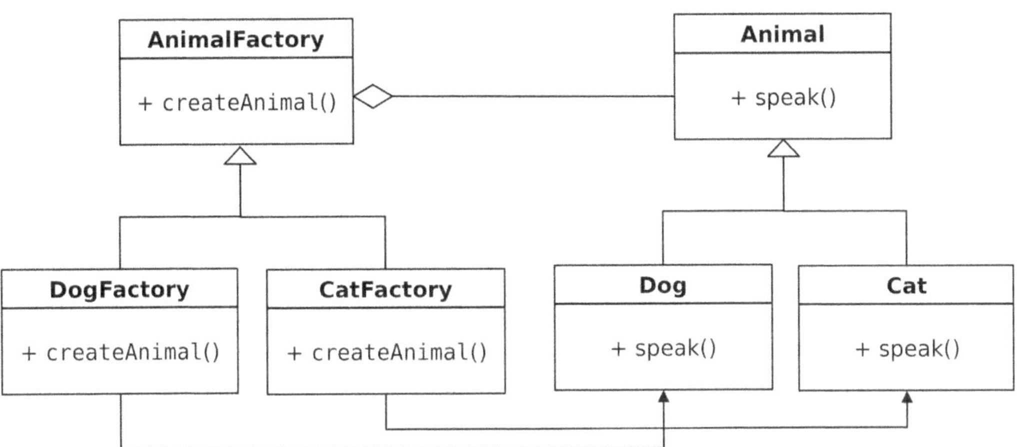

Example implementation:

```go
// Animal interface
type Animal interface {
    Speak()
}

// Concrete Dog and Cat classes
type Dog struct{}

func (d *Dog) Speak() {
    fmt.Println("Woof Woof!")
}

type Cat struct{}
```

```go
func (c *Cat) Speak() {
    fmt.Println("Meow Meow!")
}

// Creator abstract class
type AnimalFactory interface {
    CreateAnimal() Animal
}

// Concrete Creator classes
type DogFactory struct{}

func (df *DogFactory) CreateAnimal() Animal {
    return &Dog{}
}

type CatFactory struct{}

func (cf *CatFactory) CreateAnimal() Animal {
    return &Cat{}
}

// Client code
func main() {
    dogFactory := &DogFactory{}
    dog := dogFactory.CreateAnimal()
    dog.Speak()

    catFactory := &CatFactory{}
    cat := catFactory.CreateAnimal()
    cat.Speak()
}
```

Output:

```
Woof Woof!!
Meow Meow!!
```

Explanation:

1. The **Animal** interface is implemented by two concrete classes, **Dog** and **Cat**, each with its own implementation of the **Speak()** method.

2. The **AnimalFactory** interface defines a **CreateAnimal()** method, which is implemented by **DogFactory** and **CatFactory** to create instances of **Dog** and **Cat**.

3. The client code uses the factory classes to create animals and interact with them without knowing their specific class.

4. This example demonstrates how the Factory Method pattern allows the client code to create objects (**Dog** and **Cat**) without having to specify their exact class, by utilizing **DogFactory** and **CatFactory**.

Uses of the Factory Method Pattern

The Factory Method pattern has several common uses and benefits:

1. **Object Creation:** A primary use of the Factory Method pattern is to encapsulate the object creation process. This decouples client code from the specific classes it depends on, allowing you to change the object types without affecting the client code.

2. **Encapsulation of Object Creation Logic**: This pattern can encapsulate complex creation logic, such as requiring different parameters or settings for various types of objects. By abstracting this logic behind a factory interface, the creation process can be modified without affecting the client code.

3. **Dependency Injection**: The Factory Method pattern can act as a form of dependency injection, where the factory provides the dependencies required by the client. This makes the client independent of concrete implementations of its dependencies.

4. **Dynamic Object Creation**: It enables dynamic object creation based on runtime conditions or user inputs. This is useful when the specific type of object needed isn't known until the program is running.

5. **Mocking and Testing**: The pattern is valuable in testing scenarios where mock objects are needed. By using a factory interface, mock objects can easily substitute real objects during testing, helping to isolate and test the code more effectively.

6. **Customization**: Each subclass in the pattern can implement the factory method differently to create specific types of objects, making the design more flexible and customizable.

7. **Loose Coupling**: The pattern promotes loose coupling between classes. The superclass depends only on an interface, not on concrete implementations, leading to greater flexibility and easier maintenance.

Consequences

The Factory Method pattern has several benefits, but also comes with some trade-offs:

Advantages:

1. **Decoupling**: It decouples the client code from the concrete product classes, increasing flexibility and maintainability. The client interacts with the products through a factory method interface, without knowing the specific implementation.

2. **Extensibility**: New product types can be added easily by creating new subclasses that implement the factory method, adhering to the Open-Closed Principle (you can extend functionality without modifying existing code).

3. **Encapsulation**: The logic for object creation is encapsulated in the factory method, which makes the code easier to manage and understand.

4. **Code Reusability**: Shared object creation logic across multiple subclasses encourages code reuse, reducing redundancy.

5. **Dependency Injection**: By relying on an interface instead of concrete classes, the pattern supports better dependency injection, leading to more modular and testable code.

Disadvantages:

1. **Increased Complexity**: Introducing the Factory Method pattern can add complexity, especially when managing multiple product types and corresponding factory implementations.

2. **Abstraction Overhead**: Defining interfaces and abstract classes can introduce overhead and may be unnecessary in simpler object creation scenarios.

Abstract Factory Pattern

The **Abstract Factory pattern** is a Creational design pattern that provides an interface for creating families of related or dependent objects without specifying their concrete classes. This pattern enables the creation of objects that are part of a particular family, ensuring they are compatible and work seamlessly together.

Problem: In software development, systems often need to be configured with different families of related objects. For example, in a graphical user interface (GUI), you might need to create different types of buttons, windows, and other UI elements based on the operating system or theme chosen by the user. Without the Abstract Factory pattern, object creation can become complex, tightly coupled, and hard to maintain when handling multiple families of related objects.

Solution: The Abstract Factory pattern addresses this issue by introducing an abstract class or interface (the "Abstract Factory") that defines methods for creating related objects. Concrete implementations of this abstract factory represent different families of objects. Client code interacts with these factories through the abstract interface without needing to know the specific classes of the objects being created. The pattern supports coding to interfaces rather than concrete classes and follows the Open/Closed Principle, allowing new product variants to be added without changing existing code.

The **AbstractFactory** interface defines methods for creating related objects, such as **createProductA()** and **createProductB()**. The concrete factories— **ConcreteFactory1** and **ConcreteFactory2**—implement these methods to create specific products (ProductA1, ProductB1, ProductA2, ProductB2) belonging to different families.

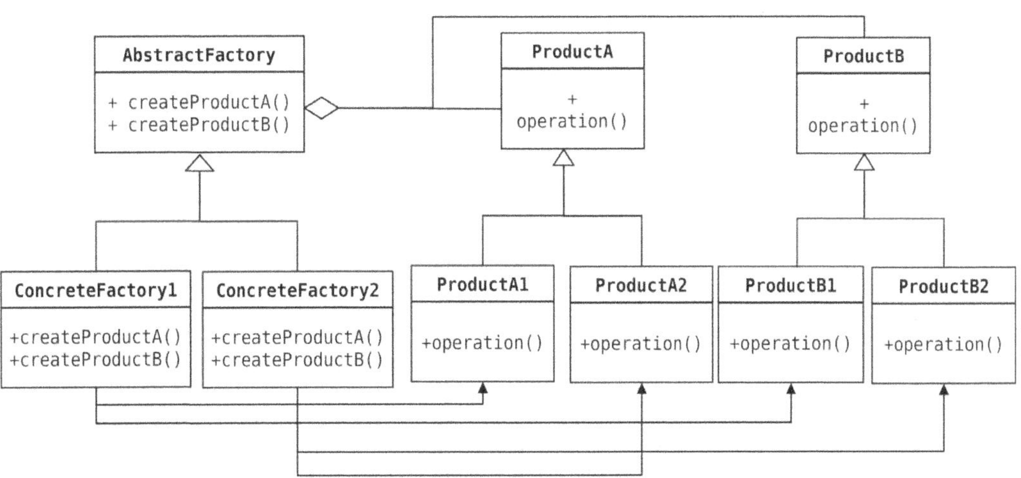

Example implementation:

```go
// ProductA interface
type ProductA interface {
    OperationA()
}

// ProductA1 struct
type ProductA1 struct{}
```

```go
func (p ProductA1) OperationA() {
    fmt.Println("ProductA1 operationA")
}

// ProductA2 struct
type ProductA2 struct{}

func (p ProductA2) OperationA() {
    fmt.Println("ProductA2 operationA")
}

// ProductB interface
type ProductB interface {
    OperationB()
}

// ProductB1 struct
type ProductB1 struct{}

func (p ProductB1) OperationB() {
    fmt.Println("ProductB1 operationB")
}

// ProductB2 struct
type ProductB2 struct{}

func (p ProductB2) OperationB() {
    fmt.Println("ProductB2 operationB")
}

// AbstractFactory interface
type AbstractFactory interface {
    CreateProductA() ProductA
    CreateProductB() ProductB
}

// ConcreteFactory1 struct
type ConcreteFactory1 struct{}

func (f ConcreteFactory1) CreateProductA() ProductA {
    return ProductA1{}
}

func (f ConcreteFactory1) CreateProductB() ProductB {
    return ProductB1{}
}
```

```go
// ConcreteFactory2 struct
type ConcreteFactory2 struct{}

func (f ConcreteFactory2) CreateProductA() ProductA {
    return ProductA2{}
}

func (f ConcreteFactory2) CreateProductB() ProductB {
    return ProductB2{}
}

// Client Code
func main() {
    factory1 := ConcreteFactory1{}
    productA1 := factory1.CreateProductA()
    productB1 := factory1.CreateProductB()
    productA1.OperationA()
    productB1.OperationB()
    factory2 := ConcreteFactory2{}
    productA2 := factory2.CreateProductA()
    productB2 := factory2.CreateProductB()
    productA2.OperationA()
    productB2.OperationB()
}
```

Output:

```
ProductA1 operationA
ProductB1 operationB
ProductA2 operationA
ProductB2 operationB
```

Explanation:

1. **ProductA** and **ProductB** are abstract product interfaces with **OperationA()** and **OperationB()** methods, respectively. Concrete implementations of these products are **ProductA1**, **ProductA2**, **ProductB1**, and **ProductB2**.

2. The **AbstractFactory** interface declares methods **createProductA()** and **createProductB()** to create related objects. These are implemented by **ConcreteFactory1** and **ConcreteFactory2** to produce specific product families.

3. Client code uses the concrete factories (**ConcreteFactory1** and **ConcreteFactory2**) to create instances of **ProductA** and **ProductB**, and then calls the product operations.

Problem: Develop0 a cross-platform GUI application that needs to support both Windows and MacOS. The application requires a consistent look and feel for each platform, which means using platform-specific components like buttons and menus. You need to implement a system that can generate these components— Windows-style buttons and menus or MacOS-style buttons and menus— depending on the platform.

The challenge is to ensure that the correct combination of components (e.g., Windows button with Windows menu, Mac button with Mac menu) is created, while keeping the client code simple and unaware of the specific classes used to create these components. This will allow you to easily extend support for other platforms in the future.

Solution: To solve this problem, we can implement the Abstract Factory Pattern. This pattern will allow us to create families of related objects (buttons and menus) without specifying their concrete classes in the client code.

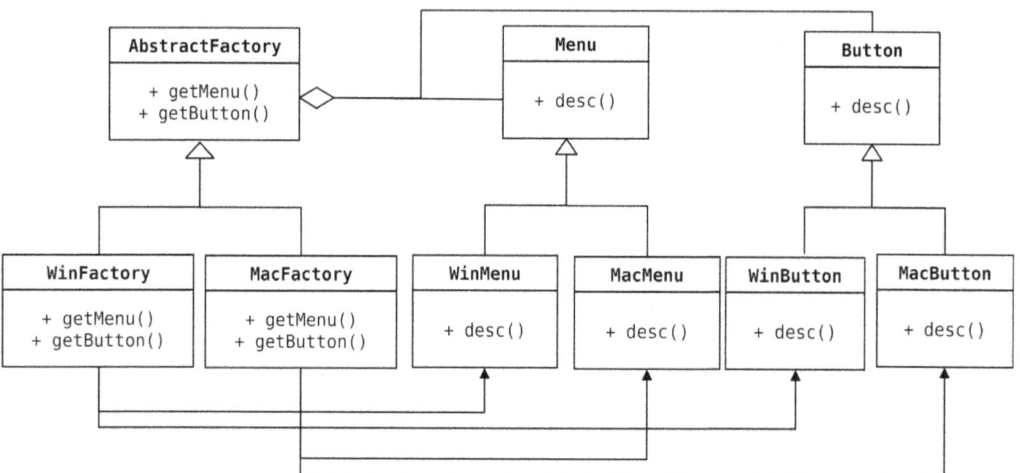

Example Implementation:

```go
// Menu interface
type Menu interface {
    Desc()
}

// WinMenu struct
type WinMenu struct{}

func (wm WinMenu) Desc() {
    fmt.Println("Win Menu!!")
}
```

```go
// MacMenu struct
type MacMenu struct{}

func (mm MacMenu) Desc() {
    fmt.Println("Mac Menu!!")
}

// Button interface
type Button interface {
    Desc()
}

// WinButton struct
type WinButton struct{}

func (wb WinButton) Desc() {
    fmt.Println("Win Button!!")
}

// MacButton struct
type MacButton struct{}

func (mb MacButton) Desc() {
    fmt.Println("Mac Button!!")
}

// AbstractFactory interface
type AbstractFactory interface {
    GetMenu() Menu
    GetButton() Button
}

// WinFactory struct
type WinFactory struct{}

func (wf WinFactory) GetMenu() Menu {
    return WinMenu{}
}

func (wf WinFactory) GetButton() Button {
    return WinButton{}
}

// MacFactory struct
type MacFactory struct{}
```

```go
func (mf MacFactory) GetMenu() Menu {
    return MacMenu{}
}

func (mf MacFactory) GetButton() Button {
    return MacButton{}
}

// Client Code
func main() {
    m := MacFactory{}
    m.GetMenu().Desc()
    m.GetButton().Desc()
    w := WinFactory{}
    w.GetButton().Desc()
    w.GetMenu().Desc()
}
```

Output:

```
Mac Menu!!
Mac Button!!
Win Menu!!
Win Button!!
```

Explanation:

1. **Menu** and **Button** are abstract interfaces, each with concrete implementations: **WinMenu**, **MacMenu**, **WinButton**, and **MacButton**.

2. The **AbstractFactory** interface defines methods **getMenu()** and **getButton()** for creating related objects. **WinFactory** and **MacFactory** are concrete factory classes that implement these methods.

3. The client code uses **MacFactory** and **WinFactory** to create menus and buttons for their respective platforms.

Uses of Abstract Factory design pattern

Here are some of the common use cases for the Abstract Factory design pattern:

1. **Creating Platform-Specific Objects**: Abstract Factory is ideal for generating related objects (e.g., UI components) for different environments (Windows, macOS, etc.) without altering client code.

2. **Encapsulation of Object Creation**: It centralizes object creation, making the codebase easier to maintain. Changing the object creation logic only requires modifying the factory, not the client.

3. **Ensuring Consistency**: All objects produced by a factory belong to the same family, ensuring they are compatible and reducing the risk of errors in the system.

4. **Adding New Object Types**: New object types can be easily added by defining a new factory class, without requiring any changes to the client code.

Consequences

The Abstract Factory pattern offers several benefits and consequences:

1. **Flexibility and Extensibility**: The pattern makes it easy to introduce new product families without modifying the existing client code. New factories can be added to generate new types of objects.

2. **Loose Coupling**: Client code is independent of the concrete classes used. It relies only on the abstract factory interface, making the design more maintainable and adaptable.

3. **Consistency**: The pattern ensures that objects created by a factory are consistent with each other and belong to the same family.

4. **Simplified Client Code**: The complexity of object creation is hidden within the factory, allowing the client to focus on its core functionality.

5. **Dependency Injection**: Abstract Factory can serve as a form of dependency injection, where the client is provided with a specific factory and works with its products without knowing their concrete types.

Builder Pattern

The **Builder design pattern** is a creational pattern used to construct complex objects step by step. It separates the construction process from the representation, enabling the same process to create different objects. This pattern is particularly effective when an object has multiple configuration options, or when creating it through a traditional constructor would result in many parameters, leading to cluttered and hard-to-maintain code.

Problem: In software development, constructing objects with numerous attributes or configuration options using traditional constructors can be cumbersome and error-prone. Having constructors with many parameters or multiple constructor overloads can make the code less readable and harder to maintain. The challenge is to create objects with various configurations without overcomplicating the object construction process.

Solution: The **Builder Pattern** solves this issue by introducing a separate Builder class that handles the object construction step by step. Each step configures a part of the object, and once all parts are set, the final product is returned. This approach makes the creation process cleaner and more manageable.

Components of the Builder Pattern:

1. **Builder**: An interface that defines the steps to build different parts of a complex object.

2. **ConcreteBuilder**: A concrete class that implements the Builder interface to build and assemble the parts.

3. **Director**: Manages the building process by coordinating with the builder.

4. **Product**: The complex object being built.

Implement the Builder Pattern class that builds a **Product**. The **Builder** interface would define methods for adding parts like the **partA** and **partB**. The **ConcreteBuilder** would implement these methods and assemble the product parts. The **Director** would manage the construction process by calling the appropriate methods from the **ConcreteBuilder**. Finally, the **Product** would be the completed product object with all its parts assembled.

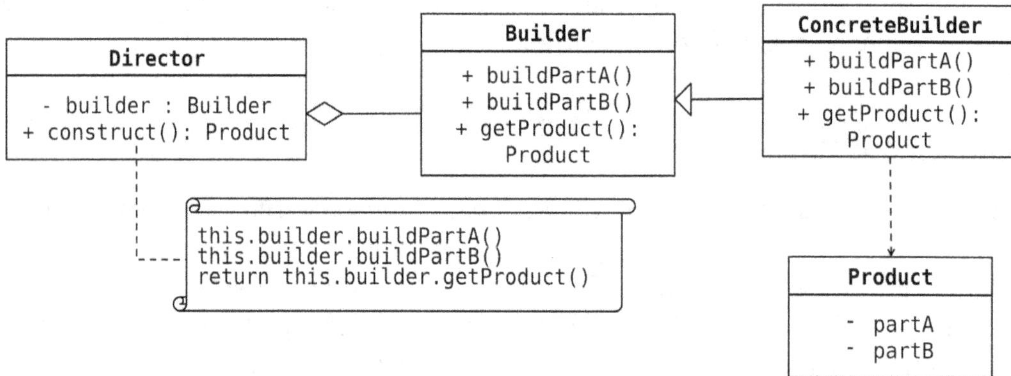

Example Implementation:

```go
// Product struct
type Product struct {
    partA, partB string
}

// String method for Product
func (p *Product) String() string {
    return fmt.Sprintf("Product : (%s, %s)", p.partA, p.partB)
}

// Builder interface
type Builder interface {
    setPartA(A string) Builder
    setPartB(B string) Builder
    getProduct() *Product
}

// ConcreteBuilder struct
type ConcreteBuilder struct {
    product *Product
}

// NewConcreteBuilder constructor
func NewConcreteBuilder() *ConcreteBuilder {
    return &ConcreteBuilder{product: &Product{partA:"AA",
partB:"BB"}}
}

// setPartA method for ConcreteBuilder
func (cb *ConcreteBuilder) setPartA(A string) Builder {
    cb.product.partA = A
    return cb
}

// setPartB method for ConcreteBuilder
func (cb *ConcreteBuilder) setPartB(B string) Builder {
    cb.product.partB = B
    return cb
}

// getProduct method for ConcreteBuilder
func (cb *ConcreteBuilder) getProduct() *Product {
    temp := cb.product
```

```go
    cb.product = &Product{partA:"AA", partB:"BB"} // assign new
product
    return temp
}

// Director struct
type Director struct {
    builder Builder
}

// NewDirector constructor
func NewDirector(builder Builder) *Director {
    return &Director{builder: builder}
}

// construct method for Director
func (d *Director) construct() *Product {
    return d.builder.setPartA("A1").setPartB("B1").getProduct()
}

// construct2 method for Director
func (d *Director) construct2() *Product {
    d.builder.setPartA("A2").setPartB("B2")
    return d.builder.getProduct()
}

// construct3 method for Director
func (d *Director) construct3() *Product {
    return d.builder.setPartA("A3").getProduct()
}

// Client Code
func main() {
    builder := NewConcreteBuilder()
    director := NewDirector(builder)

    product := director.construct()
    fmt.Println(product)

    product2 := director.construct2()
    fmt.Println(product2)

    product3 := director.construct3()
    fmt.Println(product3)
}
```

Output:

```
Product : (A1, B1)
Product : (A2, B2)
Product : (A3, B default)
```

Explanation:

1. **Product Class**: The Product class represents the object being built, which has two parts (**partA** and **partB**), each with default values.

2. **Builder Interface**: This interface defines the methods to configure the product. It includes methods for setting different parts and returning the final object.

3. **ConcreteBuilder Class**: Implements the **Builder** interface and defines the logic for configuring the parts of the product. Method chaining is used to set multiple properties in sequence.

4. **Director Class**: Manages the object creation process by calling the appropriate methods of the builder.

5. **Client Code**: The main function creates a builder and a director to orchestrate the construction process and outputs the final product.

Problem: Implement a **Builder Pattern** to construct a **House** object that consists of various parts such as walls and roofs. The construction process should be flexible to allow the creation of different types of houses, such as a wooden house or a concrete house, using the same construction steps.

The task involves:

- Defining a **HouseBuilder** interface with methods for setting walls and roofs.

- Implementing **WoodenHouseBuilder** and **ConcreteHouseBuilder** classes that follow this interface and configure the house accordingly.

- Creating a **HouseDirector** class that manages the building process by interacting with the builder.

- Producing the final **House** object using these components.

Solution: The Builder Pattern separates the house creation process into distinct steps. This allows for the construction of different types of houses using the same interface.

Example implementation:

```go
// House struct
type House struct {
    Wall string
    Roof string
}

// NewHouse constructor
func NewHouse(wall, roof string) *House {
    return &House{Wall: wall, Roof: roof}
}

// String method for House
func (h *House) String() string {
    return fmt.Sprintf("House of %s and %s", h.Wall, h.Roof)
}

// HouseBuilder interface
type HouseBuilder interface {
    setWall() HouseBuilder
    setRoof() HouseBuilder
    getHouse() *House
}

// ConcreteHouseBuilder struct
type ConcreteHouseBuilder struct {
    house *House
}

// setWall method for ConcreteHouseBuilder
func (chb *ConcreteHouseBuilder) setWall() HouseBuilder {
    chb.house.Wall = "Concrete Wall"
    return chb
}

// setRoof method for ConcreteHouseBuilder
func (chb *ConcreteHouseBuilder) setRoof() HouseBuilder {
    chb.house.Roof = "Concrete Roof"
    return chb
}
```

```go
// getHouse method for ConcreteHouseBuilder
func (chb *ConcreteHouseBuilder) getHouse() *House {
    temp := chb.house
    chb.house = &House{}
    return temp
}

// WoodenHouseBuilder struct
type WoodenHouseBuilder struct {
    house *House
}

// setWall method for WoodenHouseBuilder
func (whb *WoodenHouseBuilder) setWall() HouseBuilder {
    whb.house.Wall = "Wooden Wall"
    return whb
}

// setRoof method for WoodenHouseBuilder
func (whb *WoodenHouseBuilder) setRoof() HouseBuilder {
    whb.house.Roof = "Wooden Roof"
    return whb
}

// getHouse method for WoodenHouseBuilder
func (whb *WoodenHouseBuilder) getHouse() *House {
    temp := whb.house
    whb.house = &House{}
    return temp
}

// HouseDirector struct
type HouseDirector struct {
    builder HouseBuilder
}

// NewHouseDirector constructor
func NewHouseDirector(builder HouseBuilder) *HouseDirector {
    return &HouseDirector{builder: builder}
}

// construct method for HouseDirector
func (hd *HouseDirector) construct() *House {
    return hd.builder.setWall().setRoof().getHouse()
}
```

```go
// Client Code
func main() {
    builder := &ConcreteHouseBuilder{house: &House{}}
    director := NewHouseDirector(builder)

    house := director.construct()
    fmt.Println(house)

    // Building a wooden house using a WoodenHouseBuilder object
    builder2 := &WoodenHouseBuilder{house: &House{}}
    director2 := NewHouseDirector(builder2)

    house2 := director2.construct()
    fmt.Println(house2)
}
```

Output:

```
House of Concrete Wall and Concrete Roof
House of Wooden Wall and Wooden Roof
```

Explanation:

1. **House**: The product being built, which has two attributes: Wall and Roof.

2. **HouseBuilder Interface**: Defines methods for setting the wall and roof of the house, and a method for retrieving the completed House object.

3. **ConcreteHouseBuilder** & **WoodenHouseBuilder**: Concrete implementations of the HouseBuilder interface, which configure the house parts as either concrete or wooden.

4. **HouseDirector**: Manages the construction process by interacting with the **HouseBuilder** to build the house step by step.

5. **Client Code**: Creates houses using the **HouseDirector** and prints out the details of each house.

Uses of Builder design pattern

The **Builder design pattern** is useful in the following scenarios:

1. **Creating Complex Objects Step-by-Step**: When you need to construct an object with multiple parts, and the construction process should be independent of the object's individual components. The builder pattern allows the object to be assembled in stages, creating each part step by step.

2. **Building Different Versions of an Object with the Same Process**: If the object can have multiple variations but follows the same construction procedure. For instance, in a house-building application, various types of houses (e.g., wooden, concrete) may have different components (e.g., walls, roofs), but the overall process to construct them remains consistent.

3. **Flexible and Extensible Object Creation**: The builder pattern offers a way to create objects in a more flexible manner. It allows changes to an object's internal structure or components, enabling the creation of various types from a single builder without changing the client code.

4. **Hiding Complexity from the Client**: The builder pattern abstracts the details of object creation from the client code. By using a builder class, the complexity of constructing the object is hidden, leaving the client with a simple and intuitive interface.

Consequences

The Builder design pattern provides several advantages:

1. **Separation of Concerns**: It divides the construction process from the actual representation of the object, leading to more modular and maintainable code.

2. **Flexible Object Creation**: Different concrete builder classes can generate various representations of the same complex object, offering greater flexibility in how objects are constructed.

3. **Avoids Telescoping Constructors**: Instead of having constructors with numerous parameters (which can be confusing and difficult to manage), the builder pattern simplifies object creation by offering a clear and readable step-by-step process.

4. **Improved Code Readability**: The pattern results in more readable and self-explanatory code compared to overloaded constructors or long parameter lists, making it easier for developers to understand the object's configuration.

5. **Encapsulation of Construction Details**: The internal logic and complexity of how the object is constructed are encapsulated within the builder, ensuring that the client code only interacts with a simple and clean interface.

Prototype Pattern

The **Prototype design pattern** is a creational pattern used to create new objects by copying an existing object (known as the prototype), instead of creating them from scratch using a constructor. This pattern is useful when object creation is expensive in terms of time and resources. By using the Prototype pattern, you can efficiently create new objects by duplicating existing ones. It is also particularly useful when the exact number or type of objects needed is unknown in advance, or when the variety of objects is too large for a conventional factory pattern to handle.

Problem: In software development, there are cases where creating objects from scratch is inefficient and resource-consuming. For example, when you need multiple instances of similar objects with only slight differences, such as objects with the same structure but varying data values. Creating each object individually using traditional methods can lead to code duplication and performance issues.

Solution: To implement the Prototype pattern, you typically define an abstract **Prototype** class that declares a **clone()** method. The **clone()** method is responsible for creating and returning a copy of the current object. Concrete prototypes then implement this method by creating a new instance of the same class and copying the state of the original object.

Next, a registry or factory class is usually defined to hold references to the prototype objects. This class provides a mechanism to retrieve a clone of a prototype object by calling a method that, in turn, calls the **clone()** method of the corresponding prototype.

Overall, the Prototype pattern provides a flexible and efficient way to create new objects by duplicating existing ones. It can reduce the number of subclasses required in an application and can help create complex objects that involve a complicated initialization process.

Example implementation:

```go
// Prototype interface defines the Clone method for creating a
copy of the object.
type Prototype interface {
    Clone() Prototype
}


// ConcretePrototype1 is a concrete implementation of the
Prototype interface.
type ConcretePrototype1 struct{}
```

```go
// Creates and returns a new instance of ConcretePrototype1.
func (c *ConcretePrototype1) Clone() Prototype {
    return &ConcretePrototype1{}
}

// Returns the string representation of ConcretePrototype1.
func (c *ConcretePrototype1) String() string {
    return "ConcretePrototype1"
}

// ConcretePrototype2 is a concrete implementation of the
Prototype interface.
type ConcretePrototype2 struct{}

// Creates and returns a new instance of ConcretePrototype2.
func (c *ConcretePrototype2) Clone() Prototype {
    return &ConcretePrototype2{}
}

// Returns the string representation of ConcretePrototype2.
func (c *ConcretePrototype2) String() string {
    return "ConcretePrototype2"
}

// PrototypeRegistry holds and manages prototype objects.
type PrototypeRegistry struct {
    prototypes map[string]Prototype
}

// Creates a new instance of PrototypeRegistry.
func NewPrototypeRegistry() *PrototypeRegistry {
    return &PrototypeRegistry{
        prototypes: make(map[string]Prototype),
    }
}

// AddPrototype adds a prototype to the registry if it doesn't
already exist.
func (pr *PrototypeRegistry) AddPrototype(key string, value
Prototype) {
    if _, exists := pr.prototypes[key]; !exists {
        pr.prototypes[key] = value
    }
}
```

```go
// GetPrototype retrieves a prototype from the registry and
returns its clone.
func (pr *PrototypeRegistry) GetPrototype(key string) Prototype {
    if prototype, exists := pr.prototypes[key]; exists {
        // Use reflection to create a deep copy of the prototype
        return
reflect.New(reflect.TypeOf(prototype).Elem()).Interface().
(Prototype)
    }
    return nil
}


// Load initializes the registry with predefined prototypes.
func (pr *PrototypeRegistry) Load() {
    pr.AddPrototype("CP1", &ConcretePrototype1{})
    pr.AddPrototype("CP2", &ConcretePrototype2{})
}


// Client code
func main() {
    // Create a new registry and load predefined prototypes
    prototypeRegistry := NewPrototypeRegistry()
    prototypeRegistry.Load()

    // Retrieve clones of the prototypes from the registry
    c1 := prototypeRegistry.GetPrototype("CP1")
    c2 := prototypeRegistry.GetPrototype("CP2")

    // Print the cloned objects
    fmt.Println(c1)
    fmt.Println(c2)
}
```

Output:

```
ConcretePrototype1
ConcretePrototype2
```

Explanation:

1. In this code, **Prototype** is an interface that defines the clone method, which is implemented by the concrete prototypes **ConcretePrototype1** and **ConcretePrototype2**.

2. The **PrototypeRegistry** class acts as a registry for the prototypes and provides a way to retrieve a clone of a prototype object by calling the **GetPrototype** method, which internally invokes the **clone()** method of the corresponding prototype.

3. Therefore, the Prototype pattern allows for object creation without calling constructors, relying on object duplication instead. The **PrototypeRegistry** serves as a central manager for prototypes.

Problem: You need to efficiently create multiple instances of different shapes (e.g., **Rectangle** and **Circle**) without manually instantiating each shape object every time. Additionally, the process of creating these shape objects should be streamlined so that adding new shapes in the future is easy and requires minimal code changes. The Prototype design pattern is ideal for solving this problem because it allows you to create new objects by copying existing ones, rather than creating them from scratch.

Solution: The Prototype pattern can be used to create a **Shape** interface with two concrete classes (**Rectangle** and **Circle**). The **ShapeRegistry** class acts as a manager for prototype objects, storing the initial prototypes and providing clones of these prototypes when needed. This way, instead of creating new instances manually, the client code can request clones from the registry, thereby minimizing the effort needed to create new objects.

Example implementation:

```go
// Shape is an interface representing a shape.
type Shape interface {
    fmt.Stringer
    Clone() Shape
}

// Rectangle is a concrete implementation of the Shape interface.
type Rectangle struct{}

func (r *Rectangle) Clone() Shape {
    // Rectangle clone
    return &Rectangle{}
}

func (r *Rectangle) String() string {
    return "Rectangle."
}

// Circle is a concrete implementation of the Shape interface.
type Circle struct{}

func (c *Circle) Clone() Shape {
    // Circle clone
```

```go
    return &Circle{}
}

func (c *Circle) String() string {
    return "Circle."
}

// ShapeRegistry is a registry for managing shapes.
type ShapeRegistry struct {
    shapes map[string]Shape
}

// NewShapeRegistry creates a new instance of ShapeRegistry.
func NewShapeRegistry() *ShapeRegistry {
    return &ShapeRegistry{
        shapes: make(map[string]Shape),
    }
}

// AddShape adds a shape to the registry.
func (sr *ShapeRegistry) AddShape(key string, value Shape) {
    if _, exists := sr.shapes[key]; !exists {
        sr.shapes[key] = value
    }
}

// GetShape retrieves a shape from the registry and returns a
clone.
func (sr *ShapeRegistry) GetShape(key string) Shape {
    if shape, exists := sr.shapes[key]; exists {
        // Use reflection to create a deep copy of the shape
        return
reflect.New(reflect.TypeOf(shape).Elem()).Interface().(Shape)
    }
    return nil
}

// Load loads predefined shapes into the registry.
func (sr *ShapeRegistry) Load() {
    sr.AddShape("circle", &Circle{})
    sr.AddShape("rectangle", &Rectangle{})
}

// Client code
func main() {
    shapeRegistry := NewShapeRegistry()
```

```
    shapeRegistry.Load()

    circle := shapeRegistry.GetShape("circle")
    rectangle := shapeRegistry.GetShape("rectangle")

    fmt.Println(circle, rectangle)
}
```

Output:

```
Circle. Rectangle.
```

Explanation:

1. The Prototype pattern is used to create new objects by copying existing objects, which serve as prototypes.

2. The **Shape** interface declares the **Clone()** method, and the concrete prototypes **Circle** and **Rectangle** implement it by creating a new instance of the same type.

3. The **ShapeRegistry** class acts as a factory that holds references to these prototype objects. The **Load()** method initializes the registry by adding the prototypes.

4. Finally, client code retrieves clones of the prototypes and prints their string representations.

Uses of Prototype pattern

The Prototype pattern is widely used in software engineering to create new objects by copying existing ones. Here are some common scenarios where the Prototype pattern is beneficial:

1. When the system needs to be independent of the object creation process, composition, and representation.

2. When objects are created at runtime, allowing for more dynamic flexibility.

3. When object creation is based on a set of parameter values determined at runtime.

4. When hiding the complexity of object creation from the client is desirable.

5. When it is more efficient to copy an existing object rather than creating a new one from scratch.

6. When the number or variety of required classes is unknown beforehand or is potentially very large.

7. When new classes may need to be added dynamically during runtime.

8. When object creation is resource-intensive or time-consuming, making cloning an existing object more efficient.

Consequences

The Prototype pattern has several advantages and important considerations:

1. **Reduced Object Creation Overhead**: By cloning existing objects, the Prototype pattern minimizes the cost of initializing and configuring new objects. This can significantly improve performance and reduce resource consumption, especially for complex objects.

2. **Enhanced Flexibility**: The pattern allows the creation of new objects with variations at runtime. This enables the dynamic creation of complex objects based on different configurations or states, without the need for subclassing.

3. **Simplified Code**: Using the Prototype pattern avoids repetitive code that could result from manually creating similar objects. The cloning process encapsulates the object creation logic, leading to cleaner and more maintainable code.

4. **Support for Changing Class Hierarchies**: The Prototype pattern is beneficial in environments where class hierarchies change frequently. Since client code relies on the prototype interface rather than specific classes, changes in class hierarchies have less impact on the client code.

5. **Deep vs. Shallow Cloning**: An important consideration when implementing the Prototype pattern is whether to use shallow cloning (copying object references) or deep cloning (copying the entire object graph). The decision depends on the complexity and interrelationships of the objects. Deep cloning ensures a complete copy, while shallow cloning only duplicates the references to the object's internal data.

Summary

This chapter covered Creational Patterns, which provide solutions for object creation in software design. By focusing on how objects are instantiated, these patterns help improve code flexibility, adaptability, and maintainability. We explored several key Creational Patterns, including:

- **Singleton**: Ensures a class has only one instance and provides a global access point to it.

- **Factory Method**: Defines an interface for creating objects but lets subclasses decide which class to instantiate, promoting loose coupling.

- **Abstract Factory**: Creates families of related objects without specifying their concrete classes, ideal for systems that need to create sets of interrelated objects.

- **Builder**: Separates the construction of a complex object from its representation, allowing the same construction process to create different representations.

- **Prototype**: Uses cloning to create new objects, offering an efficient way to duplicate objects without relying on their class details.

By mastering these patterns, developers can better manage object creation, reduce dependencies, and create more scalable and maintainable systems. Understanding when and how to apply these patterns is crucial for building robust software that is both flexible and easy to modify.

Exercises

1. **Singleton Pattern based problem**: You are developing a logging system for a multi-threaded application. The system should ensure that all parts of the application write to the same log file. Implement a **Logger** class that guarantees only one instance of the logger exists throughout the system, and this instance should be accessible globally.

   Instructions:

   - Create a **Logger** class using the Singleton pattern.

   - Ensure the **Logger** class has a method **log(message: String)** that writes the message to a log file.

   - Implement thread safety to ensure that the Singleton instance is correctly handled in a multi-threaded environment.

2. **Factory Method Pattern based problem**: You are designing a game where different types of enemies (e.g., **Goblin**, **Troll**, **Dragon**) need to

be generated dynamically during gameplay. Each enemy type has unique characteristics but shares a common interface **Enemy**. Implement a **EnemyFactory** class that creates instances of different enemy types based on input.

Instructions:

- Define a common interface **Enemy** with a method **attack()**.

- Implement three classes: **Goblin**, **Troll**, and **Dragon**, each implementing the **Enemy** interface.

- Create an abstract **EnemyFactory** class with a method **createEnemy(type: String): Enemy**.

- Implement a concrete factory that overrides the **createEnemy()** method to return the appropriate **Enemy** subclass based on the input type.

3. **Abstract Factory Pattern based problem:** You are building a cross-platform UI library that needs to generate different user interface elements (e.g., **Button**, **Checkbox**, **TextField**) for different operating systems (e.g., **Windows**, **MacOS**). Each OS has its own style and behavior for these elements.

Instructions:

- Create interfaces **Button**, **Checkbox**, and **TextField** with methods relevant to each UI element.

- Implement concrete classes for each UI element corresponding to Windows and MacOS (e.g., **WindowsButton**, **MacButton**, etc.).

- Define an abstract factory **UIFactory** with methods to create each type of UI element.

- Implement two concrete factories, **WindowsFactory** and **MacFactory**, that create the Windows and MacOS versions of the UI elements, respectively.

4. **Builder Pattern based problem:** You are tasked with developing a configuration system for a computer. A **Computer** object can have various optional components like CPU, RAM, GPU, and storage. The order in which these components are added may vary depending on the user's requirements.

Instructions:

- Create a **Computer** class with attributes for CPU, RAM, GPU, and storage.

- Implement a **ComputerBuilder** class that provides methods to set each component of the **Computer** object.

- Ensure that the **ComputerBuilder** class can build and return a **Computer** object once all the desired components have been set.

5. **Prototype Pattern based problem:** You are working on a document editing application where users can create and edit different types of documents (e.g., **TextDocument**, **SpreadsheetDocument**, **PresentationDocument**). To optimize the creation process, you need a mechanism to clone existing documents instead of creating new ones from scratch.

Instructions:

- Define a **Document** interface with a method **cloneDocument()**.

- Implement concrete classes **TextDocument**, **SpreadsheetDocument**, and **PresentationDocument**, each overriding the **cloneDocument()** method to return a copy of itself.

- Create a method to demonstrate cloning a document and modifying the clone without affecting the original.

Solution of Exercises

Solution 1: Singleton Pattern:

```
type Logger struct{ file *os.File }
var instance *Logger
var once sync.Once

func GetLoggerInstance() *Logger {
    once.Do(func() {
        file, _ := os.OpenFile("logfile.txt", os.O_APPEND|
os.O_CREATE|os.O_WRONLY, 0666)
        instance = &Logger{file: file}
    })
    return instance
}
```

```go
func (l *Logger) Log(message string) { l.file.WriteString(message
+ "\n") }

func main() {
    logger := GetLoggerInstance()
    logger.Log("Log message")
}
```

Solution 2: Factory Method Pattern:

```go
type Enemy interface{ Attack() }
type Goblin struct{}
func (g Goblin) Attack() { fmt.Println("Goblin attacks!") }
type Troll struct{}
func (t Troll) Attack() { fmt.Println("Troll attacks!") }
type Dragon struct{}
func (d Dragon) Attack() { fmt.Println("Dragon attacks!") }

type EnemyFactory struct{}
func (f EnemyFactory) CreateEnemy(t string) Enemy {
    switch t {
    case "Goblin": return Goblin{};
    case "Troll": return Troll{};
    case "Dragon": return Dragon{}}
    return nil
}

func main() {
    factory := EnemyFactory{}
    factory.CreateEnemy("Dragon").Attack()
}
```

Solution 3: Abstract Factory Pattern:

```go
type Button interface{ Click() }
type Checkbox interface{ Check() }
type WindowsButton struct{}
func (WindowsButton) Click() { fmt.Println("Windows Button
clicked") }

type MacButton struct{}
func (MacButton) Click() { fmt.Println("Mac Button clicked") }

type WindowsCheckbox struct{}
```

```go
func (WindowsCheckbox) Check() { fmt.Println("Windows Checkbox
checked") }

type MacCheckbox struct{}
func (MacCheckbox) Check() { fmt.Println("Mac Checkbox
checked") }

type UIFactory interface{
    CreateButton() Button;
    CreateCheckbox() Checkbox
}

type WindowsFactory struct{}
func (WindowsFactory) CreateButton() Button { return
WindowsButton{} }
func (WindowsFactory) CreateCheckbox() Checkbox { return
WindowsCheckbox{} }

type MacFactory struct{}
func (MacFactory) CreateButton() Button { return MacButton{} }
func (MacFactory) CreateCheckbox() Checkbox { return
MacCheckbox{} }

func main() {
    factory := WindowsFactory{}
    factory.CreateButton().Click()
}
```

Solution 4: Builder Pattern:

```go
type Computer struct {
    CPU, RAM, GPU, Storage string
}

type ComputerBuilder struct {
    cpu, ram, gpu, storage string
}

func NewComputerBuilder() *ComputerBuilder {
    return &ComputerBuilder{}
}

func (b *ComputerBuilder) SetCPU(cpu string) *ComputerBuilder {
    b.cpu = cpu
    return b
}
```

```go
func (b *ComputerBuilder) SetRAM(ram string) *ComputerBuilder {
    b.ram = ram
    return b
}

func (b *ComputerBuilder) SetGPU(gpu string) *ComputerBuilder {
    b.gpu = gpu
    return b
}

func (b *ComputerBuilder) SetStorage(storage string)
*ComputerBuilder {
    b.storage = storage
    return b
}

func (b *ComputerBuilder) Build() Computer {
    return Computer{CPU: b.cpu, RAM: b.ram, GPU: b.gpu, Storage:
b.storage}
}

func main() {
    builder := NewComputerBuilder()
    computer := builder.SetCPU("i7").SetRAM("16GB").SetGPU("GTX
3080").SetStorage("1TB").Build()
    fmt.Println(computer)
}
```

Solution 5: Prototype Pattern:

```go
type Document interface{ CloneDocument() Document }
type TextDocument struct{ Content string }

func (td *TextDocument) CloneDocument() Document {
    clone := *td
    return &clone
}

func main() {
    doc := &TextDocument{Content: "Original"}
    clone := doc.CloneDocument().(*TextDocument)
    fmt.Println(clone.Content) // "Original"
}
```

Structural Patterns

Structural design patterns are a category of design patterns that focus on how classes and objects are organized to form larger components or structures. These patterns help define relationships between classes, simplify the organization of code, and make the system more flexible and maintainable.

We will begin by exploring the **Adapter Pattern**, which facilitates interoperability between classes with incompatible interfaces. By encapsulating the conversion logic within an adapter, this pattern enables seamless integration of existing components into new systems, reducing friction and fostering code reuse.

Next, the **Bridge Pattern** offers an elegant solution to managing multiple dimensions of variation in software design. By decoupling abstractions from their implementations, this pattern allows designers to handle each dimension independently, thus mitigating the explosion of class combinations that may result from combining them.

The **Composite Pattern** allows you to compose objects into tree-like structures and work with those structures as if they were individual objects. This pattern is especially useful when you have a hierarchical structure of objects and need to treat both individual objects and their compositions uniformly.

We continue with the **Decorator Pattern**, a hallmark of software design that enables dynamic extension of functionality without altering existing code. This pattern allows additional responsibilities to be attached to objects at runtime, enhancing flexibility and avoiding the drawbacks of subclass proliferation.

Next is the **Facade Pattern**, which presents a unified and simplified interface to a set of interfaces within a subsystem, shielding clients from underlying complexities. This pattern promotes clarity, encourages best practices, and enhances the ease of use for components within the system.

The **Flyweight Pattern** follows, which optimizes memory usage by sharing common data among multiple objects. It is particularly useful when dealing with large numbers of similar objects that share some intrinsic (invariant) state while maintaining some extrinsic (context-dependent) state. By sharing the intrinsic state, this pattern reduces memory consumption and improves performance.

Lastly, the **Proxy Pattern** provides a powerful mechanism for controlling access to objects and introducing additional functionalities, such as lazy initialization or access control. By placing a proxy between clients and real objects, this pattern introduces a level of indirection that can be leveraged for various purposes, such as performance optimization and security enforcement.

Adapter Pattern

The **Adapter design pattern** is a structural pattern that allows objects with incompatible interfaces to work together. It acts as a bridge between two interfaces, converting the interface of one class into the expected interface for clients. This involves creating an adapter class that serves as an intermediary between two objects. The Adapter pattern is particularly useful when integrating existing systems or libraries that cannot be easily modified to match the required interface.

Problem: In software development, situations often arise where two existing components or classes have different interfaces and cannot directly collaborate. This incompatibility may stem from different naming conventions, data formats, or method signatures. The challenge is to make these incompatible classes work together without modifying their existing code.

Solution: The Adapter design pattern addresses the compatibility issue by introducing an adapter class that acts as an intermediary. The adapter class implements the interface expected by the client and internally holds an instance of the incompatible class. The adapter translates the client's requests into appropriate calls to the methods of the encapsulated object.

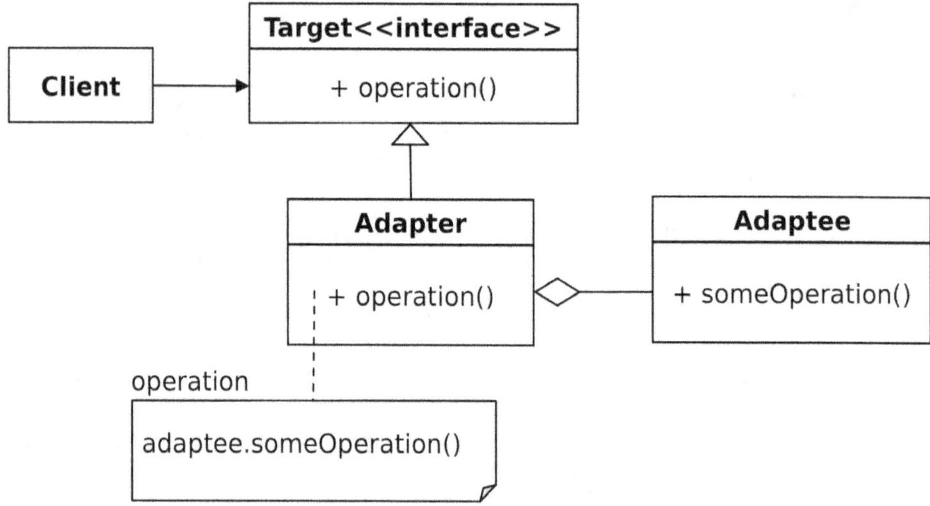

Example implementation:

```go
// DesiredInterface interface
type DesiredInterface interface {
    Operation()
}

// Adapter struct
type Adapter struct {
    adaptee *Adaptee
}

func (a *Adapter) Operation() {
    a.adaptee.SomeOperation()
}

// Adaptee struct
type Adaptee struct{}

func (a *Adaptee) SomeOperation() {
    fmt.Println("Adaptee SomeOperation() function called.")
}

// Client Code
func main() {
    adapter := Adapter{adaptee: &Adaptee{}}
    adapter.Operation()
}
```

```
Output:

Adaptee someOperation() function called.
```

Explanation:

1. In this pattern, an adapter class bridges the gap between two incompatible interfaces. In this example, the **Adaptee** class has a **SomeOperation()** method, but the client code expects an interface with an **Operation()** method. The **Adapter** class is created to provide this interface, internally using the **Adaptee** class to perform the actual operation.

2. The **DesiredInterface** abstract class defines the interface expected by the client code. The **Adapter** class implements this interface and internally uses an instance of the **Adaptee** class to perform the operation.

3. In the client code, an instance of the **Adapter** class is created, and its **Operation()** method is called. The **Adapter** class internally invokes the **SomeOperation()** method of the **Adaptee** class to perform the actual operation.

Problem: You have an existing **Rectangle** class with a method **OldDraw()**, but you want it to be compatible with a **Shape** interface that requires a **Draw()** method. The **Rectangle** class does not directly implement the **Shape** interface, and you want to integrate it into a system that uses shapes without modifying the original Rectangle class.

Solution: To achieve this, you need to use the Adapter Design Pattern. The goal is to adapt the Rectangle class so that it conforms to the Shape interface by using an adapter class.

Example implementation:

```go
// Shape interface
type Shape interface {
    Draw()
}

// Circle struct
type Circle struct {
    x, y, radius int
}

// NewCircle constructor
func NewCircle(x, y, r int) *Circle {
    return &Circle{x: x, y: y, radius: r}
}

// Draw method for Circle
func (c *Circle) Draw() {
    fmt.Println("Draw the Circle.")
}

// Rectangle struct
type Rectangle struct {
    x, y, length, width int
}

// NewRectangle constructor
func NewRectangle(x, y, l, w int) *Rectangle {
```

```go
    return &Rectangle{x: x, y: y, length: l, width: w}
}

// OldDraw method for Rectangle
func (r *Rectangle) OldDraw() {
    fmt.Println("Drawing Rectangle.")
}

// RectangleAdapter struct
type RectangleAdapter struct {
    adaptee *Rectangle
}

// NewRectangleAdapter constructor
func NewRectangleAdapter(x, y, l, w int) *RectangleAdapter {
    return &RectangleAdapter{adaptee: NewRectangle(x, y, l, w)}
}

// Draw method for RectangleAdapter
func (ra *RectangleAdapter) Draw() {
    ra.adaptee.OldDraw()
}

// Client Code
func main() {
    adapter := NewRectangleAdapter(1, 2, 3, 4)
    adapter.Draw()
}
```

Output:

```
Drawing Rectangle.
```

Explanation:

1. This code implements the Adapter pattern to adapt the interface of the **Rectangle** class to the **Shape** interface.

2. The **Shape** interface declares the **Draw()** method, which is implemented by the **Circle** class. However, the **Rectangle** class doesn't implement the **Shape** interface. To make **Rectangle** compatible with **Shape**, an adapter class **RectangleAdapter** is created that implements the **Shape** interface and internally uses the **Rectangle** class to provide the required functionality.

3. In the client code, an instance of **RectangleAdapter** is created, passing the required parameters to instantiate the **Rectangle** class. The **Draw()**

method is then called on the **RectangleAdapter**, which internally calls the **OldDraw()** method of the **Rectangle** class to draw the rectangle.

Uses of the Adapter Design Pattern

The Adapter design pattern is useful in various scenarios where incompatible interfaces need to work together. Some common uses include:

1. **Legacy Code Integration**: When integrating a legacy system with a modern one that uses a different interface, the Adapter pattern acts as a bridge between the two systems.

2. **Third-Party Library Integration**: When using a third-party library that has a different interface than your application expects, an Adapter can be created to wrap around the library and provide the expected interface.

3. **Interface Conversion**: When you have multiple components using different interfaces, the Adapter pattern can create a common interface that allows all components to interact seamlessly.

4. **Interface Simplification**: For complex interfaces, the Adapter pattern can be used to create a simplified interface that hides the underlying complexity.

5. **Platform Independence**: To make an application platform-independent, the Adapter pattern can introduce a layer between the application and platform-specific code. This layer provides a common interface that works across various platforms.

Consequences

The Adapter pattern offers several benefits and trade-offs:

1. **Compatibility**: It allows classes with different interfaces to work together, promoting code reuse and integration of existing components.

2. **Flexibility**: The pattern enables the incorporation of new classes without modifying existing client code, promoting flexibility and scalability.

3. **Maintainability**: By isolating changes in adapters, any modifications required for new classes are localized, keeping the core client code unchanged and easier to maintain.

4. **Complexity**: While useful, introducing adapters may increase code complexity by adding more classes and layers of abstraction.

5. **Performance**: The use of adapters can introduce some performance overhead due to the extra method calls involved in translating interfaces.

Bridge Pattern

The **Bridge Pattern** is a structural design pattern that decouples an abstraction from its implementation, allowing them to vary independently. In this pattern, the abstraction is a high-level component that relies on an implementor object to perform its operations. The implementor can be changed at runtime without affecting the client using the abstraction.

Problem: In software design, there are situations where a class or abstraction has multiple variants, and you want to separate the abstraction from its implementations. Traditional inheritance can lead to an explosion of classes and make the code complex and inflexible.

Solution: The Bridge pattern solves this problem by using composition instead of inheritance. It separates the abstraction and the implementation into two independent hierarchies, allowing them to evolve separately. This pattern promotes loose coupling, making the code easier to extend and maintain.

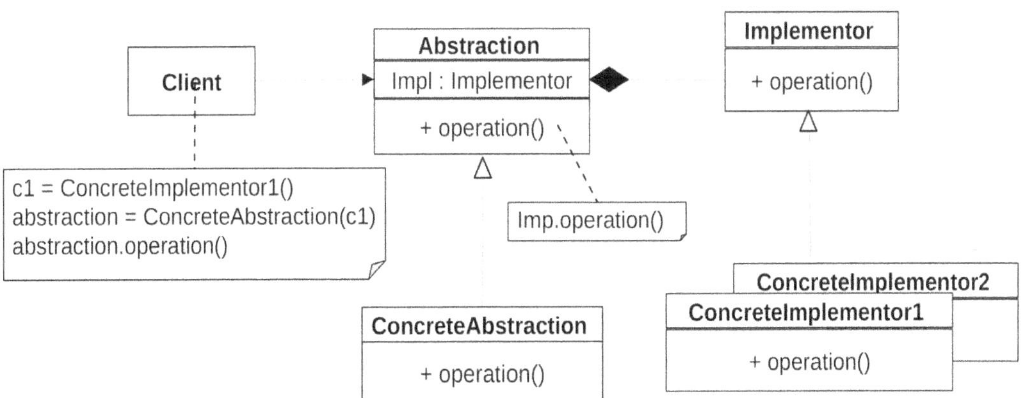

Example Implementation of the Bridge Pattern:

```go
// Implementor interface
type Implementor interface {
    Operation()
}
```

```go
// Abstraction struct
type Abstraction struct {
    imp Implementor
}

// NewAbstraction constructor
func NewAbstraction(imp Implementor) *Abstraction {
    return &Abstraction{imp: imp}
}

// Operation method for Abstraction
func (a *Abstraction) Operation() {
    a.imp.Operation()
}

// ConcreteImplementor1 struct
type ConcreteImplementor1 struct{}

// Operation method for ConcreteImplementor1
func (c *ConcreteImplementor1) Operation() {
    fmt.Println("ConcreteImplementor1 operation")
}

// ConcreteImplementor2 struct
type ConcreteImplementor2 struct{}

// Operation method for ConcreteImplementor2
func (c *ConcreteImplementor2) Operation() {
    fmt.Println("ConcreteImplementor2 operation")
}

// Client Code
func main() {
    c1 := &ConcreteImplementor1{}
    abstraction := NewAbstraction(c1)
    abstraction.Operation()
}
```

Output:

```
ConcreteImplementor1 operation
```

Explanation:

1. In this example, **Abstraction** is the abstract class, while **ConcreteAbstraction** is the concrete implementation of the abstraction. **Implementor** is the interface for the implementation classes, and

ConcreteImplementor1 and **ConcreteImplementor2** are its concrete implementations.

2. **ConcreteAbstraction** holds a reference to an instance of **Implementor** and calls its **operation()** method. **ConcreteImplementor1** and **ConcreteImplementor2** implement the Implementor interface and provide different implementations of **operation()**.

3. In the client code, an instance of **ConcreteImplementor1** is passed to **ConcreteAbstraction**. When **abstraction.operation()** is called, it uses the implementation provided by **ConcreteImplementor1** without needing to know the details of how it works.

Problem: We need to decouple the shapes (Rectangle and Circle) from their colours (Red, Green, and Blue), allowing both shapes and colours to vary independently. The objective is to make the system flexible, extendable, and maintainable without modifying existing code when new shapes or colours are added.

Solution: To solve this problem, we can use the Bridge design pattern. The Bridge pattern separates the abstraction (Shape) from its implementation (Colour) into two independent hierarchies. This allows us to add new shapes or colours without affecting each other.

Here's the step-by-step implementation using Go:

1. **Define the Colour interface**: This is the implementor interface, which will provide different colour-filling methods.

2. **Define the Shape interface**: This is the abstraction interface that all shapes will implement. Each shape will use a colour from the Colour implementor.

3. **Concrete classes for shapes (Rectangle and Circle)**: These classes implement the Shape interface and delegate the colour-filling part to the Colour interface.

4. **Concrete classes for colours (Red, Green, and Blue)**: These classes implement the Colour interface, providing specific colour values.

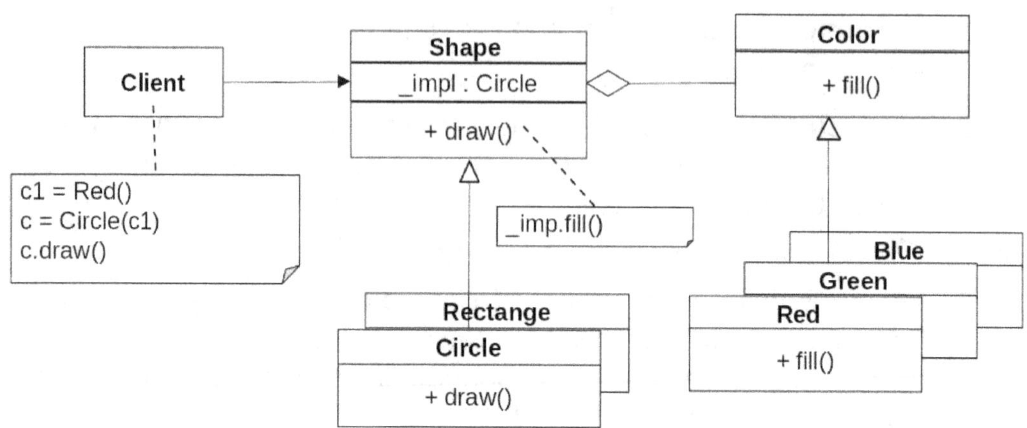

Example Implementation of the Bridge Pattern:

```go
// Colour interface (Implementor)
type Colour interface {
    Fill() string
}

// Shape interface (Abstraction)
type Shape interface {
    Draw()
}
// Rectangle struct
type Rectangle struct {
    colour Colour
}

// NewRectangle constructor
func NewRectangle(colour Colour) *Rectangle {
    return &Rectangle{colour: colour}
}

// Draw method for Rectangle
func (r *Rectangle) Draw() {
    fmt.Printf("Drawing Rectangle with colour %s\n",
r.colour.Fill())
}

// Circle struct
type Circle struct {
    colour Colour
}

// NewCircle constructor
```

```go
func NewCircle(colour Colour) *Circle {
    return &Circle{colour: colour}
}

// Draw method for Circle
func (c *Circle) Draw() {
    fmt.Printf("Drawing Circle with colour %s\n",
c.colour.Fill())
}

// Red struct
type Red struct{}

// Fill method for Red
func (r *Red) Fill() string {
    return "Red"
}

// Green struct
type Green struct{}

// Fill method for Green
func (g *Green) Fill() string {
    return "Green"
}

// Blue struct
type Blue struct{}

// Fill method for Blue
func (b *Blue) Fill() string {
    return "Blue"
}

// Client Code
func main() {
    var shape Shape
    c1 := &Red{}
    shape := NewCircle(c1)
    shape.Draw() // Output: Drawing Circle with colour Red

    c2 := &Green{}
    shape := NewRectangle(c2)
    shape.Draw() // Output: Drawing Rectangle with colour Green
}
```

Output:

```
Drawing Circle with colour Red
Drawing Rectangle with colour Green
```

Explanation:

1. **Abstraction (Shape)**: The **Shape** interface and its concrete implementations (**Rectangle** and **Circle**) represent the abstraction layer. These classes depend on an instance of the Colour interface to delegate colour operations.

2. **Implementor (Colour)**: The **Colour** interface and its concrete implementations (**Red**, **Green**, **Blue**) represent the implementation layer. These classes define the colour-filling logic used by the shapes.

3. **Client Code**: The client can create a new shape and assign a colour at runtime. This allows shapes and colours to vary independently, making the system flexible and easy to extend.

Consequences

The Bridge pattern has several advantages and consequences:

1. **Decoupling**: The key benefit of the Bridge pattern is decoupling. It allows the abstraction and implementation to change independently, providing a more flexible and maintainable codebase.

2. **Flexibility**: Since the abstraction and implementation are separated, you can easily add new variants of either without modifying existing code. This promotes adaptability in the system.

3. **Improved Extensibility**: The pattern encourages extensibility, allowing new abstractions and implementations to be introduced without altering the existing codebase, making future software evolution easier.

4. **Reduced Complexity**: The Bridge pattern mitigates the issue of class explosion that can occur with traditional inheritance hierarchies. This results in a cleaner, more manageable codebase.

5. **Enhanced Testability**: With abstractions and implementations separated, it's easier to test each component in isolation, improving unit testing and overall code reliability.

6. **Runtime Binding**: The Bridge pattern supports dynamic binding of abstraction and implementation at runtime, enabling the switching of implementations during program execution.

However, the pattern comes with some trade-offs:

1. **Initial Complexity**: Implementing the Bridge pattern can introduce complexity at the outset due to the creation of separate abstraction and implementation hierarchies.

2. **Increased Indirection**: The added level of indirection in separating the abstraction and implementation can lead to a slight performance overhead.

3. **Larger Codebase**: As the pattern requires the creation of additional abstraction and implementation classes, the codebase may increase in size.

Composite Pattern

The **Composite pattern** is a structural design pattern that allows you to compose objects into tree-like structures and work with them as if they were individual objects. It is useful when dealing with a hierarchy of objects, where individual objects and groups of objects need to be treated uniformly.

Problem: When working with complex hierarchical structures composed of both individual objects and collections of objects, it becomes difficult to treat them uniformly. Clients often need to interact with both in the same way, but traditional approaches require them to distinguish between individual objects and groups, leading to complex and error-prone code.

Solution: The Composite Design Pattern solves this problem by defining a unified interface for individual objects (leaves) and groups of objects (composites). This allows clients to treat both uniformly, making it easier to manage hierarchical structures. The pattern uses a tree-like structure where each node can be either a composite or a leaf. Composites can hold children and delegate tasks to them, while leaves perform actual work without children.

The main components of the Composite pattern include:

1. **Component**: An abstract class or interface that defines the common operations for both leaf and composite nodes.

2. **Composite**: A class representing a composite node. It can contain child components (both composites and leaves) and implements the operations by delegating them to its children.

3. **Leaf**: A class representing a leaf node, which does not have children and implements operations directly.

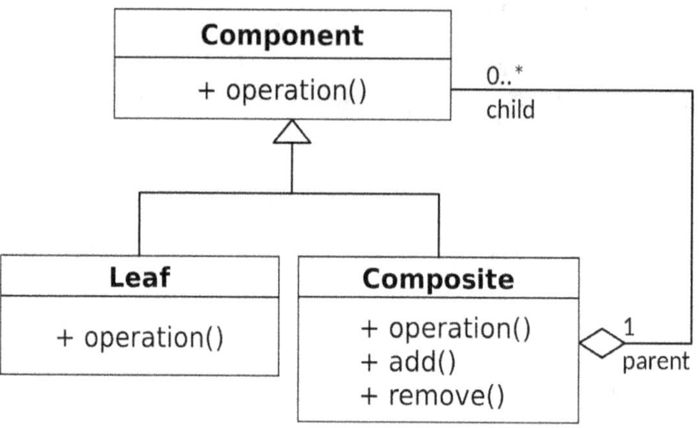

Example Implementation:

```go
// Component interface
type Component interface {
    operation()
}

// Composite struct
type Composite struct {
    children []Component
}

// NewComposite constructor for Composite
func NewComposite() *Composite {
    return &Composite{
        children: make([]Component, 0),
    }
}

// operation method for Composite
func (c *Composite) operation() {
    fmt.Println("Composite Operation")
    for _, child := range c.children {
        child.operation()
    }
```

```go
}

// add method for Composite
func (c *Composite) add(component Component) {
    c.children = append(c.children, component)
}

// remove method for Composite
func (c *Composite) remove(component Component) {
    for i, child := range c.children {
        if child == component {
            c.children = append(c.children[:i],
c.children[i+1:]...)
            break
        }
    }
}

// Leaf struct
type Leaf struct{}

// operation method for Leaf
func (l *Leaf) operation() {
    fmt.Println("Leaf Operation")
}

// Client Code
func main() {
    composite := NewComposite()
    composite.add(&Leaf{})

    composite2 := NewComposite()
    composite2.add(&Leaf{})

    composite.add(composite2)
    composite.operation()
}
```

Output:

```
Composite Operation.
Composite Operation.
Leaf Operation.
Leaf Operation.
```

Explanation:

1. This code implements the Composite pattern, enabling the creation of hierarchical structures where each object (leaf or composite) is treated uniformly.

2. The **Component** interface defines the **operation()** method that both leaves and composites implement.

3. The **Composite** class represents a composite object that can hold child components, and its **operation()** method delegates work to its children.

4. The **Leaf** class represents individual objects (leaf nodes) and implements the **operation()** method directly without any children.

5. In the client code, we create two composites, add leaf objects to them, and then invoke the **operation()** method on the root composite, which recursively calls the **operation()** method on all children.

Problem: Implement the Composite Design Pattern to manage geometric shapes (rectangles and circles) in a hierarchical manner. The goal is to create a unified interface for individual shapes (rectangles and circles) and groups of shapes (a compound shape), allowing clients to interact with them uniformly.

Solution: The Composite Design Pattern allows you to create tree structures composed of individual shapes (leaves) and groups of shapes (composites), all of which share a common interface. This pattern simplifies interaction with complex structures by treating both individual objects and groups uniformly.

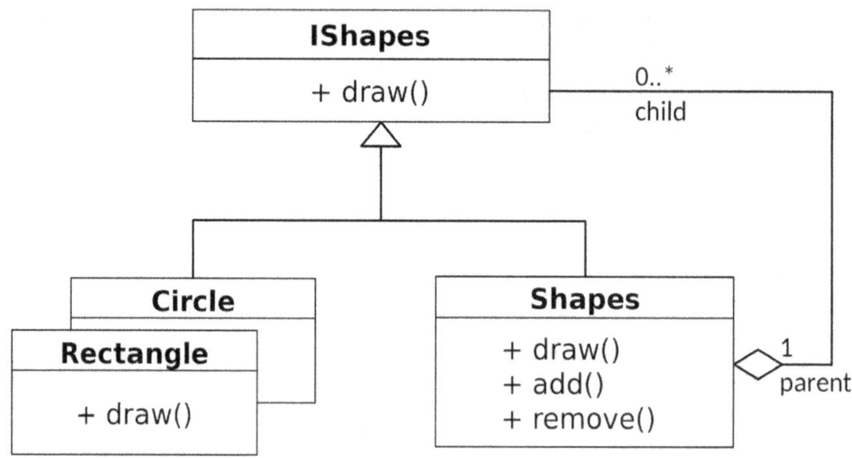

Example implementation:

```go
// IShape interface
type IShape interface {
    move(x, y int)
    draw() string
}

// Rectangle struct
type Rectangle struct {
    x, y, l, b int
}

// NewRectangle constructor for Rectangle
func NewRectangle(x, y, l, b int) *Rectangle {
    return &Rectangle{x: x, y: y, l: l, b: b}
}

// move method for Rectangle
func (r *Rectangle) move(x, y int) {
    r.x += x
    r.y += y
}

// draw method for Rectangle
func (r *Rectangle) draw() string {
    fmt.Printf("Draw a Rectangle at (%d, %d).\n", r.x, r.y)
    return "<Rectangle>"
}

// Circle struct
type Circle struct {
    x, y, radius int
}

// NewCircle constructor for Circle
func NewCircle(x, y, radius int) *Circle {
    return &Circle{x: x, y: y, radius: radius}
}

// move method for Circle
func (c *Circle) move(x, y int) {
    c.x += x
    c.y += y
}
```

```go
// draw method for Circle
func (c *Circle) draw() string {
    fmt.Printf("Draw a Circle of radius %d at (%d, %d) .\n",
c.radius, c.x, c.y)
    return "<Circle>"
}

// CompoundShape struct
type CompoundShape struct {
    children []IShape
}

// NewCompoundShape constructor for CompoundShape
func NewCompoundShape() *CompoundShape {
    return &CompoundShape{
        children: make([]IShape, 0),
    }
}

// add method for CompoundShape
func (cs *CompoundShape) add(child IShape) {
    cs.children = append(cs.children, child)
}

// remove method for CompoundShape
func (cs *CompoundShape) remove(child IShape) {
    for i, c := range cs.children {
        if c == child {
            cs.children = append(cs.children[:i],
cs.children[i+1:])
            break
        }
    }
}

// move method for CompoundShape
func (cs *CompoundShape) move(x, y int) {
    for _, child := range cs.children {
        child.move(x, y)
    }
}

// draw method for CompoundShape
func (cs *CompoundShape) draw() string {
    st := "Shapes("
    for _, child := range cs.children {
```

```
            st += child.draw()
    }
    st += ")"
    return st
}

// Client Code
func main() {
    all := NewCompoundShape()
    all.add(NewRectangle(1, 2, 1, 2))
    all.add(NewCircle(5, 3, 10))
    group := NewCompoundShape()
    group.add(NewRectangle(5, 7, 1, 2))
    group.add(NewCircle(2, 1, 2))
    all.add(group)
    fmt.Println(all.draw())
}
```

Output:

```
Draw a Circle of radius 10 at (5, 3).
Draw a Circle of radius 2 at (2, 1).
Draw a Rectangle at (5, 7).
Draw a Rectangle at (1, 2).
Shapes(<Circle>Shapes(<Circle><Rectangle>)<Rectangle>)
```

Explanation:

1. **IShape** Interface: Defines the common methods **move()** and **draw()** for both individual shapes and composite shapes.

2. **Rectangle** and **Circle** Classes: These represent individual shapes (leaves) that implement **move()** and **draw()** with their specific logic.

3. **CompoundShape** Class: This represents a composite object that can contain child shapes. It provides methods to add or remove children and delegates operations like **move()** and **draw()** to its children.

4. **Client Code:** Demonstrates how individual shapes (rectangles and circles) and groups of shapes (compound shapes) are added and operated upon uniformly.

Consequences

The Composite design pattern offers several advantages and trade-offs:

1. **Uniformity**: It provides a consistent way to handle both individual objects and composite structures, simplifying client code by eliminating the need to distinguish between them.

2. **Flexibility**: New component types can be seamlessly integrated into the system without modifying existing client code, enhancing extensibility.

3. **Hierarchical Organization**: The pattern supports the creation of complex tree-like structures, enabling clear representation of part-whole hierarchies.

4. **Increased Complexity**: While the pattern simplifies client-side interaction, it can introduce complexity within the Composite objects as they manage the hierarchy of components.

5. **Performance Impact**: Traversing a deep or complex composite structure may affect performance, especially when many elements or levels are involved.

6. **Safety Concerns**: Extra care may be needed to ensure certain operations, such as adding children, are only permitted for components that support them (e.g., preventing leaf nodes from accepting children).

Decorator Pattern

The **Decorator design pattern** is a structural pattern that allows dynamic addition of behavior to individual objects without affecting others in the same class. It provides a flexible alternative to subclassing for extending functionality at runtime.

Problem: The primary challenge addressed by the Decorator pattern is how to add new responsibilities or behaviors to objects without modifying their existing code. Subclassing, a traditional approach in object-oriented programming, has several drawbacks:

1. **Class Explosion**: Subclassing every combination of features can lead to a large number of subclasses, making code management difficult.

2. **Rigid Class Hierarchy**: Subclassing results in a fixed class hierarchy, limiting the dynamic combination of behaviors.

3. **Violation of the Open-Closed Principle**: Subclassing requires modifying existing classes, which violates the Open-Closed Principle, which states that software entities should be open for extension but closed for modification.

Solution: The **Decorator pattern** solves these issues by using composition rather than inheritance to extend functionality. A set of decorator classes wraps individual components (objects), dynamically adding new behavior. These decorators follow the same interface as the components they wrap, allowing seamless behavior extension without modifying the underlying code.

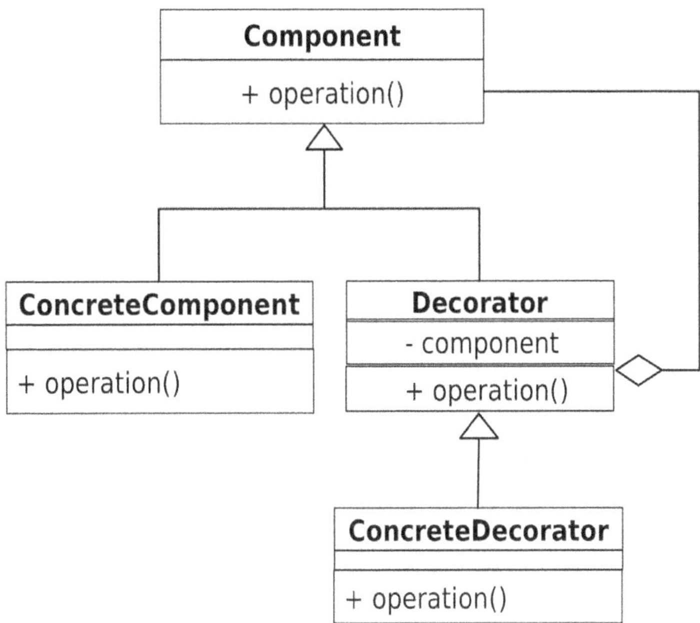

Example Implementation:

```go
// Component is the interface for the base component
type Component interface {
    Operation()
}

// ConcreteComponent is the concrete implementation of Component
type ConcreteComponent struct{}

// Operation implements the Operation method for
ConcreteComponent
func (c *ConcreteComponent) Operation() {
    fmt.Println("ConcreteComponent operation.")
}

// Decorator is the interface for the decorator
```

```go
type Decorator interface {
    Operation()
}

// BaseDecorator provides default implementation for the
Operation method
type BaseDecorator struct {
    component Component
}

// Operation implements the Operation method for BaseDecorator
func (d *BaseDecorator) Operation() {
    d.component.Operation()
}

// ConcreteDecorator1 is a concrete decorator
type ConcreteDecorator1 struct {
    BaseDecorator
}

// Operation implements the Operation method for
ConcreteDecorator1
func (d *ConcreteDecorator1) Operation() {
    fmt.Println("ConcreteDecorator1 operation start.")
    d.BaseDecorator.Operation()
    fmt.Println("ConcreteDecorator1 operation end.")
}

// ConcreteDecorator2 is another concrete decorator
type ConcreteDecorator2 struct {
    BaseDecorator
}

// Operation implements the Operation method for
ConcreteDecorator2
func (d *ConcreteDecorator2) Operation() {
    fmt.Println("ConcreteDecorator2 operation start.")
    d.BaseDecorator.Operation()
    fmt.Println("ConcreteDecorator2 operation end.")
}

// Client code
func main() {
    component := &ConcreteComponent{}
    decorator1 := &ConcreteDecorator1{BaseDecorator{component}}
    decorator2 := &ConcreteDecorator2{BaseDecorator{decorator1}}
```

```
    decorator2.Operation()
}
```

Output:

```
ConcreteDecorator2 operation start.
ConcreteDecorator1 operation start.
ConcreteComponent operation.
ConcreteDecorator1 operation end.
ConcreteDecorator2 operation end.
```

Explanation:

1. **ConcreteComponent**: Performs the core operation. The decorators extend this behavior without modifying its implementation.

2. **BaseDecorator**: Implements the **Component** interface and forwards operations to the wrapped component.

3. **ConcreteDecorator1** & **ConcreteDecorator2**: Add their own behavior before and after calling the wrapped component's operation, enhancing functionality dynamically.

4. **Client Code**: Combines the decorators, allowing them to modify the behavior of the **ConcreteComponent** dynamically.

Problem: The client wants to enhance the functionality of a simple window object by adding vertical and horizontal scroll bars. Modifying the existing **SimpleWindow** class would violate the Open/Closed Principle. The challenge is to add scroll bars to the window dynamically, without altering the class's original code.

Solution: The Decorator pattern can solve this by dynamically adding new behaviors (scroll bars) to the window object without altering its original class. The decorators wrap the SimpleWindow class to provide the additional functionality.

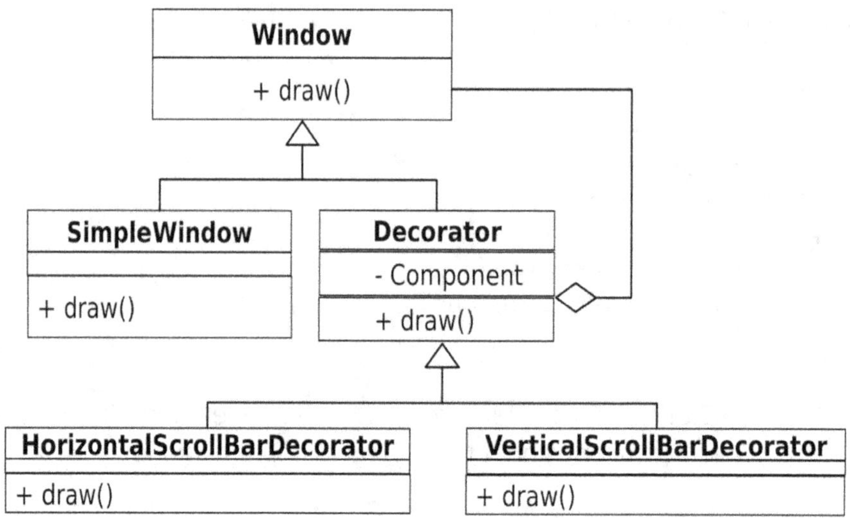

Example:

```go
// Window is the interface for windows
type Window interface {
    Draw()
}

// SimpleWindow is a simple concrete implementation of Window
type SimpleWindow struct{}

// Draw implements the Draw method for SimpleWindow
func (w *SimpleWindow) Draw() {
    fmt.Println("SimpleWindow draw.")
}

// Decorator is the interface for window decorators
type Decorator interface {
    Window
}

// BaseDecorator provides default implementation for the
Decorator interface
type BaseDecorator struct {
    component Window
}

// VerticalScrollBarDecorator is a concrete decorator for adding
a vertical scrollbar to a window
type VerticalScrollBarDecorator struct {
```

```go
        BaseDecorator
}

// Draw implements the Draw method for VerticalScrollBarDecorator
func (d *VerticalScrollBarDecorator) Draw() {
    d.component.Draw()
    fmt.Println("VerticalScrollBarDecorator draw.")
}

// HorizontalScrollBarDecorator is a concrete decorator for
adding a horizontal scrollbar to a window
type HorizontalScrollBarDecorator struct {
    BaseDecorator
}

// Draw implements the Draw method for
HorizontalScrollBarDecorator
func (d *HorizontalScrollBarDecorator) Draw() {
    d.component.Draw()
    fmt.Println("HorizontalScrollBarDecorator draw.")
}

// Client Code
func main() {
    component := &SimpleWindow{}
    decorator1 :=
&VerticalScrollBarDecorator{BaseDecorator{component}}
    decorator2 :=
&HorizontalScrollBarDecorator{BaseDecorator{decorator1}}
    decorator2.Draw()
}
```

Output:

```
SimpleWindow draw.
VerticalScrollBarDecorator draw
HorizontalScrollBarDecorator draw
```

Explanation:

1. **Window Interface**: Defines the contract for objects that can be decorated. In this example, it only includes the **draw()** method.

2. **SimpleWindow Class**: Implements the Window interface, representing the basic window without any additional features.

3. **Decorator Abstract Class**: Also implements the Window interface and serves as the base class for all decorators. It holds a reference to a

Window object and delegates the **draw()** method to the component it wraps.

4. **VerticalScrollBarDecorator and HorizontalScrollBarDecorator Classes**: These are concrete decorators that add vertical and horizontal scroll bars to the window. They extend the Decorator class and override the **draw()** method to inject their specific behavior before or after calling the **draw()** method of the wrapped component.

5. **Client Code:** In the **DecoratorPatternWindow** class, the **main()** method acts as the client code. It creates a **SimpleWindow** object and wraps it with two decorators: **VerticalScrollBarDecorator** and **HorizontalScrollBarDecorator**. When the **draw()** method is invoked on the final decorator, a chain of **draw()** calls is triggered through the decorators, each one adding its own functionality to the rendering process.

Consequences

1. **Flexible Extension**: The Decorator pattern offers flexible, dynamic behavior extension. New decorators can be added to introduce new features or combine existing ones without modifying the original class.

2. **Reduced Subclassing**: By combining decorators, the need for an explosion of subclasses is minimized, as the same functionality can be achieved through composition.

3. **Open-Closed Principle Compliance**: This pattern adheres to the Open-Closed Principle by enabling extensions to object behavior without altering existing code.

4. **Increased Complexity**: While reducing the need for subclasses, the pattern can introduce a higher number of small, individual classes, which may increase the overall complexity of the codebase.

5. **Decorator Order**: The sequence in which decorators are applied influences the final outcome. Developers must be mindful of the wrapping order to achieve the desired behavior.

6. **Performance Considerations**: Depending on the depth of the decorator chain, there may be a slight performance overhead due to the multiple levels of indirection, especially if several decorators are applied in a single object.

Flyweight Pattern

The **Flyweight design pattern** is a Structural pattern used to optimise memory usage by sharing common data among multiple objects. It is particularly useful when dealing with a large number of similar objects that have some intrinsic (invariant) state and some extrinsic (context-dependent) state. By sharing the intrinsic state, the pattern reduces the memory footprint and improves performance.

Problem: The problem that the Flyweight pattern aims to address is the excessive memory usage and inefficiency caused by creating large numbers of similar objects, each with its own unique data. This is especially common in situations where objects have some shared characteristics and a significant portion of their state can be reused across multiple instances.

Solution: The solution involves creating a FlyweightFactory that manages a pool of shared flyweight objects. These objects are shared by multiple clients, and each object is designed to be immutable and stateless. This means that the object's properties cannot be changed once it has been created, which makes it safe for sharing. When a client requests a flyweight object, the factory class checks if an instance of that object already exists in the pool. If so, it returns the existing object. If not, it creates a new object, adds it to the pool, and returns it to the client.

By using the Flyweight pattern, an application can reduce memory usage and improve performance, especially in situations where a large number of objects are created and used repeatedly. However, it's important to note that the pattern may not be suitable for all situations, and careful consideration should be given to the specific requirements of the application before implementing it.

The Flyweight pattern proposes dividing an object's state into two parts:

1. **Intrinsic State:** Represents the data that is shared among multiple objects and remains constant throughout their lifetime.

2. **Extrinsic State:** Represents the data that is unique to each individual object and can vary depending on the context.

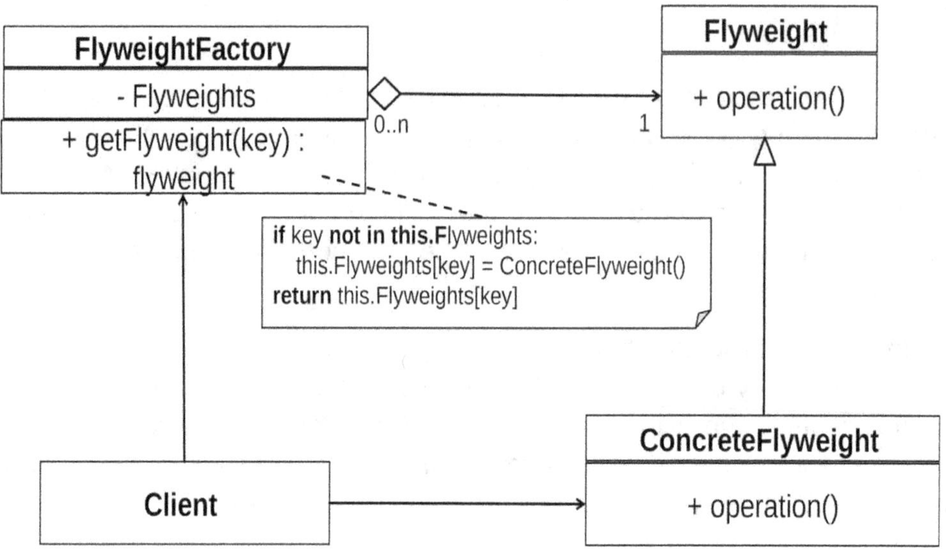

Example implementation:

```go
// Flyweight interface
type Flyweight interface {
    Operation(extrinsicState interface{})
}

// ConcreteFlyweight type
type ConcreteFlyweight struct {
    intrinsicState string
}

func (cf *ConcreteFlyweight) Operation(extrinsicState
interface{}) {
    fmt.Println("Operation inside concrete flyweight")
}

// FlyweightFactory type
type FlyweightFactory struct {
    flyweights map[string]Flyweight
}

func NewFlyweightFactory() *FlyweightFactory {
    return &FlyweightFactory{
        flyweights: make(map[string]Flyweight),
    }
}
```

```go
func (ff *FlyweightFactory) GetFlyweight(key string) Flyweight {
    if flyweight, exists := ff.flyweights[key]; exists {
        return flyweight
    }

    flyweight := &ConcreteFlyweight{intrinsicState: key}
    ff.flyweights[key] = flyweight
    return flyweight
}

func (ff *FlyweightFactory) GetCount() int {
    return len(ff.flyweights)
}

// Client Code
func main() {
    factory := NewFlyweightFactory()
    flyweight1 := factory.GetFlyweight("key")
    flyweight2 := factory.GetFlyweight("key")
    flyweight1.Operation(nil)
    fmt.Println(flyweight1, flyweight2)
    fmt.Println("Object count:", factory.GetCount())
}
```

Output:

```
Operation inside concrete flyweight
&{key} &{key}
Object count: 1
```

Explanation:

1. **Flyweight Interface**: Declares an **Operation()** method that will be implemented by concrete flyweights.

2. **ConcreteFlyweight**: Implements the **Flyweight** interface and provides the intrinsic state that is shared across objects.

3. **FlyweightFactory**: Manages the creation and reuse of flyweight objects. It keeps a map of flyweights and retrieves or creates them based on a key.

4. **Client Code**: The client requests flyweights from the factory using a specific key. The output demonstrates that both **flyweight1** and **flyweight2** refer to the same object, reducing memory usage. The factory's **GetCount()** method shows how many objects have been created.

Problem: The task is to efficiently create and manage random rectangles of various colours and positions. The challenge lies in minimizing memory usage by reusing rectangles with the same colour instead of creating new instances for each one.

Solution: The Flyweight pattern can be applied to share rectangles of the same colour, significantly reducing the memory footprint and optimizing object creation.

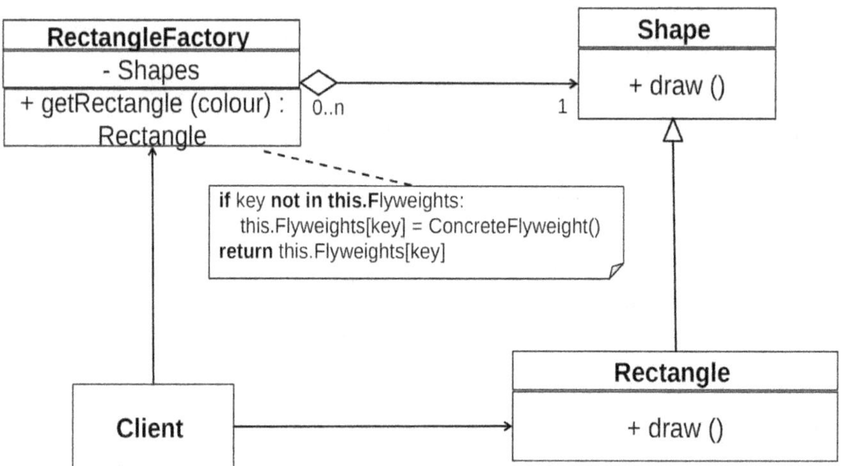

Example Implementation:

```go
// Shape interface
type Shape interface {
    Draw(x1, y1, x2, y2 int)
}

// Rectangle type
type Rectangle struct {
    colour string // Intrinsic State
}

func NewRectangle(colour string) *Rectangle {
    return &Rectangle{colour: colour}
}

func (r *Rectangle) Draw(x1, y1, x2, y2 int) {
    fmt.Printf("Draw rectangle colour:%s topleft: (%d,%d)
rightBottom: (%d,%d)\n", r.colour, x1, y1, x2, y2)
```

```go
}

// RectangleFactory type
type RectangleFactory struct {
    shapes map[string]Shape
}

func NewRectangleFactory() *RectangleFactory {
    return &RectangleFactory{
        shapes: make(map[string]Shape),
    }
}

func (rf *RectangleFactory) GetRectangle(colour string) Shape {
    if shape, exists := rf.shapes[colour]; exists {
        return shape
    }
    shape := NewRectangle(colour)
    rf.shapes[colour] = shape
    return shape
}

func (rf *RectangleFactory) GetCount() int {
    return len(rf.shapes)
}

// Client Code
func main() {
    factory := NewRectangleFactory()
    for i := 0; i < 1000; i++ {
        colour := fmt.Sprintf("%d", rand.Intn(1000))
        rect := factory.GetRectangle(colour)
        rect.Draw(rand.Intn(100), rand.Intn(100),
            rand.Intn(100), rand.Intn(100))
    }
    fmt.Println(factory.GetCount())
}
```

Explanation:

1. **Shape Interface**: Defines the **Draw()** method for all shapes.

2. **Rectangle Class**: Implements the **Shape** interface and draws a rectangle, displaying its colour and coordinates.

3. **RectangleFactory**: Acts as the flyweight factory, managing and reusing rectangle instances based on their colour. It returns an existing rectangle from the pool if available, or creates and stores a new one.

4. **Client Code**: Generates 1000 random rectangles, reusing rectangles with the same colour to optimize memory usage.

Consequences

The Flyweight pattern offers several advantages, but also has some trade-offs:

1. **Memory Efficiency**: By sharing intrinsic state across multiple objects, the pattern significantly reduces memory usage, making the application more efficient in handling large numbers of similar objects.

2. **Performance Improvement**: Since flyweight objects are reused rather than recreated, the pattern minimizes object creation and initialization overhead, resulting in better performance, particularly when managing a large number of objects.

3. **Trade-off with Processing Time**: While memory usage is optimized, managing and accessing shared flyweight objects can introduce additional processing overhead. In some cases, the extra work required to manage flyweights might slightly slow down execution. However, this trade-off is often worthwhile when memory optimization is critical.

4. **Thread Safety Considerations**: In multithreaded environments, care must be taken to ensure that flyweight objects are accessed safely. If multiple threads attempt to access or modify the same flyweight object, proper synchronization mechanisms, such as locks, need to be in place to prevent data inconsistencies or corruption.

5. **Immutable Data**: Flyweight objects are shared across different contexts, meaning that modifying their intrinsic state could affect all clients using them. To avoid unintended side effects, flyweight objects should either be immutable or their state should be carefully managed to prevent changes that impact other parts of the program.

Facade Pattern

The **Facade design pattern** is a structural design pattern that provides a simplified interface to a complex system, making it easier to interact with. It is commonly used to hide the complexities of a subsystem and present a unified, straightforward interface to client code. In this pattern, a single class serves as a simple interface to a group of classes, allowing the client to access the functionality of these classes through this facade. The facade class simplifies the interface and reduces system complexity, making it more user-friendly.

Problem: In software development, complex systems often consist of multiple interdependent classes and subsystems. When clients interact directly with these subsystems, it can result in tight coupling, increased complexity, and difficulty in maintaining and understanding the codebase. Any changes to the subsystems can also ripple through to the client code, making it challenging to adapt to modifications.

Solution: The Facade design pattern introduces a new class, the "Facade," which acts as an entry point to the subsystems. The facade provides a high-level interface that shields clients from the underlying complexities of the system. It encapsulates the interaction with the subsystems, offering a unified interface that clients can easily work with.

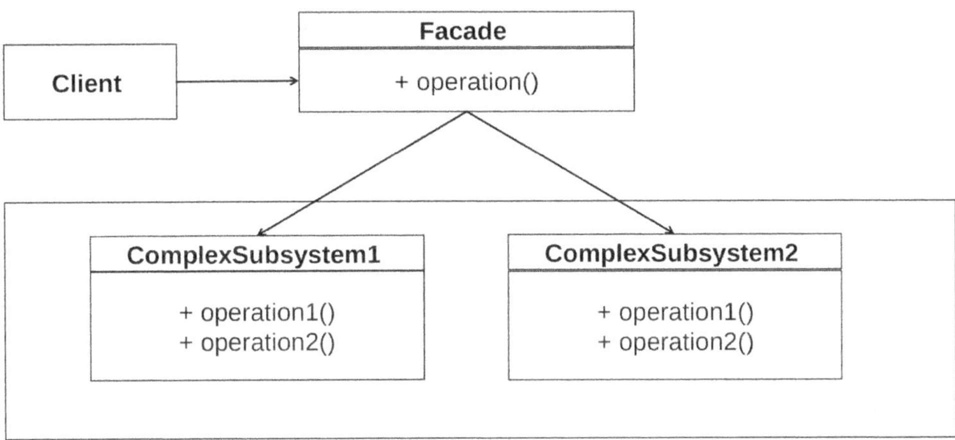

Example Implementation:

```go
// Subsystem1 represents the first subsystem
type Subsystem1 struct{}

// Operation1 implements the first operation of Subsystem1
func (s *Subsystem1) Operation1() {
    fmt.Println("Subsystem1 operation1")
}

// Operation2 implements the second operation of Subsystem1
func (s *Subsystem1) Operation2() {
    fmt.Println("Subsystem1 operation2")
}
```

```go
// Subsystem2 represents the second subsystem
type Subsystem2 struct{}

// Operation1 implements the first operation of Subsystem2
func (s *Subsystem2) Operation1() {
    fmt.Println("Subsystem2 operation1")
}

// Operation2 implements the second operation of Subsystem2
func (s *Subsystem2) Operation2() {
    fmt.Println("Subsystem2 operation2")
}

// SystemManagerFacade represents the facade for the subsystems
type SystemManagerFacade struct {
    subsystem1 *Subsystem1
    subsystem2 *Subsystem2
}

// NewSystemManagerFacade creates a new SystemManagerFacade
func NewSystemManagerFacade() *SystemManagerFacade {
    return &SystemManagerFacade{
        subsystem1: &Subsystem1{},
        subsystem2: &Subsystem2{},
    }
}

// Operation invokes operations on subsystems
func (f *SystemManagerFacade) Operation() {
    f.subsystem1.Operation1()
    f.subsystem1.Operation2()
    f.subsystem2.Operation1()
    f.subsystem2.Operation2()
}

// Client Code
func main() {
    facade := NewSystemManagerFacade()
    facade.Operation()
}
```

Explanation:

1. **Subsystem1** and **Subsystem2**: These classes represent complex subsystems. Each subsystem has two operations (**Operation1** and **Operation2**).

2. **SystemManagerFacade**: This class acts as the facade. It initializes instances of **Subsystem1** and **Subsystem2** in its constructor. The **Operation()** method is the simplified interface through which clients interact with the subsystems.

3. **Operation()**: This method, provided by the facade, internally calls the corresponding methods of **Subsystem1** and **Subsystem2** in a coordinated manner to execute the desired functionality.

4. **Client Code**: The client creates an instance of **SystemManagerFacade** (the facade) and interacts with the subsystems through the **Operation()** method, without needing to know the details of the interactions between **Subsystem1** and **Subsystem2**.

Consequences

1. **Simplified Interface**: The Facade pattern provides an easy-to-understand interface that hides subsystem complexities, simplifying system use for clients.

2. **Decoupling**: Introducing a facade decouples client code from the internal subsystems, reducing dependencies and allowing for more flexible development of both client and subsystems.

3. **Improved Code Organization**: The pattern enhances code organization by separating complex subsystem code into a dedicated facade class, promoting a clear separation of concerns and improving maintainability.

4. **Encapsulation**: The facade encapsulates interactions with subsystems, ensuring a controlled and consistent interface. Changes to subsystems are confined within the facade, minimizing their impact on client code.

5. **Reduced Learning Curve**: Developers working with the facade don't need to understand the intricacies of the entire system, lowering the learning curve for new team members.

6. **Trade-offs**: While the Facade pattern simplifies system usage, it may obscure some advanced subsystem functionalities. Striking a balance between simplicity and exposing enough capabilities for specialized use cases is essential.

Proxy Pattern

The **Proxy design pattern** is a structural design pattern that provides a surrogate or placeholder for another object, controlling access to it. By introducing an extra layer of indirection, you can manage how and when the real object is accessed. This pattern is particularly useful when you need to add extra functionality or control access to an object without modifying its core logic.

The Proxy pattern is beneficial in scenarios where creating or initializing the actual object is resource-intensive, or when you need to protect the object from unauthorized access or manipulation. By using a proxy, client code can interact with the real object indirectly, without directly handling its creation or initialization.

Problem: The Proxy pattern addresses several common scenarios:

1. **Access Control**: You may need to restrict access to an object, enforcing authentication and authorization mechanisms.

2. **Lazy Initialization**: Postpone the creation or loading of a resource-heavy object until it's actually needed, optimizing performance and resource usage.

3. **Remote Proxy**: In distributed systems or remote services, a proxy can represent an object located in a different address space.

4. **Logging and Auditing**: You might want to log method calls or track access patterns for debugging or audit purposes.

Solution: The Proxy pattern introduces a new class, the Proxy, which acts as an intermediary between the client and the actual subject (the object being proxied). The Proxy implements the same interface as the real subject, allowing clients to interact with it seamlessly, without knowing whether they're dealing with the actual object or a proxy.

The Proxy can add additional operations before or after forwarding requests to the real subject. Depending on the use case, different types of proxies may be implemented:

1. **Virtual Proxy**: Delays the creation of the real subject until it's needed, avoiding the unnecessary instantiation of resource-heavy objects.

2. **Remote Proxy**: Represents a real subject located in a different address space (e.g., a remote server).

3. **Protection Proxy**: Controls access by adding authentication or authorization checks before forwarding the request.

4. **Logging Proxy**: Logs method calls and tracks other relevant information for auditing or debugging purposes.

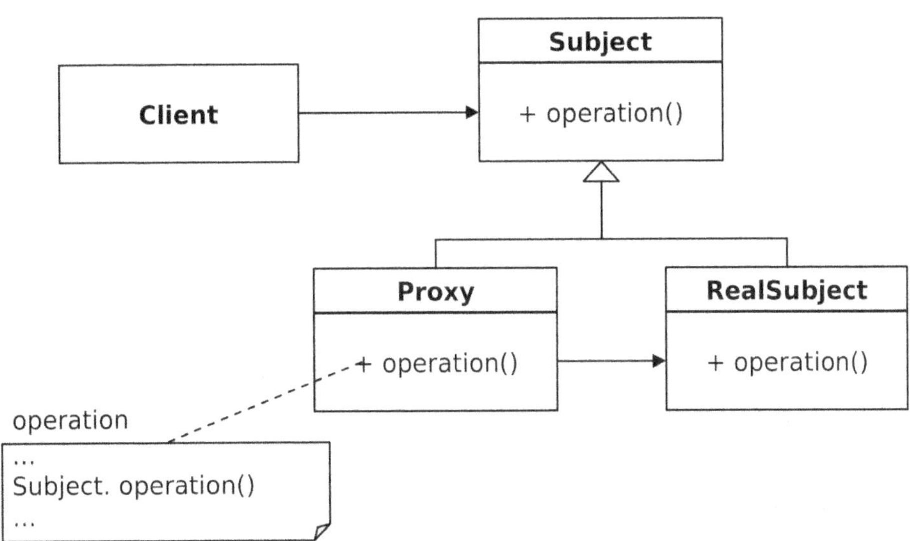

Example of the Proxy Pattern:

```go
// Subject is an interface representing a subject.
type Subject interface {
    Request()
}

// RealSubject is a concrete implementation of the Subject
interface.
type RealSubject struct{}

func (rs *RealSubject) Request() {
    fmt.Println("Concrete Subject Request Method")
}

// Proxy is a proxy implementation of the Subject interface.
type Proxy struct {
    concSub *RealSubject
}

func NewProxy() *Proxy {
    return &Proxy{
        concSub: &RealSubject{},
```

```go
        }
}

func (p *Proxy) Request() {
    p.concSub.Request()
}

// Client code
func main() {
    proxy := NewProxy()
    proxy.Request()
}
```

Output:

```
Concrete Subject Request Method
```

Explanation:

1. The **RealSubject** class represents the actual object that the client wishes to access. The **Proxy** class acts as a surrogate, managing access to the RealSubject.

2. When the **Proxy** is created, it also initializes the **RealSubject**. The **Proxy** then handles the client request and delegates the actual work to the **RealSubject**.

3. In the client code, the **Proxy** is created and its **Request()** method is called. The **Proxy** controls access to the **RealSubject**, so the client does not need to manage the creation or initialization of the **RealSubject** directly.

Problem : Implement the Proxy design pattern with lazy initialization. The problem focuses on creating a **Proxy** that acts as an intermediary for the **RealSubject**. The goal is for the **Proxy** to control access to the **RealSubject** and ensure that the **RealSubject** is instantiated only when necessary, reducing resource overhead and improving performance.

Solution: The solution involves the following steps:

1. **Define the Subject Interface**: This interface will represent the abstract contract that both the **RealSubject** and the **Proxy** will implement.

2. **Create the RealSubject**: This is the actual object that performs the real work. However, since it might be resource-intensive to create, we want to instantiate it only when needed.

3. **Implement the Proxy**: The **Proxy** will manage the access to the **RealSubject**. It ensures that the **RealSubject** is lazily instantiated only when the client explicitly calls the **Request()** method.

Example of the proxy pattern lazy initialization:

```go
// Subject is an interface representing a subject.
type Subject interface {
    Request()
}

// RealSubject is a concrete implementation of the Subject
interface.
type RealSubject struct{}

func (rs *RealSubject) Request() {
    fmt.Println("Concrete Subject Request Method")
}

// Proxy is a proxy implementation of the Subject interface.
type Proxy struct {
    subject Subject
}

func (p *Proxy) Request() {
    if p.subject == nil {
        p.subject = &RealSubject{} // Lazy Init
    }
    p.subject.Request()
}

// Client code
func main() {
    proxy := &Proxy{}
    proxy.Request()
}
```

Explanation:

1. **Subject Interface**: The **Subject** interface defines a single method **Request()** that both **RealSubject** and **Proxy** must implement.

2. **RealSubject Class**: **RealSubject** is the class that implements **Subject**. This is where the actual business logic resides, but it might be resource-intensive to create upfront.

3. **Proxy Class**: The **Proxy** class also implements **Subject** and controls access to the **RealSubject**. It contains a reference to **RealSubject**, but **RealSubject** is only created the first time **Request()** is called. This is the lazy initialization mechanism.

4. **Client Code**: In the **main** function, the client creates an instance of **Proxy** and calls its **Request()** method. The **Proxy** handles the creation of **RealSubject** and forwards the request.

Problem: The task is to implement the Proxy design pattern by creating a **LazyBookParserProxy**, which serves as a surrogate for the **ConcreteBookParser**. The **ConcreteBookParser** is a resource-heavy object that calculates the number of pages in a book. The goal is to delay the instantiation and initialization of the **ConcreteBookParser** until the number of pages is actually requested, optimizing performance and resource usage.

Solution: The solution involves creating a **LazyBookParserProxy** class that implements the **BookParser** interface. This proxy acts as a placeholder for the **ConcreteBookParser**. The **ConcreteBookParser** is only instantiated (and its heavy calculations are performed) when the client specifically requests the number of pages. Until that moment, the proxy defers the object creation.

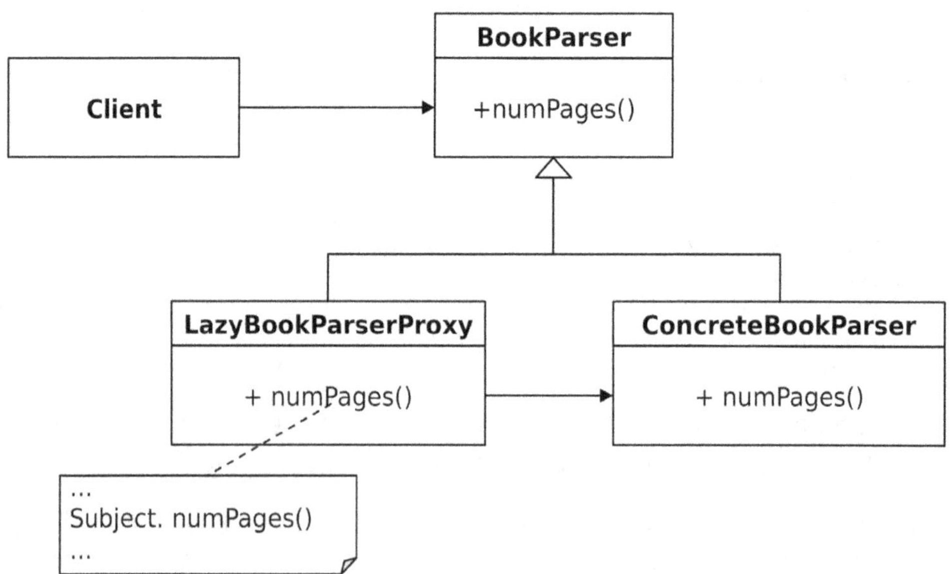

Lazy Initialization Example Using the Proxy Pattern:

```go
// BookParser is an interface representing a book parser.
type BookParser interface {
    NumPages() int
}


// ConcreteBookParser is a concrete implementation of the
BookParser interface.
type ConcreteBookParser struct {
    book        string
    numOfPages int
}


func NewConcreteBookParser(book string) *ConcreteBookParser {
    fmt.Println("Concrete Subject Request Method")
    // Number of pages calculation heavy operation.
    // Suppose this calculation comes to 1000 pages.
    return &ConcreteBookParser{
        book:        book,
        numOfPages: 1000,
    }
}


func (cbp *ConcreteBookParser) NumPages() int {
    fmt.Println("Concrete Subject Request Method")
    return cbp.numOfPages
}


// LazyBookParserProxy is a proxy implementation of the
BookParser interface.
type LazyBookParserProxy struct {
    book     string
    subject BookParser
}


func (lbp *LazyBookParserProxy) NumPages() int {
    if lbp.subject == nil {
        lbp.subject = NewConcreteBookParser(lbp.book)
    }
    return lbp.subject.NumPages()
}


// Client code
func main() {
    proxy := &LazyBookParserProxy{book: "LOTR"}
```

```
    fmt.Println(proxy.NumPages())
}
```

Explanation:

1. This code demonstrates the Proxy design pattern, where the **LazyBookParserProxy** acts as a proxy for the **ConcreteBookParser**. The **ConcreteBookParser** is a resource-intensive object that takes time to instantiate and is only created when it's actually needed. The **LazyBookParserProxy**, on the other hand, is a lightweight object used to manage access to the **ConcreteBookParser**.

2. The **BookParser** is an interface that both the **ConcreteBookParser** and **LazyBookParserProxy** implement. While the **ConcreteBookParser** performs the actual task of calculating the number of pages in a book, the **LazyBookParserProxy** delays the instantiation of the **ConcreteBookParser** until its **NumPages()** method is called for the first time.

3. In the client code, an instance of the **LazyBookParserProxy** is created, and when the **NumPages()** method is invoked, the proxy creates the **ConcreteBookParser** and returns the number of pages.

Consequences

Consequences of the Proxy Pattern:

1. **Enhanced Security**: The Protection Proxy enables you to implement access control mechanisms, offering an additional layer of security for the real object.

2. **Performance Optimization**: By using a Virtual Proxy, you can postpone the creation or initialization of the real object until it's actually required, enhancing performance and resource efficiency.

3. **Abstraction of Remote Resources**: Remote Proxies hide the complexity of interacting with remote resources, making them appear local to the client, thereby simplifying their use.

4. **Flexibility**: The Proxy pattern allows for modification or extension of the behavior of the real object without altering its core implementation, promoting separation of concerns and code reusability.

5. **Resource Management**: Proxies can help manage shared resources by controlling their usage and avoiding unnecessary resource allocation.

Summary

This chapter explored Structural Patterns, which focus on organizing classes and objects to form flexible and efficient structures. These patterns help manage relationships between components, simplify code organization, and enhance maintainability. Key patterns discussed include:

- **Adapter Pattern**: Allows incompatible interfaces to work together by wrapping one class inside an adapter that converts its interface to match what the client expects.
- **Bridge Pattern**: Decouples an abstraction from its implementation, allowing them to vary independently, reducing the complexity of managing multiple variations.
- **Composite Pattern**: Lets you treat individual objects and compositions of objects uniformly, useful for representing part-whole hierarchies.
- **Decorator Pattern**: Adds behavior to objects dynamically at runtime without modifying their code, providing a flexible alternative to subclassing.
- **Facade Pattern**: Simplifies interactions with complex subsystems by providing a single unified interface, making the system easier to use and understand.
- **Flyweight Pattern**: Reduces memory usage by sharing common data among multiple objects, ideal for large numbers of similar objects.
- **Proxy Pattern**: Controls access to objects, adding a level of indirection that can be used for lazy initialization, access control, or logging.

Exercises

1. **Adapter Pattern Problem**: You have an existing media player that plays audio files in MP3 format, but you need to integrate it with a library that only supports WAV files. Implement an adapter to allow the MP3 player to play WAV files seamlessly.

   Instructions:

   - Create an adapter class using the Adapter pattern.

   - The adapter should convert WAV files into a format that the MP3 player can handle.

   - Demonstrate how the adapter allows the MP3 player to play WAV files without modifying the original MP3 player code.

2. **Bridge Pattern Problem**: You are developing a drawing application that can render shapes in different colours and on different platforms (e.g., Windows, macOS, Linux). Use the Bridge Pattern to decouple the shape abstraction from the rendering implementation.

Instructions:

- Design a class hierarchy using the Bridge Pattern to separate shape abstractions (e.g., Circle, Rectangle) from platform-specific renderers.

- Implement the shape and renderer classes, ensuring they can be varied independently.

- Provide examples showing how new shapes and platforms can be added without modifying existing code.

3. **Composite Pattern Problem**: Develop a file system simulation where directories can contain both files and other directories. Each file and directory should have a method to display its name and size. Use the Composite Pattern to treat files and directories uniformly.

Instructions:

- Implement a File class and a Directory class using the Composite pattern.

- Ensure that directories can contain both files and other directories.

- Demonstrate how the Composite pattern allows for uniform treatment of files and directories, enabling operations like displaying contents recursively.

4. **Decorator Pattern Problem**: You have a basic TextEditor class with a display() method to show text. Extend its functionality using the Decorator Pattern to add features such as spell-checking, text formatting, and syntax highlighting.

Instructions:

- Implement decorators that can add spell-checking, text formatting, and syntax highlighting to the TextEditor.

- Apply these decorators dynamically at runtime to enhance the text editor's functionality.

- Demonstrate how different combinations of decorators can be applied to the TextEditor.

5. **Facade Pattern Problem**: You are working with a home automation system that includes multiple subsystems (e.g., lighting, heating, security). Implement a facade to provide a simplified interface to control the entire system.

   Instructions:

   - Create a HomeAutomationFacade class that offers simplified methods like activateNightMode() to control various subsystems.

   - Implement the subsystems and ensure the facade provides a unified and straightforward interface.

   - Show how the facade simplifies interactions with the complex subsystems of the home automation system.

6. **Flyweight Pattern Problem**: You are designing a graphical editor where you need to draw a large number of similar shapes (e.g., circles). Use the Flyweight Pattern to share common data among multiple shape objects while allowing for unique positions.

   Instructions:

   - Implement the Flyweight pattern to share properties like colour and radius among shape objects.

   - Ensure that each shape object can still have a unique position.

   - Demonstrate how this pattern reduces memory usage while maintaining unique attributes for each shape.

7. **Proxy Pattern Problem**: Develop an image viewer application that loads large images lazily (only when they are actually needed). Implement a virtual proxy to handle this lazy loading.

   Instructions:

   - Create a proxy class that initially displays a placeholder image.

   - Implement lazy loading of the actual image in the background when needed.

○ Demonstrate how the proxy controls access to the image object and shows the loading process with the placeholder.

Solution of Exercises

Solution 1: Adapter pattern

```go
type MP3Player interface {
    PlayMP3(fileName string)
}

type MyMP3Player struct{}

func (m *MyMP3Player) PlayMP3(fileName string) {
    fmt.Printf("Playing MP3: %s\n", fileName)
}

type WAVPlayer interface {
    PlayWAV(fileName string)
}

type WAVtoMP3Adapter struct {
    wavPlayer WAVPlayer
}

func (adapter *WAVtoMP3Adapter) PlayMP3(fileName string) {
    fmt.Printf("Converting WAV to MP3: %s\n", fileName)
    adapter.wavPlayer.PlayWAV(fileName)
}

func main() {
    adapter := &WAVtoMP3Adapter{wavPlayer: &MyWAVPlayer{}}
    adapter.PlayMP3("music.wav")
}
```

Solution 2: .Bridge Pattern

```go
type Renderer interface {
    RenderCircle(radius int)
}

type Circle struct {
    radius    int
    renderer Renderer
```

```go
}

func (c *Circle) Draw() {
      c.renderer.RenderCircle(c.radius)
}

func main() {
      (&Circle{5, &WindowsRenderer{}}).Draw()
      (&Circle{10, &LinuxRenderer{}}).Draw()
}
```

Solution 3: Composite Pattern.

```go
type FileSystemComponent interface {
      DisplayInfo()
}

type File struct { name string; size int }

func (f *File) DisplayInfo() {
      fmt.Printf("File: %s, Size: %dKB\n", f.name, f.size)
}

type Directory struct {
      name string
      components []FileSystemComponent
}

func (d *Directory) Add(c FileSystemComponent) {
      d.components = append(d.components, c)
}

func (d *Directory) DisplayInfo() {
      fmt.Printf("Dir: %s\n", d.name)
      for _, c := range d.components { c.DisplayInfo() }
}

func main() {
      root := &Directory{name: "Root"}
      root.Add(&File{"file1.txt", 10})
      root.DisplayInfo()
}
```

Solution 4: Decorator pattern.

```go
type TextEditor interface { Display() }

type BasicTextEditor struct{}

func (b *BasicTextEditor) Display() {
    fmt.Println("Text displayed.")
}

type SpellCheckDecorator struct { editor TextEditor }

func (s *SpellCheckDecorator) Display() {
    s.editor.Display();
    fmt.Println("Spell check on.")
}

func main() {
    editor := &SpellCheckDecorator{&BasicTextEditor{}}
    editor.Display()
}
```

Solution 5: Facade pattern.

```go
type LightingSystem struct{}
func (l *LightingSystem) Off() { fmt.Println("Lights off.") }

type HomeAutomationFacade struct { lighting *LightingSystem }

func (h *HomeAutomationFacade) ActivateNightMode(){
    h.lighting.Off()
}

func main() {
    facade := &HomeAutomationFacade{&LightingSystem{}}
    facade.ActivateNightMode()
}
```

Solution 6: Flyweight Pattern.

```go
type Shape interface { Draw(x, y int) }
type Circle struct { colour string; radius int }
func (c *Circle) Draw(x, y int) {
    fmt.Printf("Drawing circle at (%d, %d) colour: %s\n", x, y,
c.colour)
```

```go
}

func main() {
      circle := &Circle{colour: "red", radius: 10}
      circle.Draw(10, 10)
}
```

Solution 7: Proxy pattern.

```go
type Image interface { Display() }

type ProxyImage struct {
      realImage *RealImage;
      fileName string
}

func (proxy *ProxyImage) Display() {
      if proxy.realImage == nil {
            proxy.realImage = &RealImage{fileName:
proxy.fileName}
            fmt.Println("Loading image...")
      }
      fmt.Println("Displaying image.")
}

func main() {
      image := &ProxyImage{fileName: "large_image.jpg"}
      image.Display()
}
```

BEHAVIOURAL PATTERNS

Behavioural design patterns focus on how objects interact and communicate within a software system. These patterns define the responsibility and collaboration between objects, making the system more flexible and adaptable to change.

We begin with the **Chain of Responsibility Pattern**, which creates a series of handler objects. Each handler sequentially attempts to process a request. If one handler cannot handle the request, it passes it along to the next handler in the chain. This pattern decouples the sender and receiver, allowing multiple objects to potentially handle the request.

Next is the **Command Pattern**, which encapsulates a command as an object, enabling its execution, undoing, or queuing. This approach decouples the sender from the receiver and is particularly useful for implementing undo functionality.

Following that is the **Interpreter Pattern**, which provides a way to evaluate language grammars or expressions. It involves defining a representation of a language's grammar and implementing an interpreter to parse and evaluate expressions based on this grammar.

The **Iterator Pattern** provides a standard way to access elements of a collection sequentially without exposing its internal structure. It decouples the traversal logic from the collection, making the code more flexible and reusable.

Next, the **Mediator Pattern** introduces an object that manages communication between a set of objects (referred to as colleagues). Instead of direct communication, colleagues send messages via the mediator, promoting loose coupling and centralized control.

The **Memento Pattern** captures an object's internal state, allowing it to be saved and restored later. This pattern is useful for implementing undo functionality or maintaining a history of changes.

The **Observer Pattern** establishes a dependency between objects so that when one object changes state, all dependent objects are automatically notified and updated. This promotes loose coupling and enhances system maintainability.

The **State Pattern** allows an object to alter its behavior based on its internal state. Different states are represented by separate classes, enabling the object to transition between behaviors dynamically.

With the **Strategy Pattern**, a family of algorithms is defined, each encapsulated in its own class, making them interchangeable. This pattern allows clients to select from various algorithms without modifying the structure of the client itself.

The **Template Method** Pattern defines the framework of an algorithm in a superclass, while allowing subclasses to override specific steps. This promotes code reuse and provides a structure for implementing algorithms with variations.

Lastly, the **Visitor Pattern** separates operations from the object structure by defining visitor classes that encapsulate the operations. Objects then accept these visitors, allowing them to perform operations without modifying the object's structure.

Chain of Responsibility Pattern

The **Chain of Responsibility** pattern allows a request to be passed through a chain of objects until one of them handles it. Each object in the chain can either process the request or pass it along to the next object. This decouples the sender of the request from the receiver, making the system more flexible.

Problem: In tightly coupled systems, the sender knows exactly which receiver will handle the request, making it difficult to modify or extend the handling process. If multiple receivers can handle the request, the system becomes rigid and harder to maintain.

Solution: By promoting loose coupling, the Chain of Responsibility pattern allows multiple objects the opportunity to handle a request. The sender does not need to know which object will process the request, leading to a more flexible and extendable design.

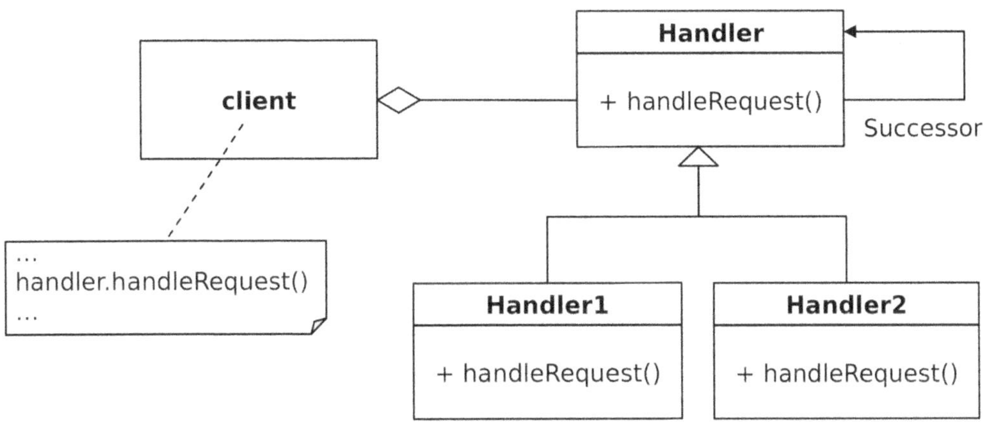

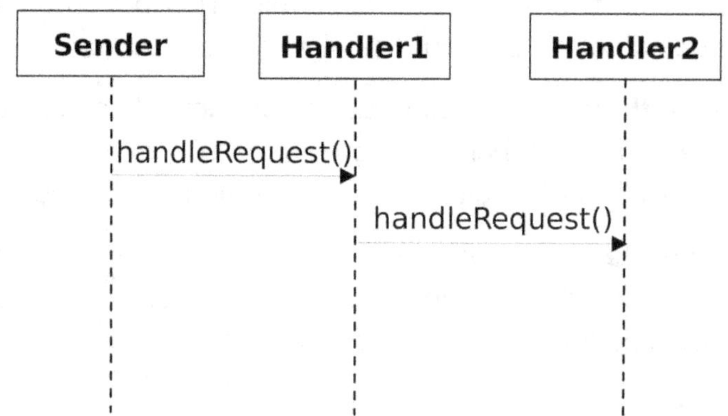

Example Implementation:

```go
// Handler defines the interface for handling requests
type Handler interface {
    HandleRequest(request string)
    SetSuccessor(successor Handler)
}

// BaseHandler implements the basic handler structure
type BaseHandler struct {
    successor Handler
}

// SetSuccessor sets the successor handler
func (h *BaseHandler) SetSuccessor(successor Handler) {
    h.successor = successor
}

// ConcreteHandler1 handles request1
type ConcreteHandler1 struct {
    *BaseHandler
}

// HandleRequest handles the request
func (ch1 *ConcreteHandler1) HandleRequest(request string) {
    if request == "request1" {
        fmt.Println("ConcreteHandler1 handles the request1.")
    } else if ch1.successor != nil {
        ch1.successor.HandleRequest(request)
    }
}
```

```go
// ConcreteHandler2 handles request2
type ConcreteHandler2 struct {
    *BaseHandler
}

// HandleRequest handles the request
func (ch2 *ConcreteHandler2) HandleRequest(request string) {
    if request == "request2" {
        fmt.Println("ConcreteHandler2 handles the request2.")
    } else if ch2.successor != nil {
        ch2.successor.HandleRequest(request)
    }
}

// ConcreteHandler3 handles request3
type ConcreteHandler3 struct {
    *BaseHandler
}

// HandleRequest handles the request
func (ch3 *ConcreteHandler3) HandleRequest(request string) {
    if request == "request3" {
        fmt.Println("ConcreteHandler3 handles the request3.")
    } else if ch3.successor != nil {
        ch3.successor.HandleRequest(request)
    }
}

// Client code
func main() {
    ch1 := &ConcreteHandler1{&BaseHandler{nil}}
    ch2 := &ConcreteHandler2{&BaseHandler{ch1}}
    ch3 := &ConcreteHandler3{&BaseHandler{ch2}}

    ch3.HandleRequest("request1")
    ch3.HandleRequest("request2")
    ch3.HandleRequest("request3")
    ch3.HandleRequest("request4")
}
```

Output:

```
ConcreteHandler1 handles the request1.
ConcreteHandler2 handles the request2.
ConcreteHandler3 handles the request3.
```

Explanation:

1. **Handler Interface**: The **Handler** interface defines the methods for handling requests and setting successors.

2. **BaseHandler**: This class provides the common functionality for managing the successor.

3. **Concrete Handlers**: Each concrete handler class (e.g., **ConcreteHandler1**, **ConcreteHandler2**, etc.) implements request processing and forwards unhandled requests to the next handler in the chain.

4. **Client Code**: Handlers are chained, and the client makes a request to the first handler, which may handle it or pass it down the chain.

Problem: You need to implement an ATM cash withdrawal system that processes withdrawal requests using a combination of available denominations (e.g., 1000, 100, 50, 10). The objective is to dispense the required cash using the fewest possible notes. If the current handler cannot fully process the request (due to an incomplete amount for its denomination), it should pass the remaining balance to the next handler in the chain.

The challenge is to structure the system in a way that minimizes tight coupling between the request and its handlers, allowing flexibility in adding or modifying denominations in the future. The Chain of Responsibility pattern provides a suitable solution to handle this scenario efficiently.

Solution: The Chain of Responsibility design pattern allows a request to pass through a chain of handlers. Each handler processes the request partially (dispensing its denomination) and passes the remaining balance to the next handler in the chain.

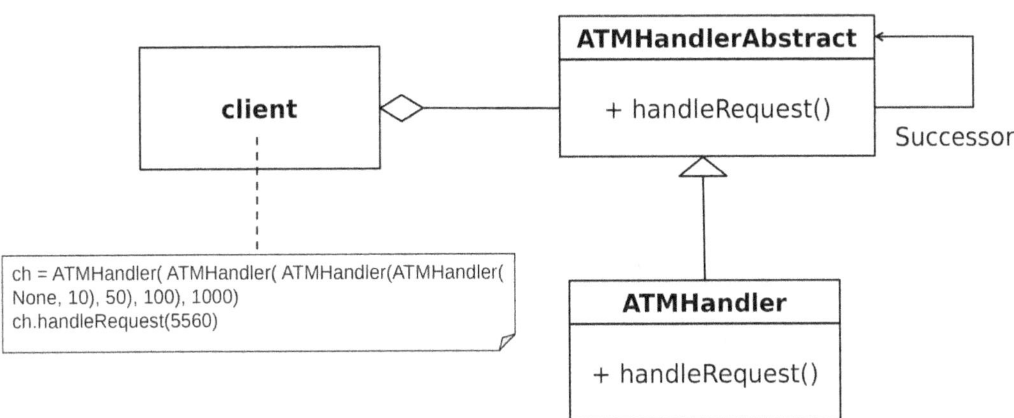

Example implementation of the Chain of Responsibility pattern :

```go
// ATMHandler interface
type ATMHandler interface {
    handleRequest(amount int)
}


// ATMHandlerConcrete struct
type ATMHandlerConcrete struct {
    successor      ATMHandler
    denomination   int
}


// NewATMHandlerConcrete constructor
func NewATMHandlerConcrete(successor ATMHandler, denomination
int) *ATMHandlerConcrete {
    return &ATMHandlerConcrete{
        successor:     successor,
        denomination: denomination,
    }
}


// handleRequest method for ATMHandlerConcrete
func (ahc *ATMHandlerConcrete) handleRequest(amount int) {
    q := amount / ahc.denomination
    r := amount % ahc.denomination

    if q != 0 {
        fmt.Printf("%d notes of %d\n", q, ahc.denomination)
    }

    if r != 0 && ahc.successor != nil {
        ahc.successor.handleRequest(r)
    }
```

```
}

// Client Code
func main() {
    ch := NewATMHandlerConcrete(
        NewATMHandlerConcrete(
            NewATMHandlerConcrete(
                NewATMHandlerConcrete(nil, 10),
                50,),100,),1000,)
    ch.handleRequest(5560)
}
```

Output:

```
5 notes of 1000
5 notes of 100
1 notes of 50
1 notes of 10
```

Explanation:

1. **ATMHandler Interface**: This interface defines the contract for all handlers. Each handler must implement the **handleRequest()** method, which is responsible for processing the request.

2. **ATMHandlerConcrete**: This struct implements the **ATMHandler** interface. It holds a reference to the next handler (**successor**) and the denomination it processes. The **handleRequest()** method calculates how many notes of the current denomination can be dispensed and passes any remaining amount to the next handler in the chain.

3. **Client Code**: The client sets up the chain of handlers from the highest denomination (1000) to the lowest (10) by passing a reference to the next handler as a successor. The chain starts with the highest denomination to minimize the number of notes dispensed.

4. **Processing the Request**: When the withdrawal request is made (e.g., 5560), the handler processes it by:

   ○ Dispensing 5 notes of 1000,

   ○ Passing the remaining 560 to the next handler, which dispenses 5 notes of 100,

   ○ Passing the remaining 60 to the next handler, which dispenses 1 note of 50,

- ○ Finally, passing the remaining 10 to the next handler, which dispenses 1 note of 10.

Consequences

The Chain of Responsibility pattern offers several benefits and consequences:

1. **Decoupling**: The Chain of Responsibility pattern decouples the client from knowing exactly which handler will process the request. This allows for easy modification of the handling process without affecting the client code.

2. **Flexibility**: The pattern allows the dynamic addition, modification, or removal of handlers in the chain. This flexibility helps adapt the system to handle different types of requests or changing business rules.

3. **Reduced Coupling**: By passing requests through a chain of handlers, the system reduces tight coupling between the sender and receivers, leading to more maintainable and adaptable code.

4. **Fallback Mechanism**: If none of the handlers in the chain can process the request, a fallback mechanism can be introduced to handle the case where no handler is suitable (e.g., an error message or special handler for invalid amounts).

Command Pattern

The **Command Design Pattern** is a behavioural design pattern that allows you to encapsulate a request as an object. This approach decouples the sender of the request from the receiver, making it easier to parameterize objects with different requests, queue or log requests, and support undoable operations.

Problem: In many software applications, it's necessary to decouple the sender of a request from the receiver. For example, you may want to design a system where different objects can request actions without needing to know how those actions are implemented. Additionally, you might need to support undo and redo functionality in your application.

Direct coupling between the sender and receiver can lead to several issues:

- The sender becomes dependent on the implementation details of the receiver.

- Adding or modifying functionality becomes cumbersome, as it requires changes to both the sender and receiver.

- Implementing undo and redo functionality can be complex and prone to errors if not properly handled.

Solution: The Command Design Pattern solves these problems by introducing an intermediary object known as the "command" that encapsulates the request and its associated action. The pattern typically consists of the following components:

1. **Command**: This is an interface or abstract class that defines a common structure for all command objects. It declares an **execute()** method to carry out the action.

2. **ConcreteCommand**: These are implementations of the Command interface. Each ConcreteCommand binds a specific action to a receiver, holding a reference to the receiver and implementing the **execute()** method by calling the appropriate operation on the receiver.

3. **Invoker**: The class that holds the Command object and triggers its execution by calling **execute()**.

4. **Receiver**: The class that knows how to perform the actual action associated with the command.

5. **Client**: The class that creates **ConcreteCommand** objects, sets the appropriate receivers, and binds them to Invokers.

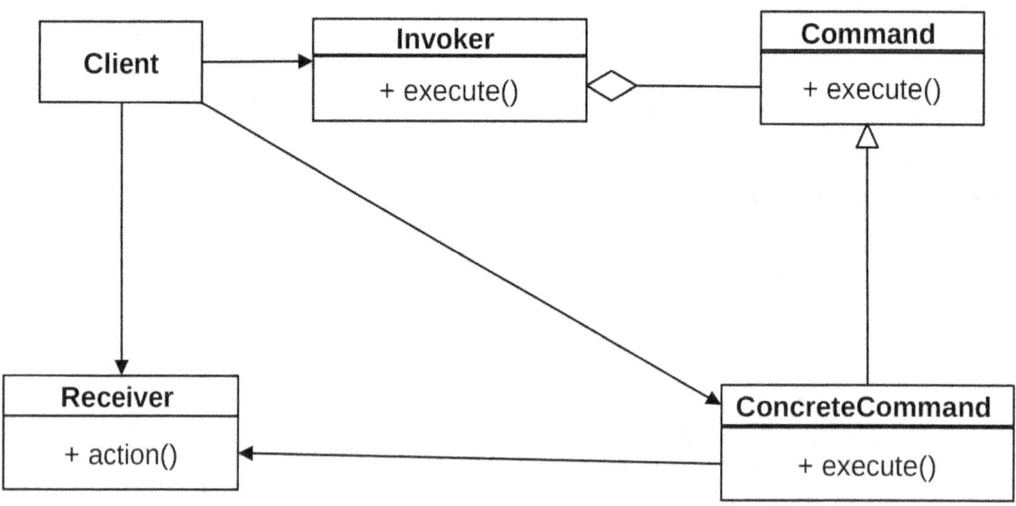

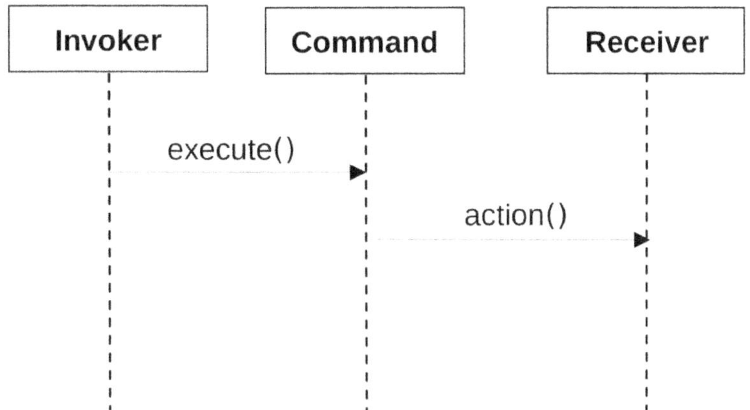

Example Implementation:

```go
// Command interface
type Command interface {
    execute()
    unexecute()
}

// Invoker struct
type Invoker struct {
    commands []Command
}

// setCommand method for Invoker
func (i *Invoker) setCommand(command Command) {
    i.commands = append(i.commands, command)
}

// executeCommands method for Invoker
func (i *Invoker) executeCommands() {
    for _, command := range i.commands {
        command.execute()
    }
}

// unexecuteCommands method for Invoker
func (i *Invoker) unexecuteCommands() {
    for _, command := range i.commands {
        command.unexecute()
    }
}

// ConcreteCommand struct
```

```go
type ConcreteCommand struct {
    receiver Receiver
}

// NewConcreteCommand constructor
func NewConcreteCommand(receiver Receiver) *ConcreteCommand {
    return &ConcreteCommand{
        receiver: receiver,
    }
}

// execute method for ConcreteCommand
func (c *ConcreteCommand) execute() {
    c.receiver.action("Action 1")
}

// unexecute method for ConcreteCommand
func (c *ConcreteCommand) unexecute() {
    c.receiver.action("Action 2")
}

// Receiver struct
type Receiver struct{}

// action method for Receiver
func (r *Receiver) action(action string) {
    fmt.Println(action)
}

// Client Code
func main() {
    receiver := &Receiver{}
    concreteCommand := NewConcreteCommand(*receiver)
    invoker := &Invoker{}

    invoker.setCommand(concreteCommand)
    invoker.executeCommands()
    invoker.unexecuteCommands()
}
```

Output:

```
Action 1
Action 2
```

Explanation: The code implements the Command Design Pattern, which separates the sender and receiver of a request using the **Invoker**, **Command**,

and **Receiver** classes. Let's go through the code step by step and explain its functionality:

1. **Invoker (Remote Control):**

   - The **Invoker** acts as a remote control. It holds a list of commands and provides methods to both execute and undo (unexecute) them via **executeCommands()** and **unexecuteCommands()**.

2. **Command Interface:**

   - The **Command** interface defines two methods: **execute()** and **unexecute()**. Any class implementing this interface must provide concrete implementations for these methods.

3. **ConcreteCommand:**

   - This is the implementation of the **Command** interface. The **ConcreteCommand** knows about a specific action that the **Receiver** will perform. It calls the Receiver's **action()** method in both the **execute()** and **unexecute()** methods, with different action strings.

4. **Receiver:**

   - The `Receiver` class is responsible for executing the actual action. It has an `action()` method that takes an action string as input and prints it.

5. **Client Code:** In the client code:

   - A **Receiver** instance is created to perform actions.

   - A **ConcreteCommand** is instantiated, passing the **Receiver** to it.

   - The **ConcreteCommand** is added to the **Invoker**.

   - The **Invoker** first executes the command, triggering **Receiver** to print "Action 1".

   - The **Invoker** then undoes the command, causing the **Receiver** to print "Action 2".

Problem : Implementing a Stock Trading System, We need to design a simple stock trading system capable of placing "buy" and "sell" orders. The challenge is to decouple the code responsible for executing these orders from the code that initiates them. Additionally, we want the flexibility to introduce new types of orders in the future without altering the existing codebase.

Solution: To address this problem, we can use the Command Design Pattern. This pattern helps in decoupling the sender of a request from the receiver by introducing a command object that encapsulates the request details and the associated action.

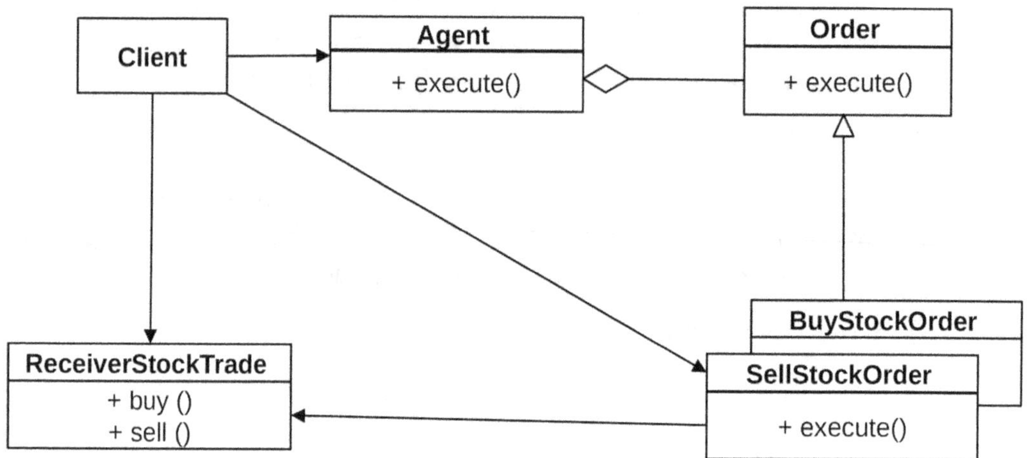

Example implementation of the Command pattern :

```go
// Agent struct (Invoker)
type Agent struct{}

// placeOrder method for Agent
func (a *Agent) placeOrder(command Order) {
    command.execute()
}

// Order interface
type Order interface {
    execute()
}

// BuyStockOrder struct
type BuyStockOrder struct {
    stock *ReceiverStockTrade
}

// NewBuyStockOrder constructor
func NewBuyStockOrder(stock *ReceiverStockTrade) *BuyStockOrder {
    return &BuyStockOrder{
        stock: stock,
    }
}
```

```go
// execute method for BuyStockOrder
func (b *BuyStockOrder) execute() {
    b.stock.buy()
}

// SellStockOrder struct
type SellStockOrder struct {
    stock *ReceiverStockTrade
}

// NewSellStockOrder constructor
func NewSellStockOrder(stock *ReceiverStockTrade)*SellStockOrder{
    return &SellStockOrder{
        stock: stock,
    }
}

// execute method for SellStockOrder
func (s *SellStockOrder) execute() {
    s.stock.sell()
}

// ReceiverStockTrade struct (Receiver)
type ReceiverStockTrade struct{}

// buy method for ReceiverStockTrade
func (r *ReceiverStockTrade) buy() {
    fmt.Println("Buy stocks")
}

// sell method for ReceiverStockTrade
func (r *ReceiverStockTrade) sell() {
    fmt.Println("Sell stocks")
}

// Client Code
func main() {
    trader := &ReceiverStockTrade{}
    buyStock := NewBuyStockOrder(trader)
    sellStock := NewSellStockOrder(trader)

    agent := &Agent{}
    agent.placeOrder(buyStock)
    agent.placeOrder(sellStock)
}
```

Output:

```
Buy stocks
Sell stocks
```

Explanation: This code that implements the Command Design Pattern to address the problem statement. Let's break down the code step by step:

1. **Agent (Invoker)**: Manages the order placement by calling the **execute()** method on command objects.

2. **Order (Command Interface)**: Provides a common interface with an **execute()** method for concrete commands.

3. **BuyStockOrder / SellStockOrder** (**ConcreteCommands**): Implement the **Order** interface to perform specific actions (**buy** and **sell**) on the Receiver.

4. **ReceiverStockTrade (Receiver)**: Implements the actual stock trading actions.

5. **Client Code**: Creates instances of commands and the receiver, and uses the agent to execute these commands.

Consequences

The Command Design Pattern offers several advantages and has certain consequences:

1. **Decoupling**: It decouples the sender from the receiver, enabling them to evolve independently. The sender does not need to understand how a request is handled, which simplifies maintenance and modifications.

2. **Undo/Redo Functionality**: Since commands encapsulate actions, it becomes easier to implement undo and redo functionality. By maintaining a history of executed commands, you can revert or reapply actions as needed.

3. **Flexibility**: New commands can be introduced without altering existing code, making the system more flexible and extensible. This promotes scalability and allows for easier adjustments to meet changing requirements.

4. **Logging and Auditing**: Commands can be logged for auditing purposes, facilitating the tracking of operations performed within the system. This is valuable for monitoring and analyzing system behavior.

5. **Complexity**: The pattern adds additional classes and abstraction layers, which can increase code complexity. This may lead to a higher maintenance effort and require more careful management of the codebase.

Interpreter Pattern

The **Interpreter pattern** is a behavioural design pattern used to define a grammar for a language and provide an interpreter to interpret sentences in that language. This pattern is particularly useful when working with domain-specific languages (DSLs). It allows you to define a grammar and then implement an interpreter to evaluate expressions or statements written in that DSL.

Problem: The Interpreter pattern is valuable when you need to evaluate expressions in a domain-specific language and want to avoid complex, nested conditional statements or repetitive if-else blocks. For instance, if you're building a simple language to process date expressions like "today," "tomorrow," "next week," and "last month," manually handling these expressions with conditional statements can quickly become cumbersome and hard to maintain.

Solution:The Interpreter pattern suggests creating a class for each grammar rule or terminal/non-terminal expression. These classes implement an **interpret()** method to process or evaluate the expression. The expressions can be composed in a way that represents the grammar of the language.

The pattern typically includes the following components:

1. **Context:** Contains the information on which the expressions operate.

2. **AbstractExpression:** An interface or abstract class that defines the **interpret()** method.

3. **TerminalExpression:** Concrete classes implementing the **AbstractExpression** for terminal expressions in the grammar.

4. **NonTerminalExpression:** Concrete classes implementing the **AbstractExpression** for non-terminal expressions in the grammar.

5. **Client:** Builds the abstract syntax tree (AST) of the expressions and invokes the **interpret()** method on the root of the tree.

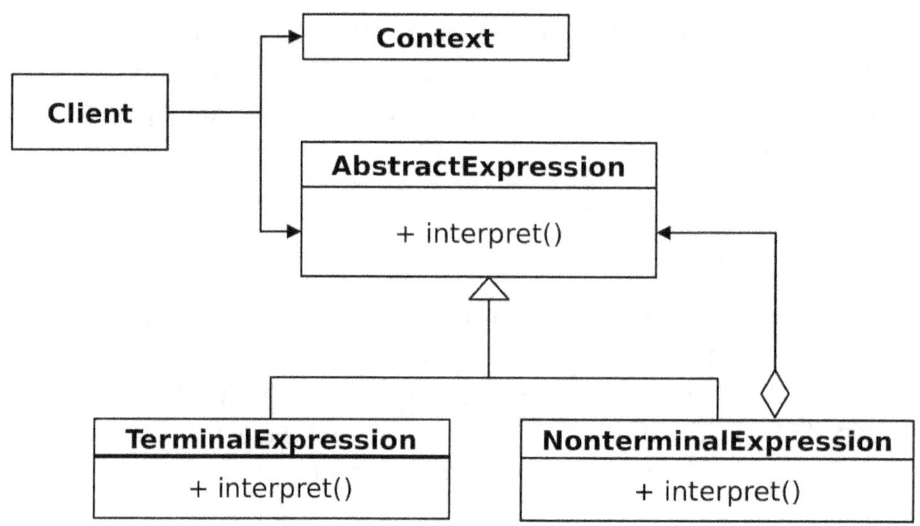

Example Implementation:

```go
// AbstractExpression interface
type AbstractExpression interface {
    interpret()
}

// NonterminalExpression struct
type NonterminalExpression struct {
    expression AbstractExpression
}

func (n *NonterminalExpression) interpret() {
    fmt.Println("NonterminalExpression:interpret")
    n.expression.interpret()
}

// TerminalExpression struct
type TerminalExpression struct{}

func (t *TerminalExpression) interpret() {
    fmt.Println("TerminalExpression:interpret")
}

// Client code
func main() {
    tree := &NonterminalExpression{
        expression: &TerminalExpression{},
    }
    tree.interpret()
}
```

Output:

```
NonTerminalExpression:interpret
TerminalExpression:interpret
```

Explanation: This code snippet demonstrates the implementation of the Interpreter design pattern. Let's go through the explanation of each part of the code:

1. **AbstractExpression:** This interface defines the **interpret()** method that must be implemented by all expressions in the grammar. It dictates how each expression is evaluated.

2. **NonTerminalExpression:** This concrete class represents a non-terminal expression in the grammar. It holds an **AbstractExpression**, which could be either a terminal or another non-terminal expression. Its **interpret()** method delegates the interpretation to the contained expression.

3. **TerminalExpression:** This concrete class represents a terminal expression that cannot be decomposed further. Its **interpret()** method simply prints text.

4. **Client Code:** Here, we create a **NonterminalExpression** that contains a **TerminalExpression**. The interpretation process starts at the root and recursively evaluates the contained sub-expressions.

Problem : Create an interpreter for a simple mathematical language that can evaluate expressions involving addition. The language should support two types of expressions:

- Terminal expressions (numbers).

- Non-terminal expressions (addition of two expressions).

The goal is to implement the Interpreter Design Pattern to evaluate these expressions and return the result.

Solution: We will use the Interpreter pattern to solve this problem. The steps are as follows:

1. **Define an interface for expressions**: This interface will have a method **interpret()** that all concrete classes must implement.

2. **Implement Terminal Expression**: A terminal expression will represent a number in our mathematical language and return its value.

3. **Implement Non-Terminal Expression**: A non-terminal expression will represent the addition of two expressions. It will interpret both the left and right expressions and return their sum.

4. **Create a context (optional)**: This can be used to store variables and their values, making the interpreter more flexible for future use cases like variable assignments.

5. **Client Code**: In the client code, we will construct an expression tree representing a mathematical expression and call the **interpret()** method to evaluate it.

Example Implementation:

```go
// Expression interface
type Expression interface {
    interpret(context *Context) int
}

// NumberExpression struct
type NumberExpression struct {
    number int
}

func (n *NumberExpression) interpret(context *Context) int {
    return n.number
}


// AddExpression struct
type AddExpression struct {
    left  Expression
    right Expression
}

func (a *AddExpression) interpret(context *Context) int {
    return a.left.interpret(context) + a.right.interpret(context)
}

// Context struct
type Context struct {
    variables map[string]int
}

func (c *Context) setVariable(variable string, value int) {
    if c.variables == nil {
```

```go
        c.variables = make(map[string]int)
    }
    c.variables[variable] = value
}

func (c *Context) getVariable(variable string) int {
    return c.variables[variable]
}

// Client code
func main() {
    context := &Context{}
    context.setVariable("x", 10)
    context.setVariable("y", 5)

    // Create the expression tree: x + (y + 2)
    expression := &AddExpression{
        left: &NumberExpression{number:
context.getVariable("x")},
        right: &AddExpression{
            left:  &NumberExpression{number:
context.getVariable("y")},
            right: &NumberExpression{number: 2},
        },
    }

    result := expression.interpret(context)
    fmt.Printf("Result: %d\n", result) // Output: Result: 17
}
```

Explanation:

1. **Expression Interface:** The **Expression** interface declares the **interpret()** method, which all expressions must implement.

2. **NumberExpression (Terminal Expression):** This class represents a number and simply returns its value when **interpret()** is called.

3. **AddExpression (Non-Terminal Expression):** This class represents the addition of two expressions. It takes two expressions (left and right) as input, calls their **interpret()** methods, and returns the sum of their values.

4. **Client Code:** In the client code, an expression tree representing the mathematical expression 10 + (5 + 2) is built using instances of **NumberExpression** and AddExpression. The **interpret()** method is then called to evaluate the expression, yielding the result 17.

Consequences

The Interpreter pattern provides a range of benefits but also comes with certain trade-offs.

Benefits:

1. **Flexibility**: The grammar can be easily modified or extended by adding new classes to represent additional expressions.

2. **Improved Readability**: It simplifies complex grammatical rules, resulting in more readable and maintainable code.

3. **Separation of Concerns**: By separating grammar definitions from parsing logic, the pattern improves the overall organization and structure of the code.

Trade-offs:

1. **Increased Complexity**: For larger or frequently changing grammars, the pattern can lead to a significant increase in complexity, making it harder to manage.

2. **Performance Overheads**: The efficiency of the pattern may decrease with more complex grammars and larger abstract syntax trees (AST), making it unsuitable for high-performance requirements in certain cases.

Iterator Pattern

The **Iterator pattern** is a **Behavioural design pattern** that enables sequential access to the elements of a collection without exposing its internal structure. It abstracts the traversal logic from the collection itself, allowing for flexible, maintainable, and reusable code.

Problem: When dealing with complex data structures (e.g., lists, arrays, trees), traditional loops can become cumbersome and tightly coupled with the collection's internal representation. This approach increases code duplication and reduces flexibility, especially if the structure of the collection changes.

Solution: The Iterator pattern solves this by decoupling the iteration process from the collection itself. It provides a clean way to traverse elements sequentially without exposing the underlying data structure.

The pattern consists of the following components:

1. **Iterator:** This is an interface that defines methods like **hasNext()** to check if there are more elements in the collection, and **next()** to retrieve the next element.

2. **ConcreteIterator:** This is a specific implementation of the Iterator interface for a particular collection. It keeps track of the current position during iteration.

3. **Iterable (Aggregate):** This is an interface that defines a method **createIterator()** to instantiate an Iterator for the collection.

4. **ConcreteIterable (ConcreteAggregate):** This is a specific implementation of the Iterable interface that creates and returns a **ConcreteIterator** for the collection.

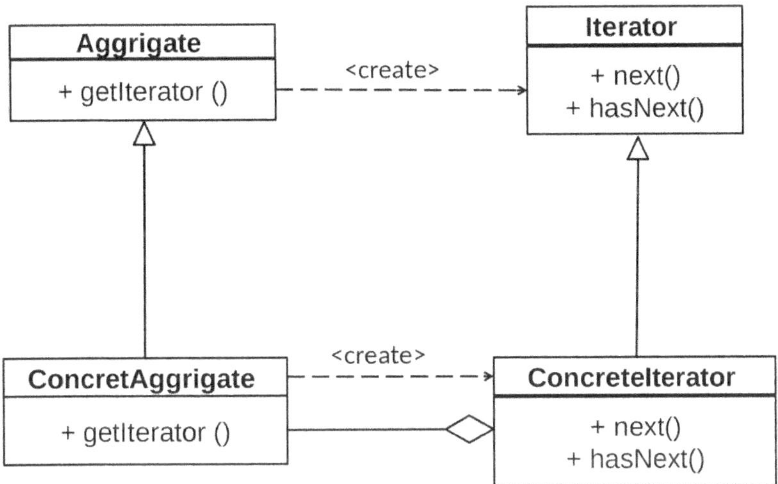

Example Implementation:

```go
// Aggregate interface
type Aggregate interface {
    getIterator() Iterator
}

// ConcreteAggregate struct
type ConcreteAggregate struct {
    data []int
}

func (ca *ConcreteAggregate) addData(val int) {
    ca.data = append(ca.data, val)
}
```

```go
func (ca *ConcreteAggregate) getIterator() Iterator {
    return &ConcreteIterator{aggregate: ca, index: 0}
}

// Iterator interface
type Iterator interface {
    next() int
    hasNext() bool
}

// ConcreteIterator struct
type ConcreteIterator struct {
    aggregate *ConcreteAggregate
    index     int
}

func (ci *ConcreteIterator) next() int {
    if ci.index >= len(ci.aggregate.data) {
        panic("StopIteration")
    }
    val := ci.aggregate.data[ci.index]
    ci.index++
    return val
}

func (ci *ConcreteIterator) hasNext() bool {
    return ci.index < len(ci.aggregate.data)
}

// Client code
func main() {
    aggregate := &ConcreteAggregate{}
    for i := 0; i < 5; i++ {
        aggregate.addData(i)
    }

    iterator := aggregate.getIterator()
    for iterator.hasNext() {
        fmt.Print(iterator.next(), " ")
    }
}
```

Output:

```
0 1 2 3 4
```

Explanation:

1. **Aggregate Interface**: The **Aggregate** interface defines the method **getIterator()**, implemented by **ConcreteAggregate**. The **ConcreteAggregate** maintains a list of data and returns a **ConcreteIterator** for traversing the data.

2. **Iterator Interface**: The **Iterator** interface defines the methods **next()** and **hasNext()**, implemented by **ConcreteIterator**. The **ConcreteIterator** traverses the elements in **ConcreteAggregate**.

3. **Client Code**: The client uses the **Iterator** to sequentially traverse the elements in the **ConcreteAggregate**.

Problem : LinkedList with Iterator Pattern, Implement a simple linked list and provide the ability to iterate over its elements using the Iterator design pattern

Solution: The code defines a **LinkedList** class with methods **addTail()** and **addHead()** for adding elements. It also implements a **LinkedListIterator** to allow the client to traverse the list sequentially.

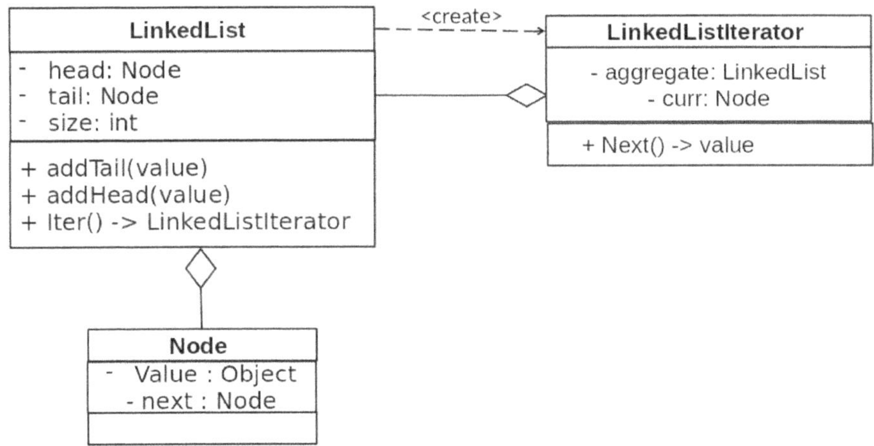

Example Implementation:

```go
// Node struct representing elements of linked list
type Node struct {
    value int
    next  *Node
}


// LinkedList struct representing a linked list
type LinkedList struct {
```

```go
    head *Node
    tail *Node
    size int
}

// AddTail adds a new node to the tail of the linked list
func (ll *LinkedList) AddTail(value int) {
    newNode := &Node{value: value, next: nil}
    if ll.head == nil {
        ll.head = newNode
    } else {
        ll.tail.next = newNode
    }

    ll.tail = newNode
    ll.size++
}

// AddHead adds a new node to the head of the linked list
func (ll *LinkedList) AddHead(value int) {
    newNode := &Node{value: value, next: ll.head}
    if ll.head == nil {
        ll.tail = newNode
    }
    ll.head = newNode
    ll.size++
}

// LinkedListIterator struct representing an iterator for the
linked list
type LinkedListIterator struct {
    aggregate *LinkedList
    curr      *Node
}

// NewLinkedListIterator creates a new iterator for the linked
list
func NewLinkedListIterator(aggregate *LinkedList)
*LinkedListIterator {
    return &LinkedListIterator{
        aggregate: aggregate,
        curr:      aggregate.head,
    }
}

// Next returns the next element in the iteration
```

```go
func (li *LinkedListIterator) Next() int {
    if li.curr == nil {
        return -1 // Use a sentinel value to indicate the end of
the iteration
    }
    val := li.curr.value
    li.curr = li.curr.next
    return val
}

// Client code
func main() {
    aggregate := &LinkedList{}
    for i := 0; i < 5; i++ {
        aggregate.AddHead(i)
    }

    iterator := NewLinkedListIterator(aggregate)

    for val := iterator.Next(); val != -1; val = iterator.Next(){
        fmt.Print(val, " ")
    }
}
```

Output:

4 3 2 1 0

Explanation:

1. **Node**: Represents an element in the linked list with a **value** and pointer to the **next** node.

2. **LinkedListIterator**: Implements the iterator for **LinkedList**, providing **Next()** to traverse the list.

3. **LinkedList**: Adds new nodes using **AddTail()** or **AddHead()**, and creates an iterator.

4. **Client Code**: Creates a **LinkedList**, adds elements, and iterates through it using the iterator.

Consequences

The Iterator design pattern offers several advantages and consequences:

1. **Decoupling**: The pattern decouples client code from the underlying collection, as interactions occur solely through the Iterator interface. This enhances code flexibility and maintainability.

2. **Single Responsibility Principle**: By separating iteration logic from the collection itself, the pattern adheres to the Single Responsibility Principle, resulting in more modular and organized code.

3. **Simplified Client Code**: The Iterator pattern simplifies client code by providing a uniform method to access elements, independent of the collection's internal implementation.

4. **Support for Multiple Iterators**: The pattern enables multiple iterators to operate on the same collection simultaneously without conflicts.

5. **Easier Extension**: Adding new collection types or custom iterators is more straightforward because the iteration logic is isolated from the collection's implementation.

6. **Performance Considerations**: Although the Iterator pattern introduces some overhead due to additional interfaces and objects, the benefits of improved flexibility and maintainability generally outweigh this cost.

Mediator Pattern

The **Mediator design pattern** is a behavioural pattern that promotes loose coupling between components by centralizing their communication through a mediator object. It reduces direct dependencies between objects, making the system more maintainable and extendable. Let's explore the problem it solves, the solution it provides, and the consequences of using it.

Problem: In a complex system, components often need to communicate with one another. Direct communication between these components can lead to a tightly coupled design, where any change to one component may require changes to others. This interdependency makes the code harder to maintain and extend. Moreover, the direct communication paths between objects can make it difficult to understand the system's flow.

Solution: The **Mediator pattern** introduces a mediator object that acts as a central hub for communication. Instead of components communicating directly, they interact via the mediator, which encapsulates the communication logic. This reduces interdependencies and simplifies the overall design.

Key Components:

1. **Mediator**: Defines an interface for communication and implements the communication logic.

2. **Concrete Mediator**: Implements the mediator interface and coordinates communication.

3. **Colleague**: Defines an interface for the components needing communication.

4. **Concrete Colleague**: Implements the colleague interface and communicates via the mediator.

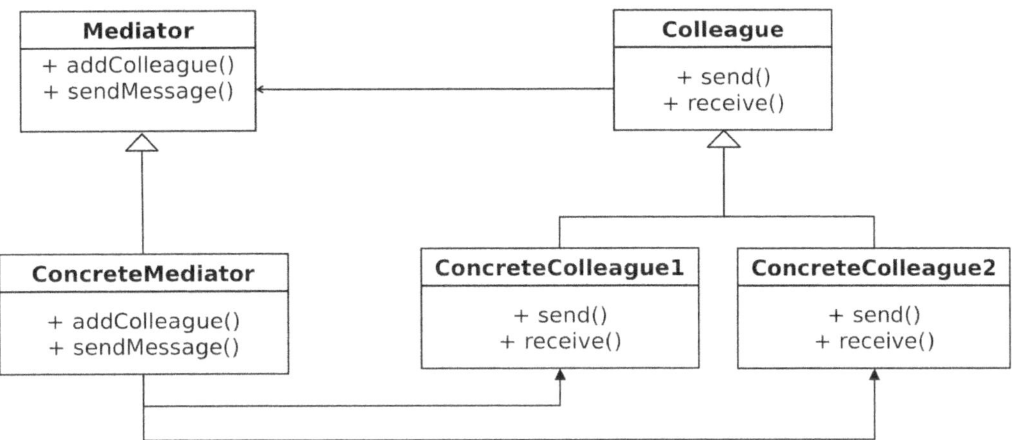

Example Implementation:

```go
// Mediator interface
type Mediator interface {
    addColleague(colleague Colleague)
    sendMessage(message string, colleagueID string)
}

// ConcreteMediator struct
type ConcreteMediator struct {
    colleagues map[string]Colleague
}

func (m *ConcreteMediator) addColleague(colleague Colleague) {
    m.colleagues[colleague.getID()] = colleague
}
```

```go
func (m *ConcreteMediator) sendMessage(message string,
colleagueID string) {
    fmt.Printf("Mediator pass Message: %s\n", message)
    m.colleagues[colleagueID].receive(message)
}

// Colleague interface
type Colleague interface {
    getID() string
    send(message string, to string)
    receive(message string)
}

// ConcreteColleague1 struct
type ConcreteColleague1 struct {
    mediator Mediator
    id       string
}

func (c *ConcreteColleague1) getID() string {
    return c.id
}

func (c *ConcreteColleague1) send(message string, to string) {
    fmt.Printf("%s Sent Message: %s\n", c.id, message)
    c.mediator.sendMessage(message, to)
}

func (c *ConcreteColleague1) receive(message string) {
    fmt.Printf("%s Received Message %s\n", c.id, message)
}

// ConcreteColleague2 struct
type ConcreteColleague2 struct {
    mediator Mediator
    id       string
}

func (c *ConcreteColleague2) getID() string {
    return c.id
}

func (c *ConcreteColleague2) send(message string, to string) {
    fmt.Printf("%s Sent Message: %s\n", c.id, message)
    c.mediator.sendMessage(message, to)
}
```

```go
func (c *ConcreteColleague2) receive(message string) {
    fmt.Printf("%s Received Message %s\n", c.id, message)
}

// Client code
func main() {
    mediator := &ConcreteMediator{
        colleagues: make(map[string]Colleague),
    }

    first := &ConcreteColleague1{
        mediator: mediator,
        id:       "First",
    }
    mediator.addColleague(first)

    second := &ConcreteColleague2{
        mediator: mediator,
        id:       "Second",
    }
    mediator.addColleague(second)

    first.send("Hello, World!", "Second")
}
```

Output:

```
First Sent Message : Hello, World!
Mediator pass Message : Hello, World!
Second Received Message Hello, World!
```

Explanation:

1. **Mediator Interface**: This code defines a **Mediator** interface with methods **addColleague()** and **sendMessage()**, implemented by the **ConcreteMediator** class. The **ConcreteMediator** manages a map of colleagues and facilitates their communication.

2. **Colleague Interface**: The **Colleague** interface is defined with methods **send()** and **receive()**, which are implemented by **ConcreteColleague1** and **ConcreteColleague2**. These classes communicate via the mediator instead of directly with each other.

3. **Client Code**: The client code creates a **ConcreteMediator** object and two **ConcreteColleague** objects, adding them to the mediator. A message is sent from the first colleague to the second using the **send()**

method, which invokes the mediator's **sendMessage()** method to relay the message.

Problem : Design a simple chat room application using the Mediator design pattern. The goal is to create a system where participants in the chat room can communicate with each other through a central mediator (**ChatRoom** class) instead of direct interaction. The **ChatRoom** class serves as a central communication hub, allowing participants (instances of the **Participant** class) to either send messages to specific participants or broadcast messages to all participants.

Solution: To implement the chat room using the Mediator pattern, we will define two interfaces: **IChatRoom** for the mediator and **IParticipant** for the participants. We will then create classes that implement these interfaces. The **ChatRoom** class will manage the participants and handle message broadcasting and sending. The **Participant** class will represent each chat room participant and use the **ChatRoom** to communicate.

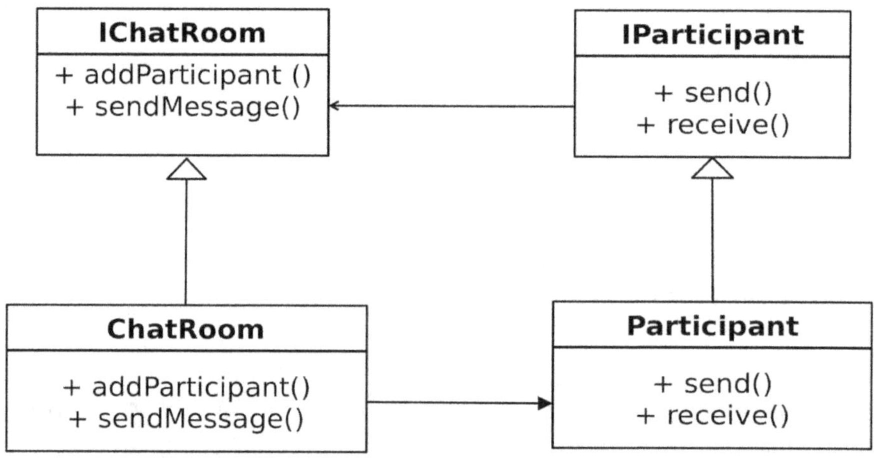

Example Implementation:

```go
// IChatRoom interface
type IChatRoom interface {
    AddParticipant(participant *Participant)
    Broadcast(message, origin string)
    SendMessage(message, to string)
}

// ChatRoom struct implementing IChatRoom
```

```go
type ChatRoom struct {
    participants map[string]*Participant
}
// AddParticipant adds a participant to the chat room
func (cr *ChatRoom) AddParticipant(participant *Participant) {
    cr.participants[participant.name] = participant
}

// Broadcast sends a message to all participants except the
origin
func (cr *ChatRoom) Broadcast(message, origin string) {
    fmt.Printf("ChatRoom broadcast Message: %s\n", message)
    for name, p := range cr.participants {
        if name != origin {
            p.Receive(message)
        }
    }
}

// SendMessage sends a message from one participant to another
func (cr *ChatRoom) SendMessage(message, to string) {
    cr.participants[to].Receive(message)
}

// IParticipant interface
type IParticipant interface {
    Broadcast(message string)
    Send(message, to string)
    Receive(message string)
}

// Participant struct implementing IParticipant
type Participant struct {
    name     string
    chatRoom *ChatRoom
}

// NewParticipant creates a participant and adds to the chatroom
func NewParticipant(name string, chatRoom *ChatRoom) *Participant
{
    participant := &Participant{name: name, chatRoom: chatRoom}
    chatRoom.AddParticipant(participant)
    return participant
}

// Broadcast sends a message to all participants
```

```go
func (p *Participant) Broadcast(message string) {
    fmt.Printf("%s broadcast Message: %s\n", p.name, message)
    p.chatRoom.Broadcast(message, p.name)
}

// Send sends a message from one participant to another
func (p *Participant) Send(message, to string) {
    fmt.Printf("%s sent Message: %s\n", p.name, message)
    p.chatRoom.SendMessage(message, to)
}

// Receive receives a message
func (p *Participant) Receive(message string) {
    fmt.Printf("%s received Message: %s\n", p.name, message)
}

// Client code
func main() {
    chatRoom := &ChatRoom{participants:
make(map[string]*Participant)}
    James := NewParticipant("James", chatRoom)
    Michael := NewParticipant("Michael", chatRoom)
    NewParticipant("Robert", chatRoom)
    Michael.Send("Good Morning.", "James")
    James.Broadcast("Hello, World!")
}
```

Output:

```
Michael sent Message : Good Morning.
James received Message : Good Morning.
James broadcast Message : Hello, World!
ChatRoom broadcast Message : Hello, World!
Michael received Message : Hello, World!
Robert received Message : Hello, World!
```

Explanation:

1. **IChatRoom Interface:**

   ○ **AddParticipant(participant *Participant)**: Adds a new participant to the chat room.

   ○ **Broadcast(message, origin string)**: Broadcasts a message to all participants except the originator.

   ○ **SendMessage(message, to string)**: Sends a direct message to a specific participant.

2. **ChatRoom Class:**

   - Implements the **IChatRoom** interface.

   - **Maintains a map** of participants to manage all chat room members.

   - **Handles message broadcasting and sending** through **Broadcast()** and **SendMessage()** methods.

3. **IParticipant Interface:**

   - **Broadcast(message string)**: Allows a participant to broadcast a message to all others.

   - **Send(message, to string)**: Allows a participant to send a message to a specific participant.

   - **Receive(message string)**: Handles receiving a message for a participant.

4. **Participant Class:**

   - Implements the **IParticipant** interface.

   - **Sends messages through the chat room** mediator using **Send()** and **Broadcast()** methods.

   - **Receives messages** and displays them using the **Receive()** method.

5. **Client Code:**

   - Creates an instance of **ChatRoom** to act as the mediator.

   - Adds participants (**James**, **Michael**, and **Robert**) to the chat room.

   - Demonstrates messaging functionality by sending direct messages and broadcasting to all participants.

Consequences

1. **Decoupling**: The Mediator pattern effectively decouples components from one another, fostering a more flexible and maintainable design. Each component only needs to be aware of the mediator rather than other components. This simplification reduces interdependencies, streamlining the system's architecture and enhancing modularity.

2. **Centralized Control**: The mediator centralizes control over the communication between components. This concentration of

communication logic in one place can make the system easier to understand and debug, as all interactions are managed through the mediator, providing a clear overview of component interactions.

3. **Scalability and Extensibility**: The pattern enhances scalability and extensibility by making it easier to add new components to the system. New components only need to interact with the mediator to communicate with existing components, minimizing the risk of bugs and reducing the complexity associated with system expansion.

4. **Increased Complexity**: While the Mediator pattern simplifies component interactions, it introduces an additional layer of abstraction. This can increase overall system complexity, especially in smaller projects where direct communication might suffice. It is crucial to apply the pattern judiciously, particularly in situations where the complexity of direct interactions justifies the need for a mediator.

5. **Single Point of Failure**: The mediator, being the central communication hub, can become a single point of failure. If the mediator encounters issues or becomes overloaded, the entire system's communication flow may be disrupted. This risk must be carefully managed to ensure system reliability and robustness.

Memento Pattern

The **Memento pattern** is a behavioural design pattern that enables saving and restoring an object's state. It's particularly useful when you need to implement undo-redo functionality in an application.

Problem: The challenge lies in preserving the internal state of an object and allowing it to be restored at a later time without violating encapsulation. In certain situations, objects need to be able to revert to previous states, track changes, or support rollback mechanisms.

Solution: In this pattern, the object whose state needs to be saved is referred to as the "Originator." The state of the Originator is stored in a "Memento" object, which contains all the necessary information to restore the Originator to a previous state. The Memento object is then managed by a "Caretaker," which is responsible for storing and handling the mementos.

The Memento pattern has three key components:

1. **Originator**: The object whose state is saved and restored. The Originator creates a Memento that captures its current state.

2. **Memento**: This object holds the Originator's state. The Memento is created by the Originator, ensuring it accurately captures a snapshot of the state.

3. **Caretaker**: This object manages the Memento. It stores multiple Memento objects, allowing the Originator to restore to various points in time.

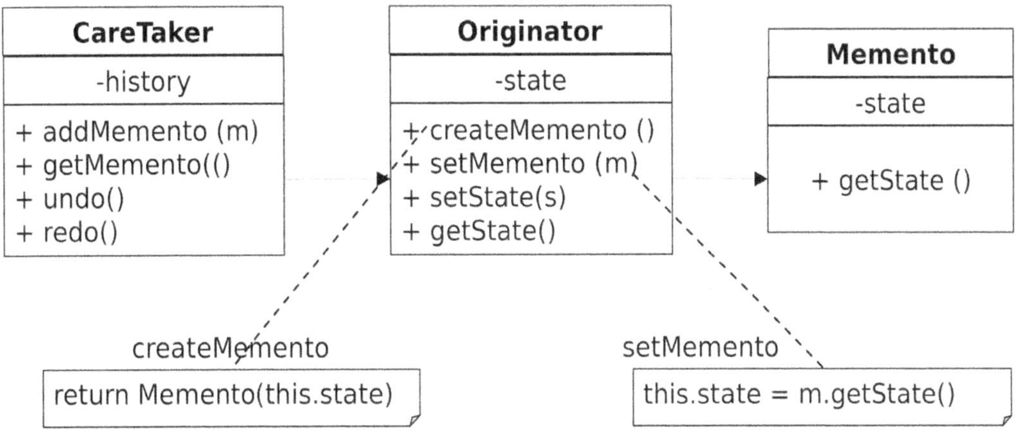

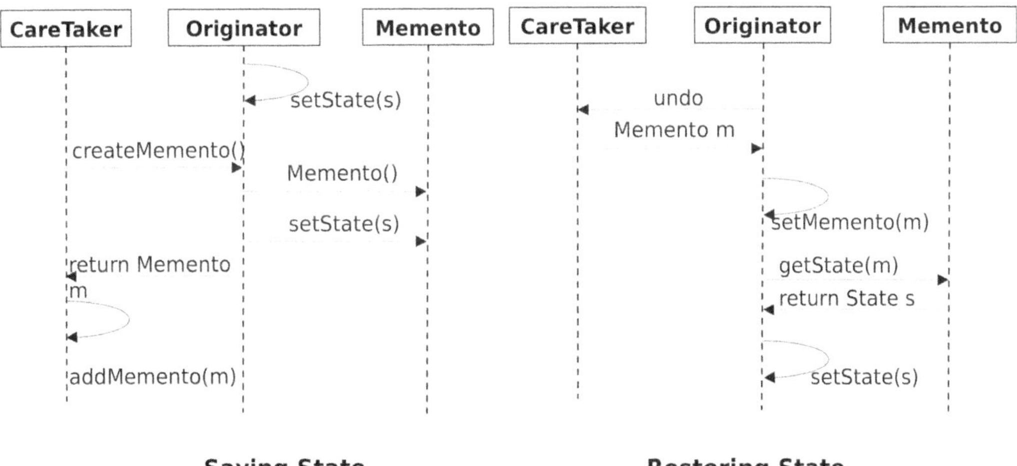

Saving State   **Restoring State**

Example Implementation of the Memento Pattern:

```go
// Memento struct - wrapper around state
type Memento struct {
    state string
}
```

```go
func (m *Memento) GetState() string {
    return m.state
}

// Originator struct
type Originator struct {
    state string
}

func (o *Originator) SetState(state string) {
    o.state = state
}

func (o *Originator) GetState() string {
    return o.state
}

func (o *Originator) CreateMemento() *Memento {
    return &Memento{state: o.state}
}

func (o *Originator) SetMemento(m *Memento) {
    o.state = m.GetState()
}

// CareTaker struct - manages history
type CareTaker struct {
    history []Memento
    top     int
    max     int
}

func NewCareTaker() *CareTaker {
    return &CareTaker{
        history: make([]Memento, 0),
        top:     -1,
        max:     -1,
    }
}

func (c *CareTaker) AddMemento(m *Memento) {
    c.top++
    c.max = c.top
    if c.top <= len(c.history)-1 {
        c.history[c.top] = *m
    } else {
```

```go
        c.history = append(c.history, *m)
    }
}

func (c *CareTaker) GetMemento(index int) *Memento {
    return &c.history[index]
}

func (c *CareTaker) Undo() *Memento {
    fmt.Println("Undoing state.")
    if c.top <= 0 {
        c.top = 0
        return c.GetMemento(0)
    }

    c.top--
    return c.GetMemento(c.top)
}

func (c *CareTaker) Redo() *Memento {
    fmt.Println("Redoing state.")
    if c.top >= len(c.history)-1 || c.top >= c.max {
        return c.GetMemento(c.top)
    }

    c.top++
    return c.GetMemento(c.top)
}

// Client code
func main() {
    originator := &Originator{}
    careTaker := NewCareTaker()

    originator.SetState("State 1")
    careTaker.AddMemento(originator.CreateMemento())
    fmt.Println(originator.GetState())
    originator.SetState("State 2")
    careTaker.AddMemento(originator.CreateMemento())
    fmt.Println(originator.GetState())
    originator.SetState("State 3")
    careTaker.AddMemento(originator.CreateMemento())
    fmt.Println(originator.GetState())

    originator.SetMemento(careTaker.Undo())
    fmt.Println(originator.GetState())
```

```
    originator.SetMemento(careTaker.Undo())
    fmt.Println(originator.GetState())
    originator.SetMemento(careTaker.Redo())
    fmt.Println(originator.GetState())
    originator.SetMemento(careTaker.Redo())
    fmt.Println(originator.GetState())
}
```

Output:

```
State 1
State 2
State 3
Undoing state.
State 2
Undoing state.
State 1
Redoing state.
State 2
Redoing state.
State 3
```

Explanation:

1. This is an implementation of the Memento pattern. It consists of three classes: **Originator**, **Memento**, and **CareTaker**.

2. The **Originator** class is the class whose object state needs to be saved and restored. It has methods for setting and getting the state, creating a **Memento** object with the current state, and restoring the state from a **Memento** object.

3. The **Memento** class represents the saved state of the **Originator**. It has a **getState()** method for getting the saved state.

4. The **CareTaker** class is responsible for managing the saved states. It has a history list to store the **Memento** objects and methods for adding a new **Memento**, getting a **Memento** at a specified index, undoing the last state change, redoing the last undone state change, and getting the number of saved states.

5. In the usage example, we create an instance of **Originator**, set its initial state to "State 1", and save it using the **createMemento()** method. We

add the **Memento** object to the **CareTaker** using the **addMemento()** method.

6. We then change the state of the **Originator** to "State 2" and save it again, followed by changing it to "State 3" and saving it again.

7. We then call the **undo()** method of the **CareTaker** twice to restore the **Originator** to its previous states. We call the **redo()** method of the **CareTaker** twice to redo the last undone state changes.

Consequences

The Memento pattern offers several benefits for system design:

1. **Encapsulation**: The pattern ensures that the internal state of the Originator remains encapsulated and hidden from external clients. This preserves the integrity of the object and its state.

2. **Undo/Redo Functionality**: The pattern simplifies the implementation of undo and redo features by maintaining a stack of Mementos. It allows objects to revert to previous states and track state history efficiently.

3. **Isolation of State**: State is encapsulated within Memento objects, making it easier to manage different snapshots of an object's state and handle their lifecycle independently.

4. **Flexibility**: Clients can save the state of an object at any desired point, offering a flexible mechanism for state management.

5. **Snapshot Support**: The pattern facilitates taking snapshots of an object's state at regular intervals or specific events. This is useful in scenarios such as version control systems or data recovery.

However, there are some potential downsides to using the Memento pattern:

1. **Memory Overhead**: Storing multiple Mementos can consume significant memory, especially if the state of the Originator is large or complex.

2. **Performance Concerns**: Creating and managing Mementos can introduce overhead, particularly if the state changes frequently or if there are many state transitions.

3. **Managing Memento Lifecycles**: The Caretaker must properly manage the lifecycle of Mementos to prevent resource leaks or unexpected behavior.

Observer Pattern

The **Observer design pattern** is a behavioural pattern in software design that enables an object, known as the subject, to notify its dependents, called observers, whenever there is a change in its state. When the state of the subject changes, all registered observers are automatically informed and updated. This pattern facilitates loose coupling between the subject and its observers, as they are not aware of each other's existence.

Problem: In software development, certain scenarios require multiple objects to be informed when another object changes. Direct coupling between these objects can lead to several issues:

1. **Tight coupling**: When objects are directly dependent on each other, a change in one object may necessitate changes in many other objects, reducing flexibility and maintainability.

2. **Scalability**: As the number of objects needing notifications grows, managing dependencies becomes increasingly complex, making it difficult to add new observers.

3. **Inefficiency**: Without a proper notification mechanism, observers may rely on inefficient polling methods to check for updates, leading to performance issues.

Solution: The Observer pattern addresses these problems by decoupling the subject from its observers. It is particularly useful when there is a one-to-many relationship between objects, where the state of one object affects several others. This pattern is commonly used in GUI programming, where components need to be notified of changes in other components, and in event-driven systems, where events trigger changes in the system's state.

Main Components:

1. **Subject**: The object whose state is monitored. It maintains a list of registered observers and provides methods to add, remove, and notify them.

2. **Observer**: An interface defining the contract for objects that need to be notified of changes in the subject's state, typically including an **update()** method called by the subject when a change occurs.

3. **Concrete Subject**: An implementation of the subject interface that maintains the state and sends notifications to registered observers upon state changes.

4. **Concrete Observer**: An implementation of the observer interface that defines how the observer reacts to updates from the subject.

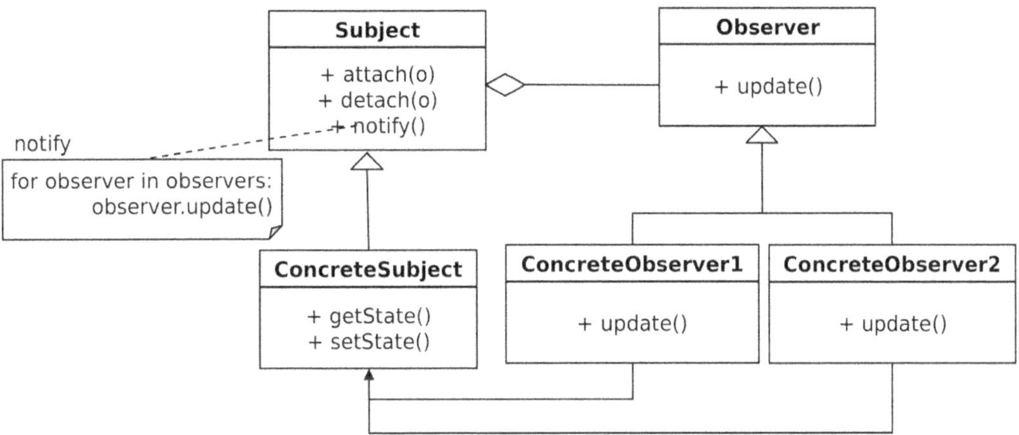

Example Implementation:

```go
// Subject interface
type Subject interface {
    Attach(observer Observer)
    Detach(observer Observer)
    Notify()
}

// ConcreteSubject struct
type ConcreteSubject struct {
    state     string
    observers []Observer
}

func (s *ConcreteSubject) Attach(observer Observer) {
    observer.SetSubject(s)
    s.observers = append(s.observers, observer)
}
```

```go
func (s *ConcreteSubject) Detach(observer Observer) {
    for i, obs := range s.observers {
        if obs == observer {
            observer.SetSubject(nil)
            s.observers = append(s.observers[:i],
s.observers[i+1:]...)
            break
        }
    }
}

func (s *ConcreteSubject) Notify() {
    for _, observer := range s.observers {
        observer.Update()
    }
}

func (s *ConcreteSubject) GetState() string {
    return s.state
}

func (s *ConcreteSubject) SetState(state string) {
    s.state = state
    s.Notify()
}

// Observer interface
type Observer interface {
    Update()
    SetSubject(subject Subject)
}

// ConcreteObserver struct
type ConcreteObserver struct {
    subject Subject
}

func (o *ConcreteObserver) Update() {
    state := o.subject.(*ConcreteSubject).GetState()
    fmt.Printf("%s notified to Observer\n", state)
}

func (o *ConcreteObserver) SetSubject(subject Subject) {
    o.subject = subject
}
```

```go
// Client code
func main() {
    subject := &ConcreteSubject{}
    observer1 := &ConcreteObserver{}
    observer2 := &ConcreteObserver{}

    subject.Attach(observer1)
    subject.Attach(observer2)

    subject.SetState("First state")
    subject.SetState("Second state")
}
```

Output:

```
First state notified to Observer1
First state notified to Observer2
Second state notified to Observer1
Second state notified to Observer2
```

Explanation:

1. This implementation defines a one-to-many dependency between objects where changes in the state of the subject automatically notify and update its observers.

2. The **Subject** interface provides methods to manage observers. The **ConcreteSubject** class maintains its state and notifies observers when it changes.

3. The Observer interface defines the **update()** method, while **ConcreteObserver** implements how observers react to notifications.

4. The client code creates a **ConcreteSubject** and attaches multiple **ConcreteObserver** instances. Changing the subject's state triggers notifications to the observers.

Problem : how can we implement a **Publisher-Subscriber (Observer) pattern** where a publisher can broadcast messages to multiple subscribers, but only to those who are interested in specific topics? How do the roles of publisher and subscriber interact in terms of topics, and how can we efficiently manage and notify subscribers based on their topic subscriptions?

Solution: To implement the Publisher-Subscriber pattern with topics, we define two main components: **Publisher** and **Subscriber.**

Publisher:

- **Role:** Manages a list of subscribers for each topic (e.g., "news", "sports").

- **Responsibilities:**

  - **Subscribe:** Registers subscribers to specific topics, adding them to the list of subscribers for that topic.

  - **Unsubscribe:** Removes subscribers from specific topics, deleting them from the list of subscribers for that topic.

  - **Notify:** Sends messages to all subscribers of a topic when new information is available, calling each subscriber's **Update()** method.

Subscriber:

- **Role:** An entity that registers interest in one or more topics and receives notifications when new messages are published to those topics.

- **Responsibilities:**

  - **Receive Updates:** Implements an **Update()** method that is called by the publisher when there is a new message for a subscribed topic.

  - **Manage Subscriptions:** Chooses to subscribe or unsubscribe from topics based on its interests.

Example Implementation:

```go
// Publisher interface
type Publisher interface {
    Subscribe(subs Subscriber, topic string)
    Unsubscribe(subs Subscriber, topic string)
    Notify(data string, topic string)
}

// ConcretePublisher struct
type ConcretePublisher struct {
    topicSubscribers map[string][]Subscriber
}

func (p *ConcretePublisher) Subscribe(subs Subscriber, topic
string) {
    if p.topicSubscribers == nil {
        p.topicSubscribers = make(map[string][]Subscriber)
```

```go
    }

    p.topicSubscribers[topic] = append(p.topicSubscribers[topic],
subs)
    fmt.Printf("Subscribing: %s to topic: %s\n", subs.GetID(),
topic)
}

func (p *ConcretePublisher) Unsubscribe(subs Subscriber, topic
string) {
    if subscribers, ok := p.topicSubscribers[topic]; ok {
        for i, s := range subscribers {
            if s == subs {
                p.topicSubscribers[topic] =
append(subscribers[:i], subscribers[i+1:]...)
                break
            }
        }
    }

    fmt.Printf("Unsubscribing: %s to topic: %s\n", subs.GetID(),
topic)
}

func (p *ConcretePublisher) Notify(data string, topic string) {
    if subscribers, ok := p.topicSubscribers[topic]; ok {
        fmt.Printf("Publishing: %s in topic: %s\n", data, topic)
        for _, subscriber := range subscribers {
            subscriber.Update(data)
        }
    }
}

// Subscriber interface
type Subscriber interface {
    Update(data string)
    GetID() string
}

// ConcreteSubscriber struct
type ConcreteSubscriber struct {
    id string
}

func (s *ConcreteSubscriber) Update(data string) {
    fmt.Printf("Subscriber %s got :: %s\n", s.id, data)
```

```go
}

func (s *ConcreteSubscriber) GetID() string {
    return s.id
}

// Client code
func main() {
    pub := &ConcretePublisher{}

    sub1 := &ConcreteSubscriber{id: "Subscriber1"}
    sub2 := &ConcreteSubscriber{id: "Subscriber2"}
    sub3 := &ConcreteSubscriber{id: "Subscriber3"}

    pub.Subscribe(sub1, "topic1")
    pub.Subscribe(sub2, "topic2")
    pub.Subscribe(sub3, "topic2")

    pub.Notify("Topic 1 data", "topic1")
    pub.Notify("Topic 2 data", "topic2")

    pub.Unsubscribe(sub3, "topic2")
    pub.Notify("Topic 2 data", "topic2")
}
```

Output:

```
Subscribing: Subscriber1 to topic: topic1
Subscribing: Subscriber2 to topic: topic2
Subscribing: Subscriber3 to topic: topic2
Publishing: Topic 1 data in topic: topic1
Subscriber Subscriber1 got :: Topic 1 data
Publishing: Topic 2 data in topic: topic2
Subscriber Subscriber2 got :: Topic 2 data
Subscriber Subscriber3 got :: Topic 2 data
Unsubscribing: Subscriber3 to topic: topic2
Publishing: Topic 2 data in topic: topic2
Subscriber Subscriber2 got :: Topic 2 data
```

Explanation:

1. **Publisher Class**: The **Publisher** class serves as the central component responsible for managing subscriptions. It maintains a list of subscribers for each topic and provides methods to allow subscribers to subscribe to or unsubscribe from specific topics. Additionally, it includes functionality to notify all subscribers when new data is published for a particular topic.

2. **Subscriber Class**: The **Subscriber** class represents an entity interested in receiving updates about specific topics. It contains an **update()** method, which is called by the publisher whenever new data is available on the topics the subscriber is subscribed to.

3. **Client Code**: In the client code, we first create an instance of the **Publisher** class and several instances of the **Subscriber** class. We use the **subscribe()** method of the **Publisher** class to associate subscribers with various topics. Next, when we publish data to these topics using the **Publisher's notifySubscribers()** method, all relevant subscribers are notified of the new data.

4. **Unsubscribing Subscribers**: Finally, we demonstrate the unsubscribe functionality by removing a subscriber from a topic using the **Publisher's unsubscribe()** method. When we publish additional data after this, the unsubscribed subscriber does not receive any further notifications, confirming the unsubscribe action.

Problem: The provided code aims to implement a Publisher-Subscriber (Observer) pattern, where a **Publisher** (in this case, a **Courses** class) manages subscribers (**Student** instances) that are interested in specific topics (courses). The problem is to effectively manage subscriptions and notifications such that when the publisher sends a message about a specific course, all subscribers to that course receive the update. This requires mechanisms for subscribing to and unsubscribing from topics and ensuring notifications are sent to the appropriate subscribers.

Solution: To solve this, we use the Publisher-Subscriber pattern to create a flexible system where students can subscribe to or unsubscribe from various courses, and receive notifications about any updates related to the courses they are interested in.

The implementation involves two primary components:

1. **Courses (Publisher)**: Maintains a list of subscribed students for each course (topic) and manages adding or removing students from these lists.

2. **Student (Subscriber)**: Represents the entities interested in receiving updates about specific courses. When notified, a student receives the message associated with a course update.

Example Implementation:

```go
package main

import "fmt"

// Courses struct acts as the Publisher
type Courses struct {
    courseStudents map[string]map[*Student]struct{}
}

// NewCourses initializes a new Courses instance
func NewCourses() *Courses {
    return &Courses{
        courseStudents: make(map[string]map[*Student]struct{}),
    }
}

// Subscribe adds a student to the list of subscribers for a
given course
func (c *Courses) Subscribe(subject string, student *Student) {
    if _, ok := c.courseStudents[subject]; !ok {
        c.courseStudents[subject] = make(map[*Student]struct{})
    }
    c.courseStudents[subject][student] = struct{}{}
}

// Unsubscribe removes a student from the list of subscribers for
a given course
func (c *Courses) Unsubscribe(subject string, student *Student) {
    if students, ok := c.courseStudents[subject]; ok {
        delete(students, student)
        if len(students) == 0 {
            delete(c.courseStudents, subject)
        }
    }
}

// Publish sends a message to all students subscribed to a
particular course
func (c *Courses) Publish(subject, message string) {
    if students, ok := c.courseStudents[subject]; ok {
        for student := range students {
            student.Notify(subject, message)
        }
    } else {
        fmt.Printf("No subscribers for subject '%s'.\n", subject)
```

```go
        }
}

// Student struct acts as the Subscriber
type Student struct {
    Name string
}

// NewStudent initializes a new Student instance
func NewStudent(name string) *Student {
    return &Student{Name: name}
}

// Notify method to receive messages from Courses
func (s *Student) Notify(subject, message string) {
    fmt.Printf("%s received message on subject '%s': %s\n",
s.Name, subject, message)
}

// Client code
func main() {
    courses := NewCourses()
    john := NewStudent("John")
    eric := NewStudent("Eric")
    jack := NewStudent("Jack")

    courses.Subscribe("English", john)
    courses.Subscribe("English", eric)
    courses.Subscribe("Maths", eric)
    courses.Subscribe("Science", jack)

    courses.Publish("English", "Tomorrow class at 11")
    courses.Publish("Maths", "Tomorrow class at 1")

    // Unsubscribe Eric from English
    courses.Unsubscribe("English", eric)

    courses.Publish("English", "Updated schedule for English")
}
```

Output:

```
John received message on subject 'English': Tomorrow class at 11
Eric received message on subject 'English': Tomorrow class at 11
Eric received message on subject 'Maths': Tomorrow class at 1
John received message on subject 'English': Updated schedule for
English
```

Explanation:

1. **Courses Struct**: Represents the publisher that holds a mapping of course names (**subject**) to their respective sets of subscribed students (**courseStudents**). The map uses pointers to **Student** instances to track subscribers.

2. **Subscribe Method**: Allows a **Student** to subscribe to a particular course (subject). It adds the student to the set of subscribers for that course, creating a new set if it doesn't already exist.

3. **Unsubscribe Method**: Allows a **Student** to unsubscribe from a particular course. It removes the student from the set of subscribers and deletes the set if it becomes empty.

4. **Publish Method**: Sends a message to all subscribers of a given course by calling their **Notify()** method. If no subscribers exist for a course, it prints a message stating there are no subscribers.

5. **Student Struct**: Represents a subscriber that has a **Name** and a **Notify()** method to receive messages.

6. **Notify() Method**: Defines how a **Student** receives messages about updates to courses they are subscribed to. It prints the message received for a given subject.

7. **Client Code (main function)**: Demonstrates the functionality by creating instances of **Courses** and **Student**, subscribing students to various courses, publishing messages, and unsubscribing students.

Consequences

The Observer design pattern offers the following advantages:

1. **Loose Coupling**: Decouples the subject and observers, making it easier to add or remove observers without altering the subject's code.

2. **Reusability**: Observers can be reused in various contexts since they are independent of the subject's implementation.

3. **Maintainability**: Changing the subject's state does not require modifications in observer classes, improving code maintainability.

4. **Real-Time Updates**: Observers receive real-time updates when the subject's state changes, enabling synchronous communication.

However, the pattern can lead to some potential challenges:

1. **Performance Impact**: With many observers, notifying all of them on each state change can lead to performance overhead.

2. **Notification Order**: The order in which observers are notified may not be guaranteed, which could be problematic in some scenarios.

3. **Memory Management**: Proper management of observers' lifecycle is essential to avoid memory leaks.

State Pattern

The **State design pattern** is a behavioural design pattern that enables an object to change its behavior when its internal state changes. This pattern is useful when an object has multiple possible states, each requiring different behavior. Instead of embedding all behaviors within the object itself, the State pattern encapsulates the behavior for each state in separate classes.

Problem: In software design, certain objects can have multiple states, with their behavior varying depending on the current state. Managing these states and their interactions can become complex and error-prone, especially as the number of states and associated behaviors increases. This complexity can lead to code that is difficult to maintain, understand, and extend.

Solution: The State pattern addresses this problem by encapsulating each state of an object into a separate class, which makes it easier to manage and maintain state-specific behavior. This pattern allows an object to change its behavior dynamically when its state changes, without altering its class. It also promotes a clean separation between state-related logic and the core functionality of the object.

The pattern consists of four key components:

1. **Context**: The class that holds the current state and behavior dependent on that state. It delegates the behavior to the current state object.

2. **State**: An abstract class or interface that defines the behavior for each state. This is implemented by the concrete state classes.

3. **ConcreteState**: A class that implements the behavior specific to a particular state.

4. **Client**: The class that interacts with the Context and State objects to perform actions.

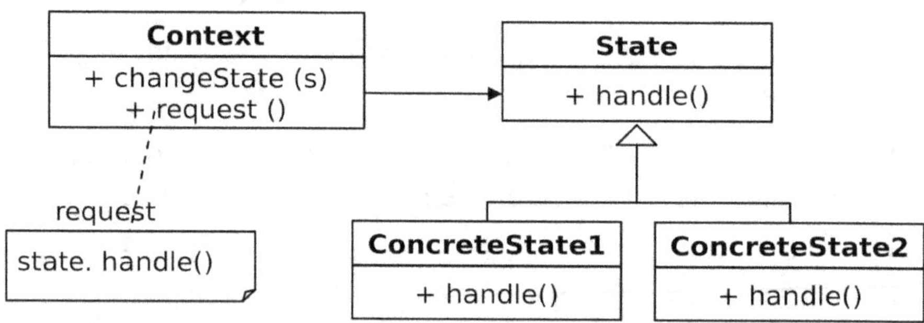

Example Implementation:

```go
type Context struct {
    currentState State
}

func NewContext(state State) *Context {
    return &Context{
        currentState: state,
    }
}

func (c *Context) changeState(state State) {
    c.currentState = state
}

func (c *Context) request() {
    c.currentState.handle(c)
}

type State interface {
    handle(context *Context)
}

type ConcreteState1 struct{}

func (cs1 *ConcreteState1) handle(context *Context) {
    fmt.Println("ConcreteState1 handle")
    context.changeState(&ConcreteState2{})
}

type ConcreteState2 struct{}

func (cs2 *ConcreteState2) handle(context *Context) {
```

```go
        fmt.Println("ConcreteState2 handle")
        context.changeState(&ConcreteState1{})
}

// Client code
func main() {
    state1 := &ConcreteState1{}
    context := NewContext(state1)
    context.request()
    context.request()
}
```

Output:

```
ConcreteState1 handle
ConcreteState2 handle
```

Explanation:

1. In this pattern, an object's behavior is determined by its current state, which can change dynamically based on certain conditions. The pattern separates the behavior of the object from its state, allowing for different behaviors to be implemented by simply changing the object's state.

2. In the implementation provided, the **Context** class holds a **State** object representing the current state of the context. The **State** interface defines the methods that concrete state classes, such as **ConcreteState1** and **ConcreteState2**, must implement.

3. The **Context** class has a method to change its state and a method to request that the current state handles a specific action. When the **request()** method is called, it invokes the **handle()** method of the current state, which may then update the context's state.

4. In this example, the initial state of the context is **ConcreteState1**. When the **request()** method is first called, **ConcreteState1's handle()** method is executed, printing "ConcreteState1 handle" and changing the context's state to **ConcreteState2**. The next call to **request()** invokes **ConcreteState2's handle()** method, printing "ConcreteState2 handle" and switching the context's state back to **ConcreteState1**. This cycle can continue indefinitely.

Problem: You need to implement a simple **BulbControl** system that manages a bulb's state using the State Design Pattern. The goal is to allow the bulb to toggle between "On" and "Off" states smoothly, with each state represented by a separate class. The state transitions should be controlled through the **BulbControl** class, encapsulating the behavior associated with each state.

Solution: The State Design Pattern is applied to create a modular and maintainable solution. The pattern defines a **BulbState** interface representing the state of the bulb, and two concrete classes, **On** and **Off**, that implement this interface. The BulbControl class maintains the current state and allows toggling between states.

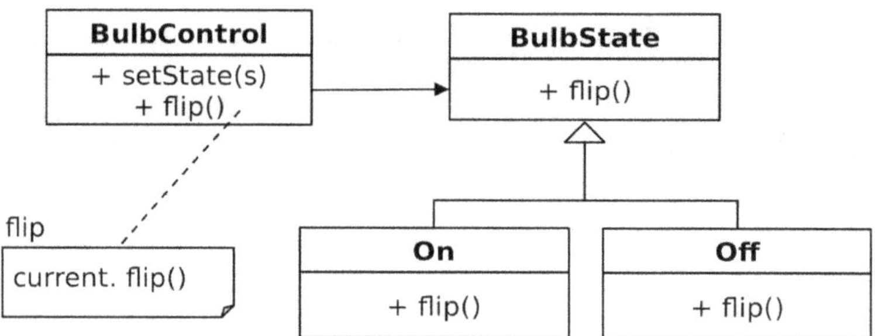

Example Implementation:

```go
type BulbControl struct {
    current BulbState
}

func NewBulbControl() *BulbControl {
    return &BulbControl{
        current: &Off{},
    }
}

func (bc *BulbControl) setState(state BulbState) {
    bc.current = state
}

func (bc *BulbControl) flip() {
    bc.current.flip(bc)
}

func (bc *BulbControl) toString() string {
    return bc.current.toString()
}

type BulbState interface {
    flip(bc *BulbControl)
    toString() string
```

```go
}

type On struct{}

func (o *On) flip(bc *BulbControl) {
    bc.setState(&Off{})
}

func (o *On) toString() string {
    return "On"
}

type Off struct{}

func (off *Off) flip(bc *BulbControl) {
    bc.setState(&On{})
}

func (off *Off) toString() string {
    return "Off"
}

// Client code
func main() {
    c := NewBulbControl()
    c.flip()
    fmt.Println(c.toString())
    c.flip()
    fmt.Println(c.toString())
}
```

Output:

```
On
Off
```

Explanation:

1. **State Pattern Implementation**: The code implements the State Design Pattern using a BulbControl class to manage the state of a bulb. The **BulbState** interface defines the contract for bulb states, while the **On** and **Off** classes implement the specific behavior for each state.

2. **State Transitions**: The **BulbControl** class keeps track of the current state and allows the state to be toggled between **On** and **Off** using the **flip()** method. The **toString()** method provides a string representation of the current state.

3. **Encapsulation of Behavior:** By encapsulating state-specific behavior in separate classes, the State Pattern allows for easy modification or extension of states without affecting the core logic of the **BulbControl** class.

Consequences

The State design pattern offers the following advantages:

1. **Modularity and Flexibility**: The State Pattern enhances modularity by representing each state as a separate class. This design makes it straightforward to add or modify states without affecting other states or the main context class. As a result, the design is more flexible and extensible, allowing for easier scaling and adaptability.

2. **Maintainability**: By isolating the behavior for each state within its own class, the State Pattern improves maintainability. Changes to a specific state's behavior can be made independently, reducing the risk of unintended side effects or bugs in other parts of the codebase. This isolation ensures that modifying or extending the behavior of a particular state is straightforward and does not impact the entire system.

3. **Readability and Understandability**: The explicit definition of states and their transitions in separate classes makes the code more readable and understandable. This clarity helps developers comprehend the flow of the program and the conditions under which different behaviors are executed, making it easier to follow and debug.

4. **Complexity Management**: The State Pattern effectively manages complexity by encapsulating state-specific behavior within dedicated classes. This approach avoids large, state-dependent switch or conditional statements, leading to cleaner and more maintainable code. It also helps in avoiding lengthy and nested switch/case or if/else structures, which can be challenging to read and maintain.

However, the pattern can lead to some potential challenges:

1. **Potential Overhead**: One downside of the State Pattern is the potential overhead introduced by additional classes. Each state is represented by a separate class, which may lead to a slight increase in memory usage and complexity in the class hierarchy, especially if there are many states.

2. **Increased Number of Classes**: The State Pattern can result in a higher number of classes, which may complicate the system's architecture,

particularly for smaller applications. Managing a large number of classes can become burdensome, and it might be overkill for simple use cases where a straightforward conditional check could suffice.

3. **Appropriate Use Cases**: While the State Pattern is beneficial for objects with multiple states and complex behavior changes, it may introduce unnecessary overhead for simpler objects. In cases where an object has few states or minimal state-dependent behavior, the pattern could complicate the codebase more than it simplifies it. The added complexity might not justify the benefits, making the pattern less suitable for simple scenarios.

Strategy Pattern

The **Strategy Design Pattern** is a behavioural design pattern that enables an object to change its behavior at runtime by encapsulating a family of algorithms and choosing one based on client requests or specific conditions.

Problem: In software development, you might face scenarios where multiple algorithms or strategies could be used to solve a problem. Without the Strategy pattern, you would likely end up writing multiple versions of the same code, using conditional statements to pick the right behavior. This can lead to code duplication, reduced maintainability, and increased complexity.

Solution: The Strategy pattern solves this by separating the different algorithms into individual classes, each implementing a common interface. These classes represent specific strategies. The client interacts with an abstraction (an interface or an abstract class), which delegates the behavior selection to a concrete strategy at runtime.

The pattern consists of three main components:

1. **Context**: The object whose behavior can change based on the selected algorithm. It holds a reference to a Strategy object and delegates the work to it.

2. **Strategy**: An interface or abstract class that defines the algorithm. The Context uses this to call the algorithm without knowing which specific strategy is being used.

3. **Concrete Strategy**: The implementation of the Strategy interface. This class encapsulates a specific algorithm or behavior that the Context will use.

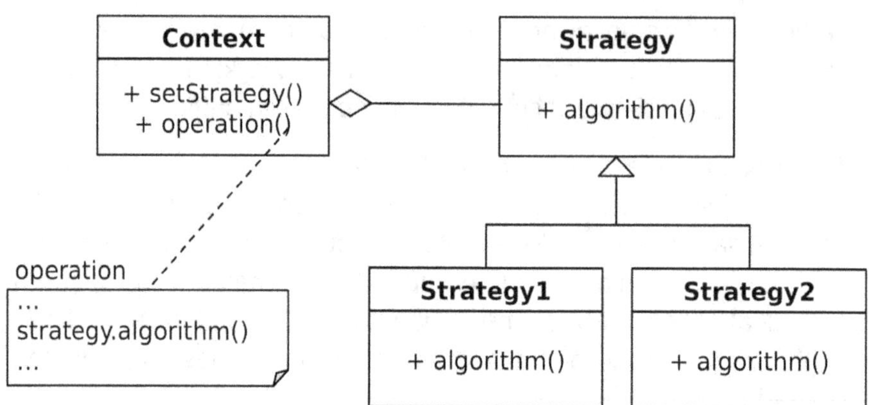

Example Implementation :

```go
type Strategy interface {
    execute(data int)
}


type ConcreteStrategy1 struct{}

func (cs1 *ConcreteStrategy1) execute(data int) {
    fmt.Println("ConcreteStrategy1 execute")
}


type ConcreteStrategy2 struct{}

func (cs2 *ConcreteStrategy2) execute(data int) {
    fmt.Println("ConcreteStrategy2 execute")
}


type Context struct {
    strategy Strategy
}


func NewContext(strategy Strategy) *Context {
    return &Context{
        strategy: strategy,
    }
}


func (c *Context) setStrategy(strategy Strategy) {
    c.strategy = strategy
}


func (c *Context) execute() {
    data := 1
```

```go
        c.strategy.execute(data)
}

// Client code
func main() {
    c := NewContext(&ConcreteStrategy1{})
    c.execute()
    c.setStrategy(&ConcreteStrategy2{})
    c.execute()
}
```

Output:

```
ConcreteStrategy1 execute
ConcreteStrategy2 execute
```

Explanation:

The code provided implements the Strategy design pattern. Let's go through the classes and their roles:

1. **Strategy (Interface)**: This interface declares a method **execute(data int)** that all concrete strategy classes must implement.

2. **ConcreteStrategy1 and ConcreteStrategy2 (Concrete Classes)**: These are specific implementations of the Strategy interface. Each one provides its own version of the **execute(data int)** method, which in this case, simply prints a message indicating which strategy is in use.

3. **Context (Context Class)**: The Context class is the one that uses the strategies. It maintains a reference to a Strategy object and provides methods to change the strategy at runtime. The constructor initializes the strategy, which defaults to **ConcreteStrategy1**, but can be set to another strategy during instantiation or later through the **setStrategy()** method. The **execute()** method calls the current strategy's **execute(data int)** method with a predefined **data** value, but this could be any relevant data in a real-world scenario.

4. **Client Code:** The client creates an instance of the Context class with **ConcreteStrategy1** as the initial strategy. When **c.execute()** is called, it prints "ConcreteStrategy1 execute." The strategy is then switched to **ConcreteStrategy2**, and **c.execute()** is called again, now printing "ConcreteStrategy2 execute" because the strategy has been changed.

Problem: You need to implement two sorting algorithms—Bubble Sort and Selection Sort—but want the flexibility to switch between these algorithms at runtime without modifying the existing codebase. The goal is to allow the client to dynamically choose which sorting algorithm to use based on specific conditions or preferences.

Solution: Use the Strategy Design Pattern to encapsulate each sorting algorithm within its own class, implementing a common interface. This approach allows the client to switch sorting algorithms easily without altering the core logic.

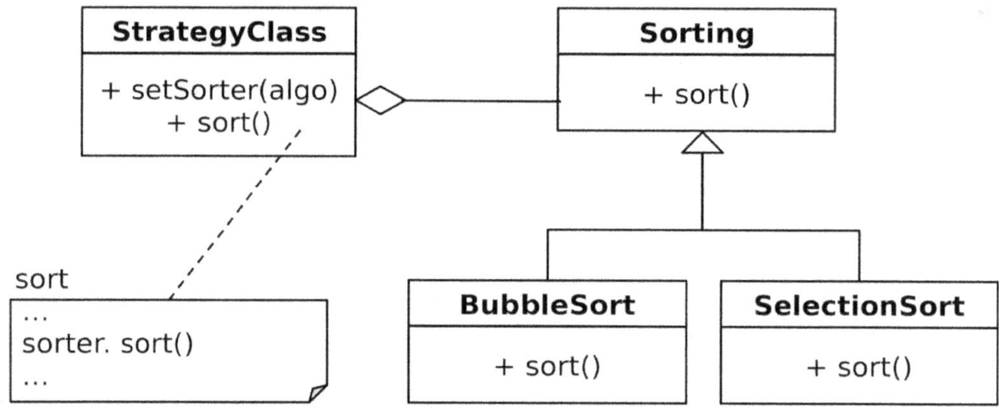

Example implementation:

```go
type Sorting interface {
    sort(numbers []int)
}


type BubbleSort struct{}


func (bs *BubbleSort) sort(numbers []int) {
    // Bubble Sort Algorithm
    fmt.Println("Bubble Sort Algorithm executed.")
    size := len(numbers)
    for i := 0; i < size-1; i++ {
        for j := 0; j < size-i-1; j++ {
            if numbers[j] > numbers[j+1] {
                // Swapping
                temp := numbers[j]
                numbers[j] = numbers[j+1]
                numbers[j+1] = temp
            }
        }
    }
}
```

```go
type SelectionSort struct{}

func (ss *SelectionSort) sort(numbers []int) {
    // Selection Sort Algorithm
    fmt.Println("Selection Sort Algorithm executed.")
    size := len(numbers)
    for i := 0; i < size-1; i++ {
        maxIndex := 0
        for j := 1; j < size-i; j++ {
            if numbers[j] > numbers[maxIndex] {
                maxIndex = j
            }
        }
        temp := numbers[size-1-i]
        numbers[size-1-i] = numbers[maxIndex]
        numbers[maxIndex] = temp
    }
}

type StrategyClass struct {
    sorter Sorting
}

func NewStrategyClass(algo Sorting) *StrategyClass {
    return &StrategyClass{
        sorter: algo,
    }
}

func (sc *StrategyClass) setSorter(algo Sorting) {
    sc.sorter = algo
}

func (sc *StrategyClass) sort(a []int) {
    sc.sorter.sort(a)
}

// Client code
func main() {
    a := []int{4, 5, 3, 2, 6, 7, 1, 8, 9, 10}
    s := NewStrategyClass(&BubbleSort{})
    s.sort(a)
    fmt.Println(a)

    a = []int{4, 5, 3, 2, 6, 7, 1, 8, 9, 10}
```

```
        s.setSorter(&SelectionSort{})
        s.sort(a)
        fmt.Println(a)
}
```

Output:

```
Bubble Sort Algorithm executed.
[1, 2, 3, 4, 5, 6, 7, 8, 9, 10]
Selection Sort Algorithm executed.
[1, 2, 3, 4, 5, 6, 7, 8, 9, 10]
```

Explanation:

1. **Sorting Interface**: The **Sorting** interface defines a method **sort(numbers []int)**, which all sorting algorithms must implement. This interface serves as a contract for different sorting strategies.

2. **BubbleSort and SelectionSort Classes**: These are concrete implementations of the **Sorting** interface. Each class contains its own sorting logic: **BubbleSort** uses the Bubble Sort algorithm, while **SelectionSort** uses the Selection Sort algorithm. Both print a message when executed.

3. **StrategyClass (Context)**: The **StrategyClass** acts as the context in the Strategy Pattern. It holds a reference to a **Sorting** instance and allows the client to set a specific sorting strategy using the **setSorter()** method. The **sort()** method calls the **sort** function of the current strategy.

4. **Client Code**: The client initializes an array and sorts it using the default sorting strategy (Bubble Sort) by creating an instance of **StrategyClass** with **BubbleSort**. After sorting and printing the array, the client switches to **SelectionSort** using **setSorter** and sorts a new array, which is then printed.

Consequences

By employing the Strategy pattern, you gain several benefits:

1. **Simplified Code Maintenance**: Each sorting algorithm is isolated within its own class, making it easy to modify or extend without affecting the client code.

2. **Improved Code Reusability**: Each strategy can be reused across different parts of the application or even in other projects.

3. **Runtime Flexibility**: The client can dynamically switch between different sorting algorithms at runtime, offering adaptability to changing requirements.

4. **Easy Extension**: Adding a new sorting algorithm is straightforward. Simply create a new class that implements the Sorting interface.

5. **Better Testing**: Independent strategies make it easier to write unit tests for each algorithm in isolation, ensuring that each works correctly on its own.

Template Method Pattern

The **Template Method Pattern** is a behavioural design pattern that defines the framework of an algorithm in a base class, allowing subclasses to override specific steps without altering the algorithm's overall structure. Essentially, it creates a template in an abstract class that outlines the steps of a process, with some steps implemented in the base class and others left for subclasses to define.

Problem: When developing algorithms or processes that share a common structure but require varying implementations for certain steps, developers face the challenge of balancing code reuse with flexibility. Without a well-structured design, code duplication can become a significant issue, leading to maintenance challenges and inconsistencies. Additionally, tightly coupling different parts of the algorithm can make the code hard to extend and maintain.

Solution: The Template Method Pattern solves this problem by introducing an abstract class (or interface) that defines a "template method," which outlines the skeleton of the algorithm. This method calls various abstract or hook methods, which subclasses implement to customize specific steps. The key idea is to separate the unchanging parts of the algorithm from the parts that can vary, encapsulating them in different methods. This approach promotes code reuse while allowing the algorithm's structure to remain intact when the implementation of specific steps changes.

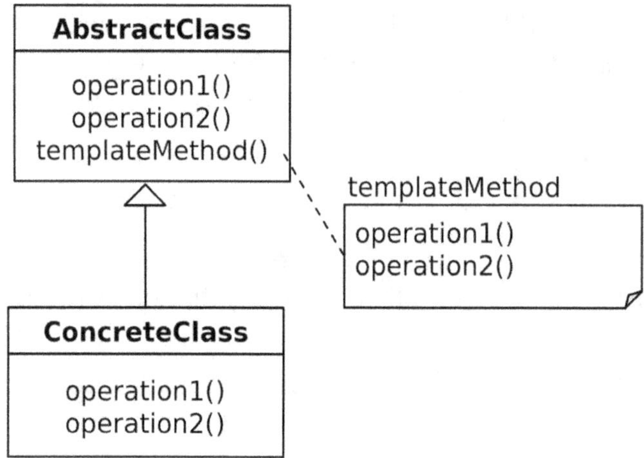

Example Implementation:

```go
// AbstractClass is the abstract class defining the template
method.
type AbstractClass interface {
    templateMethod()
    operation1()
    operation2()
}

// ConcreteClass1 is a concrete implementation of AbstractClass.
type ConcreteClass1 struct{}

func (c *ConcreteClass1) templateMethod() {
    c.operation1()
    c.operation2()
}

func (c *ConcreteClass1) operation1() {
    fmt.Println("Concrete Class 1 : Operation 1")
}

func (c *ConcreteClass1) operation2() {
    fmt.Println("Concrete Class 1 : Operation 2")
}

// ConcreteClass2 is another concrete implementation of
AbstractClass.
type ConcreteClass2 struct{}

func (c *ConcreteClass2) templateMethod() {
    c.operation1()
    c.operation2()
```

```go
}

func (c *ConcreteClass2) operation1() {
    fmt.Println("Concrete Class 2 : Operation 1")
}

func (c *ConcreteClass2) operation2() {
    fmt.Println("Concrete Class 2 : Operation 2")
}

// Client code
func main() {
    concreteClass := &ConcreteClass1{}
    concreteClass.templateMethod()
}
```

Output:

```
Concrete Class 1 : Operation 1
Concrete Class 1 : Operation 2
```

Explanation:

1. In this example, the abstract class **AbstractClass** defines a **templateMethod()** that outlines the algorithm by calling two abstract methods: **operation1()** and **operation2()**.

2. The concrete subclasses **ConcreteClass1** and **ConcreteClass2** implement these abstract methods, each providing their own specific behavior.

3. When the client code creates an instance of **ConcreteClass1** and calls the **templateMethod()**, it outputs "Concrete Class 1 : Operation 1" and "Concrete Class 1 : Operation 2". This demonstrates that the algorithm's structure, as defined in the abstract class, is followed, while the specific steps are determined by the subclass implementation.

Problem: You need to implement a system for adding data to different destinations, such as a file or a database. While the overall process of adding data follows the same general steps (open, add, close), the implementation details vary depending on the destination. Without a structured approach, this could lead to code duplication and a lack of flexibility. How can you design a solution that encapsulates the common steps while allowing customization for each destination?

Solution: The Template Method design pattern can be applied to this problem. You create an abstract class **AddDataTemplate** that defines a template method **addData()**. This method outlines the steps to add data by calling abstract methods **open()**, **add()**, and **close()**. The specific implementations of these steps are provided by subclasses like **AddDataToFile** and **AddDataToDB**, which handle the details of adding data to a file and a database, respectively.

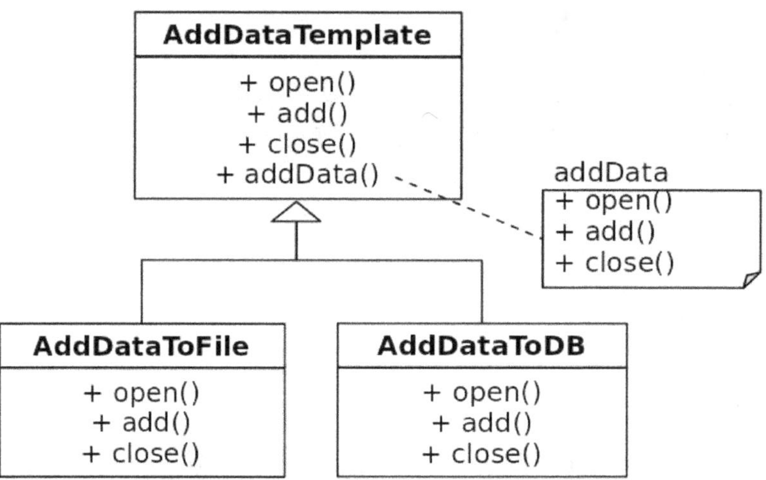

Example implementation:

```go
// AddDataTemplate is the abstract class defining the template
method.
type AddDataTemplate interface {
    addData()
    open()
    add()
    close()
}

// AddDataToFile is a concrete implementation of AddDataTemplate
for adding data to a file.
type AddDataToFile struct{}

func (a *AddDataToFile) addData() {
    a.open()
    a.add()
    a.close()
}

func (a *AddDataToFile) open() {
```

```go
        fmt.Println("Open file.")
}

func (a *AddDataToFile) add() {
    fmt.Println("Add data to file.")
}

func (a *AddDataToFile) close() {
    fmt.Println("Close file.")
}

// AddDataToDB is another concrete implementation of
AddDataTemplate for adding data to a database.
type AddDataToDB struct{}

func (a *AddDataToDB) addData() {
    a.open()
    a.add()
    a.close()
}

func (a *AddDataToDB) open() {
    fmt.Println("Open Database.")
}

func (a *AddDataToDB) add() {
    fmt.Println("Add data to Database.")
}

func (a *AddDataToDB) close() {
    fmt.Println("Close Database.")
}

// Client code
func main() {
    o := &AddDataToDB{}
    o.addData()
}
```

Output:

```
Open Database.
Add data to Database.
Close Database.
```

Explanation:

1. The **AddDataTemplate** interface defines the template method **addData()** which outlines the algorithm by calling three methods: **open()**, **add()**, and **close()**. These methods are abstract, meaning that they must be implemented by subclasses.

2. The **AddDataToFile** and **AddDataToDB** classes provide specific implementations for the abstract methods. **AddDataToFile** handles adding data to a file, while **AddDataToDB** manages adding data to a database.

3. The client code creates an instance of **AddDataToDB** and calls the **addData()** method. This triggers the sequence of method calls defined in the template method, resulting in the output "Open database. Add data to database. Close database."

Consequences

List of advantages of the Template Method pattern:

1. **Code Reusability**: The Template Method pattern enhances code reusability by encapsulating the shared structure of an algorithm within a single template method. Subclasses are responsible for providing the specific implementations for certain steps, which promotes the reuse of existing code and reduces redundant effort.

2. **Flexibility**: This pattern offers flexibility by allowing subclasses to override only the necessary steps of an algorithm. This enables customization without altering the core structure, making it simpler to adapt the algorithm to a variety of scenarios.

3. **Reduction of Code Duplication**: By centralizing the common parts of the algorithm in one location, the Template Method pattern minimizes code duplication. This results in cleaner, more maintainable code, as changes to the common structure need only be made in one place.

4. **Clear Separation of Concerns**: The pattern distinctly separates the high-level algorithm from the details of its steps, fostering a clear division of responsibilities. This separation enhances readability and makes it easier to understand the algorithm's overall flow.

5. **Inversion of Control**: The Template Method pattern inverts the control flow by placing the algorithm's structure within the abstract class. Rather

than allowing subclasses to dictate the flow, the template method orchestrates the sequence by invoking specific methods defined in the subclasses.

List of trade-offs of the Template Method pattern:

1. **Limited Runtime Flexibility**: A downside of the Template Method pattern is its lack of runtime flexibility. Since the algorithm's structure is set at compile time, making dynamic changes to the algorithm's flow or behavior can be challenging without modifying the base class.

2. **Increased Complexity**: Introducing an abstract class with multiple subclasses can increase the overall complexity of the codebase. This added complexity might not be justified for simpler algorithms that don't require a flexible structure.

3. **Dependency on Subclass Behavior**: The pattern relies on subclasses to correctly implement the specific steps of the algorithm. If a subclass incorrectly overrides a method, it can lead to unexpected behaviors, making the system harder to debug and maintain.

Visitor Pattern

The **Visitor design pattern** is a behavioural design pattern that enables you to add new behaviors or operations to a group of classes without altering their existing code. By decoupling the algorithm from the object structure it operates on, the pattern allows for easier extension of class functionality.

Problem: In object-oriented programming, adding new operations or functionalities to each class within a complex class hierarchy can be cumbersome. This approach often violates the Open/Closed Principle—a key principle in SOLID design that suggests classes should be open for extension but closed for modification. Moreover, modifying existing classes introduces the risk of unintended side effects, potentially breaking existing functionality.

Solution: The Visitor pattern addresses this problem by introducing a separate set of visitor classes that encapsulate new operations or functionalities. Rather than modifying the classes themselves, you define new operations by creating concrete visitor classes that can "visit" each class in the object structure.

This pattern comprises two main components:

1. **Visitor**: An interface or abstract class that defines the operations to be performed on the elements.

2. **Element**: A class that defines an accept method, which takes a visitor as a parameter and calls the visitor's method, passing itself as an argument.

Using the Visitor pattern, you can add new operations to elements without changing their implementation. Simply define new visitor classes that implement the visitor interface and introduce the desired behaviors. This approach allows for the easy addition of new functionalities to existing classes without altering their source code.

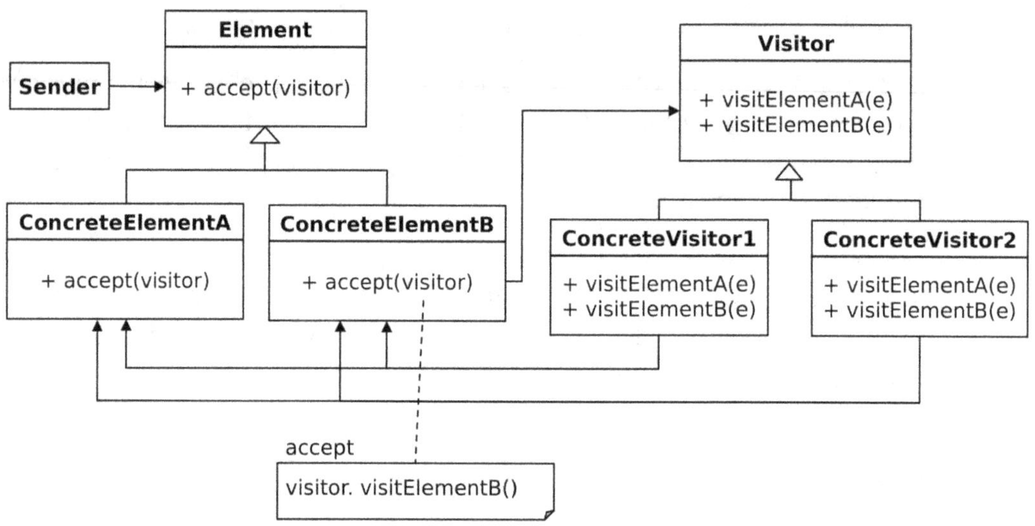

Example implementation :

```go
// Element is the abstract class defining the accept method.
type Element interface {
    accept(visitor Visitor)
}


// ConcreteElementA is a concrete implementation of Element for
element A.
type ConcreteElementA struct{}

func (e *ConcreteElementA) accept(visitor Visitor) {
    visitor.visitElementA(e)
}


// ConcreteElementB is another concrete implementation of Element
for element B.
type ConcreteElementB struct{}

func (e *ConcreteElementB) accept(visitor Visitor) {
    visitor.visitElementB(e)
}
```

```go
// Visitor is the abstract class defining the visit methods.
type Visitor interface {
    visitElementA(elementA *ConcreteElementA)
    visitElementB(elementB *ConcreteElementB)
}

// ConcreteVisitor1 is a concrete implementation of Visitor.
type ConcreteVisitor1 struct{}

func (v *ConcreteVisitor1) visitElementA(elementA
*ConcreteElementA) {
    fmt.Println("ConcreteVisitor1 visitElementA() method
called.")
}

func (v *ConcreteVisitor1) visitElementB(elementB
*ConcreteElementB) {
    fmt.Println("ConcreteVisitor1 visitElementB() method
called.")
}

// ConcreteVisitor2 is another concrete implementation of
Visitor.
type ConcreteVisitor2 struct{}

func (v *ConcreteVisitor2) visitElementA(elementA
*ConcreteElementA) {
    fmt.Println("ConcreteVisitor2 visitElementA() method
called.")
}

func (v *ConcreteVisitor2) visitElementB(elementB
*ConcreteElementB) {
    fmt.Println("ConcreteVisitor2 visitElementB() method
called.")
}

func main() {
    // Client Code
    visitor1 := &ConcreteVisitor1{}
    elementA := &ConcreteElementA{}
    elementA.accept(visitor1)
    elementB := &ConcreteElementB{}
    elementB.accept(visitor1)
}
```

Output:

```
ConcreteVisitor1 visitElementA() method called.
ConcreteVisitor1 visitElementB() method called.
```

Explanation:

1. The **Element** interface defines the **accept()** method, which accepts a visitor as an argument and calls the appropriate **visit()** method on the visitor.

2. **ConcreteElementA** and **ConcreteElementB** implement the **Element** interface and override the **accept()** method to call the specific **visit()** method on the visitor.

3. The **Visitor** interface declares **visit()** methods for each type of element it might encounter. **ConcreteVisitor1** and **ConcreteVisitor2** implement these methods to perform specific actions on the elements they visit.

4. In the client code, an instance of **ConcreteVisitor1** is used to visit **ConcreteElementA** and **ConcreteElementB**. The visitor's **visit()** methods are called for each element, allowing the visitor to perform the specified actions on the elements.

Problem: Implement the Visitor design pattern to manage different shapes (such as Circle and Rectangle) within an "ObjectsStructure" class. The goal is to enable the addition of new operations (visitors) without modifying the shape classes themselves.

Solution: The code defines several classes to implement the Visitor pattern:

1. **Shape (abstract class)**: Represents a generic shape and defines an abstract accept method that must be implemented by its subclasses.

2. **Circle (subclass of Shape)**: Represents a circle with specific coordinates (x, y) and a radius.

3. **Rectangle (subclass of Shape)**: Represents a rectangle with coordinates (x, y), width, and height.

4. **Visitor (abstract class)**: Defines methods for visiting different shape classes.

5. **XMLVisitor (subclass of Visitor)**: Implements the visitor interface to generate XML representations for circles and rectangles.

6. **TextVisitor (subclass of Visitor)**: Implements the visitor interface to generate text representations for circles and rectangles.

7. **ObjectsStructure**: Represents a collection of shapes and provides methods to add shapes, set a visitor, and apply the visitor to all shapes.

Example Implementation:

```go
// Shape is the abstract class defining the accept method.
type Shape interface {
    Accept(visitor Visitor) string
}

// Circle is a concrete implementation of Shape for circles.
type Circle struct {
    x, y, radius int
}

func (c *Circle) Accept(visitor Visitor) string {
    return visitor.VisitCircle(c)
}

// Rectangle is another concrete implementation of Shape for
rectangles.
type Rectangle struct {
    x, y, width, height int
}

func (r *Rectangle) Accept(visitor Visitor) string {
    return visitor.VisitRectangle(r)
}

// Visitor is the abstract class defining the visit methods.
type Visitor interface {
    VisitCircle(circle *Circle) string
    VisitRectangle(rectangle *Rectangle) string
}

// XMLVisitor is a concrete implementation of Visitor for
generating XML representation.
type XMLVisitor struct{}

func (v *XMLVisitor) VisitCircle(circle *Circle) string {
```

```go
        return fmt.Sprintf("<circle>\n  <x>%d</x>\n  <y>%d</y>\n
<radius>%d</radius>\n</circle>", circle.x, circle.y,
circle.radius)
}

func (v *XMLVisitor) VisitRectangle(rectangle *Rectangle) string
{
        return fmt.Sprintf("<rectangle>\n  <x>%d</x>\n  <y>%d</y>\n
<width>%d</width>\n  <height>%d</height>\n</rectangle>",
rectangle.x, rectangle.y, rectangle.width, rectangle.height)
}

// TextVisitor is another concrete implementation of Visitor for
generating text representation.
type TextVisitor struct{}

func (v *TextVisitor) VisitCircle(circle *Circle) string {
    return fmt.Sprintf("Circle ( (x : %d, y : %d), radius : %d)",
circle.x, circle.y, circle.radius)
}

func (v *TextVisitor) VisitRectangle(rectangle *Rectangle) string
{
        return fmt.Sprintf("Rectangle ( (x : %d, y : %d), width : %d,
height : %d)", rectangle.x, rectangle.y, rectangle.width,
rectangle.height)
}

// ObjectsStructure is the structure holding a collection of
shapes.
type ObjectsStructure struct {
    shapes   []Shape
    visitor Visitor
}

func (os *ObjectsStructure) AddShapes(shape Shape) {
    os.shapes = append(os.shapes, shape)
}

func (os *ObjectsStructure) SetVisitor(visitor Visitor) {
    os.visitor = visitor
}

func (os *ObjectsStructure) Accept() {
    for _, shape := range os.shapes {
        fmt.Println(shape.Accept(os.visitor))
    }
}
```

```go
}

func main() {
    os := &ObjectsStructure{}
    os.AddShapes(&Rectangle{6, 7, 8, 9})
    os.AddShapes(&Circle{6, 7, 8})

    os.SetVisitor(&XMLVisitor{})
    os.Accept()

    os.SetVisitor(&TextVisitor{})
    os.Accept()
}
```

Output:

```
<rectangle>
  <x>6</x>
  <y>7</y>
  <width>8</width>
  <height>9</height>
</rectangle>
<circle>
  <x>6</x>
  <y>7</y>
  <radius>8</radius>
</circle>

Rectangle ( (x : 6, y : 7), width : 8, height : 9)
Circle ( (x : 6, y : 7), radius : 8)
```

Explanation:

1. **Shape Interface and Implementations**: The **Shape** interface defines the **Accept()** method, which is implemented by each concrete shape type (**Circle** and **Rectangle**). This method takes a **Visitor** and calls the corresponding visit method (**VisitCircle** or **VisitRectangle**) on the visitor.

2. **Visitor Interface and Implementations**: The **Visitor** interface defines methods for visiting each shape type. **XMLVisitor** and **TextVisitor** implement this interface, providing different ways of processing the shapes (such as generating XML or text representations).

3. **ObjectsStructure**: This struct holds a collection of shapes and provides methods to add shapes and set a visitor. The **Accept()** method iterates through all shapes, calling their **Accept()** method with the current visitor.

4. **Test Code**: In the test code, shapes are added to the **ObjectsStructure**, and two different visitors (**XMLVisitor** and **TextVisitor**) are used to generate different representations of the shapes, demonstrating the flexibility of the Visitor pattern.

Consequences

The Visitor pattern offers several benefits:

1. **Extensibility**: You can add new operations without modifying existing classes, adhering to the Open/Closed Principle.

2. **Separation of Concerns**: The Visitor pattern separates algorithms from the object structure, improving code organization and maintainability.

3. **Single Responsibility Principle:** Each visitor encapsulates a specific operation, ensuring responsibilities remain well-defined.

However, there are some trade-offs:

1. **Complexity**: The pattern can introduce complexity, particularly if the object structure is subject to frequent changes or new operations are added.

2. **Dependency on Class Hierarchy**: A stable class hierarchy is often necessary, as adding new classes can be cumbersome.

3. **Performance Overhead**: The use of double dispatch in some languages may introduce a slight performance overhead due to the additional function calls required.

Summary

In this chapter, we covered Behavioral Patterns, which focus on the interactions and responsibilities between objects in a system, enhancing flexibility and adaptability. Key patterns include:

1. **Chain of Responsibility**: Passes a request along a chain of handlers, each having the chance to process it, reducing dependencies between sender and receiver.

2. **Command**: Encapsulates a request as an object, allowing for parameterization and queuing of requests, and enabling undoable operations.

3. **Interpreter**: Defines a grammatical representation for a language and provides an interpreter to process it, useful for parsing languages.

4. **Iterator**: Provides a way to access elements of a collection sequentially without exposing its underlying structure.

5. **Mediator**: Centralizes communication between objects, reducing direct dependencies and simplifying object interactions.

6. **Memento**: Captures an object's state to allow it to be restored later, useful for implementing undo functionality.

7. **Observer**: Sets up a dependency where an object automatically notifies and updates dependents when its state changes.

8. **State**: Alters an object's behavior when its internal state changes, allowing dynamic change in behavior.

9. **Strategy**: Encapsulates interchangeable algorithms inside a family of classes, letting clients choose the algorithm at runtime.

10. **Template** Method: Defines the steps of an algorithm, allowing subclasses to override specific steps without changing its structure.

11. **Visitor**: Separates operations from object structures by using visitors to perform actions, making it easy to add new operations.

Exercises

1. **Chain of Responsibility Pattern Problem**: Implement a request processing system with handlers (AuthenticationHandler, AuthorizationHandler, LoggingHandler). Each handler decides to process or pass the request.

   Instructions:

   - Create a base handler interface with methods for processing requests and setting the next handler.

   - Implement handlers that either handle requests or pass them on.

   - Show a request being processed through the chain.

2. **Command Pattern Problem**: Develop a remote control application that executes commands (like turning lights on/off, setting a thermostat) and supports undo operations.

Instructions:

- Define a Command interface with execute and undo.

- Implement command classes (TurnOnLightCommand, TurnOffLightCommand, SetThermostatCommand).

- Create a RemoteControl class to execute and undo commands.

- Demonstrate using the remote control without knowing command specifics.

3. **Interpreter Pattern Problem**: Create an interpreter for a mini-language supporting addition, subtraction, multiplication, and division.

Instructions:

- Define an Expression interface with interpret.

- Implement classes (NumberExpression, AddExpression, etc.) for operations.

- Build a parser for expression trees.

- Show the interpreter evaluating expressions.

4. **Iterator Pattern Problem**: Build an iterator for a linked list to allow sequential access without exposing the list's structure.

Instructions:

- Define an Iterator interface with hasNext() and next().

- Create a LinkedList class and an iterator for it.

- Demonstrate iterating through the linked list.

5. **Mediator Pattern Problem**: Design a messaging app where users interact via a ChatRoom mediator.

Instructions:

- Create a ChatRoom interface for user communication.

- Implement a concrete ChatRoom class to manage users.

- Define a User class that communicates via the mediator.

- Show users sending messages through the mediator.

6. **Memento Pattern Problem**: Implement a text editor with undo functionality using the Memento pattern.

Instructions:

- Define a Memento class to store the editor's state.
- Create a TextEditor class with methods to save and restore state.
- Demonstrate undo functionality by restoring previous states.

7. **Observer Pattern Problem**: Develop a stock monitoring system where observers (e.g., traders) get notified of stock price changes.

   Instructions:

   - Create a Subject interface for attaching/detaching observers.
   - Implement a Stock class and observer classes (Trader, Analyst).
   - Show observers reacting to stock price changes.

8. **State Pattern Problem**: Create a traffic light control system using states (Red, Green, Yellow).

   Instructions:

   - Define a State interface for transitions.
   - Implement state classes (RedState, GreenState, YellowState).
   - Create a TrafficLight class that changes states.
   - Demonstrate state transitions.

9. **Strategy Pattern Problem**: Design a sorting app that allows choosing different sorting algorithms (Bubble Sort, Quick Sort, etc.).

   Instructions:

   - Define a SortStrategy interface with a sort method.
   - Implement sorting algorithms as strategy classes.
   - Create a Sorter class that uses a strategy.
   - Show sorting with different algorithms.

10. **Template Method Pattern Problem**: Implement a game framework using a base class to define the sequence of actions.

    Instructions:

    - Create an abstract Game class with a template method.
    - Implement game classes (Chess, Football) with specific steps.

○ Demonstrate different games using the framework.

11. **Visitor Pattern Problem**: Create a document editor that processes elements (paragraphs, images) with visitors.

Instructions:

○ Define an Element interface with accept.

○ Implement element classes (Paragraph, Image).

○ Create a Visitor interface and implement (PrintVisitor, SpellCheckVisitor).

○ Show processing with different visitors.

Solution of Exercises

Solution 1: Chain of Responsibility Pattern

```go
type Handler interface {
    SetNext(Handler)
    HandleRequest(string)
}


type BaseHandler struct{ next Handler }
func (h *BaseHandler) SetNext(next Handler) { h.next = next }
func (h *BaseHandler) HandleRequest(req string) { if h.next !=
nil { h.next.HandleRequest(req) } }

type AuthHandler struct{ BaseHandler }
func (h *AuthHandler) HandleRequest(req string) {
    if req == "auth" { fmt.Println("Auth handled") } else
{ h.BaseHandler.HandleRequest(req) }
}

type LogHandler struct{ BaseHandler }
func (h *LogHandler) HandleRequest(req string) {
    if req == "log" { fmt.Println("Log handled") } else
{ h.BaseHandler.HandleRequest(req) }
}

// Usage
auth := &AuthHandler{}
log := &LogHandler{}
auth.SetNext(log)
auth.HandleRequest("auth")
```

```go
auth.HandleRequest("log")
```

Solution 2: Command Pattern

```go
type Command interface { Execute(); Undo() }

type Light struct{ on bool }
func (l *Light) On() { l.on = true; fmt.Println("Light On") }
func (l *Light) Off() { l.on = false; fmt.Println("Light Off") }

type LightOnCommand struct{ light *Light }
func (c *LightOnCommand) Execute() { c.light.On() }
func (c *LightOnCommand) Undo() { c.light.Off() }

type RemoteControl struct{ cmd Command }
func (r *RemoteControl) SetCommand(cmd Command) { r.cmd = cmd }
func (r *RemoteControl) PressButton() { r.cmd.Execute() }
func (r *RemoteControl) PressUndo() { r.cmd.Undo() }

// Usage
light := &Light{}
onCommand := &LightOnCommand{light}
remote := &RemoteControl{}
remote.SetCommand(onCommand)
remote.PressButton()
remote.PressUndo()
```

Solution 3: Interpreter Pattern

```go
type Expression interface { Interpret() int }

type Number struct{ value int }
func (n *Number) Interpret() int { return n.value }

type Add struct{ left, right Expression }
func (a *Add) Interpret() int { return a.left.Interpret() +
a.right.Interpret() }

// Usage
expr := &Add{&Number{2}, &Number{3}}
fmt.Println(expr.Interpret()) // Output: 5
```

Solution 4: Iterator Pattern

```go
type Iterator interface {
    HasNext() bool
    Next() int
}

type LinkedList struct {
    data []int
}

type LinkedListIterator struct {
    list *LinkedList
    index int
}

func (it *LinkedListIterator) HasNext() bool {
    return it.index < len(it.list.data)
}

func (it *LinkedListIterator) Next() int {
    value := it.list.data[it.index]
    it.index++
    return value
}

// Usage
list := &LinkedList{data: []int{1, 2, 3}}
it := &LinkedListIterator{list: list}

for it.HasNext() {
    fmt.Println(it.Next()) // Output: 1 2 3
}
```

Solution 5: Mediator Pattern

```go
type Mediator interface {
    ShowMessage(user *User, message string)
}

type ChatRoom struct{}

func (c *ChatRoom) ShowMessage(user *User, message string) {
    fmt.Printf("[%s]: %s\n", user.name, message)
}
```

```go
type User struct {
    name     string
    mediator Mediator
}

func (u *User) SendMessage(message string) {
    u.mediator.ShowMessage(u, message)
}

// Usage
mediator := &ChatRoom{}
user1 := &User{"Alice", mediator}
user2 := &User{"Bob", mediator}
user1.SendMessage("Hi Bob!")
user2.SendMessage("Hello Alice!")
```

Solution 6: Memento Pattern

```go
type EditorState struct { content string }

type Editor struct {
    content string
}

func (e *Editor) CreateState() *EditorState {
    return &EditorState{content: e.content}
}

func (e *Editor) Restore(state *EditorState) {
    e.content = state.content
}

// Usage
editor := &Editor{}
editor.content = "Hello"
saved := editor.CreateState()
editor.content = "World"
editor.Restore(saved)
fmt.Println(editor.content) // Output: Hello
```

Problem 7: Observer Pattern

```go
type Observer interface { Update(price float64) }
```

```go
type Stock struct {
    observers []Observer
    price float64
}

func (s *Stock) Attach(o Observer) { s.observers =
append(s.observers, o) }
func (s *Stock) Notify() { for _, o := range s.observers
{ o.Update(s.price) } }
func (s *Stock) SetPrice(price float64) { s.price = price;
s.Notify() }

type Trader struct { name string }
func (t *Trader) Update(price float64) { fmt.Printf("%s notified
of price: %f\n", t.name, price) }

// Usage
stock := &Stock{}
trader := &Trader{name: "Alice"}
stock.Attach(trader)
stock.SetPrice(100.0) // Output: Alice notified of price:
100.000000
```

Solution 8: State Pattern

```go
type State interface {
    HandleLight(light *TrafficLight)
}

type RedState struct{}
func (r *RedState) HandleLight(light *TrafficLight) {
    fmt.Println("Red Light")
    light.SetState(&GreenState{})
}

type GreenState struct{}
func (g *GreenState) HandleLight(light *TrafficLight) {
    fmt.Println("Green Light")
    light.SetState(&YellowState{})
}

type YellowState struct{}
func (y *YellowState) HandleLight(light *TrafficLight) {
    fmt.Println("Yellow Light")
    light.SetState(&RedState{})
}
```

```go
type TrafficLight struct{ state State }
func (t *TrafficLight) SetState(s State) { t.state = s }
func (t *TrafficLight) Change() { t.state.HandleLight(t) }

// Usage
light := &TrafficLight{state: &RedState{}}
light.Change() // Output: Red Light
light.Change() // Output: Green Light
light.Change() // Output: Yellow Light
```

Solution 9: Strategy Pattern

```go
type SortStrategy interface { Sort([]int) }

type BubbleSort struct{}
func (b *BubbleSort) Sort(arr []int) { fmt.Println("Bubble
sorting") }

type QuickSort struct{}
func (q *QuickSort) Sort(arr []int) { fmt.Println("Quick
sorting") }

type Sorter struct{ strategy SortStrategy }
func (s *Sorter) SetStrategy(strategy SortStrategy) { s.strategy
= strategy }
func (s *Sorter) Sort(arr []int) { s.strategy.Sort(arr) }

// Usage
sorter := &Sorter{}
sorter.SetStrategy(&BubbleSort{})
sorter.Sort([]int{3, 2, 1}) // Output: Bubble sorting
sorter.SetStrategy(&QuickSort{})
sorter.Sort([]int{3, 2, 1}) // Output: Quick sorting
```

Problem 10: Template Method Pattern

```go
type Game interface {
    Initialize()
    StartPlay()
    EndPlay()
}

type BaseGame struct{}
```

```go
func (b *BaseGame) Play() {
    b.Initialize()
    b.StartPlay()
    b.EndPlay()
}

type Chess struct{ BaseGame }
func (c *Chess) Initialize() { fmt.Println("Chess Game
Initialized") }
func (c *Chess) StartPlay()  { fmt.Println("Chess Game
Started") }
func (c *Chess) EndPlay()     { fmt.Println("Chess Game Ended") }

// Usage
game := &Chess{}
game.Play()
```

Solution 11: Visitor Pattern

```go
type Element interface { Accept(Visitor) }

type Paragraph struct{}
func (p *Paragraph) Accept(v Visitor) { v.VisitParagraph(p) }

type Visitor interface { VisitParagraph(*Paragraph) }

type PrintVisitor struct{}
func (p *PrintVisitor) VisitParagraph(paragraph *Paragraph) {
    fmt.Println("Printing paragraph")
}

// Usage
p := &Paragraph{}
v := &PrintVisitor{}
p.Accept(v) // Output: Printing paragraph
```

Concurrency Patterns

Concurrency patterns are techniques and solutions in software design that manage and coordinate the execution of multiple threads or processes simultaneously. These patterns address the complexities of concurrent programming, where different parts of a program run independently and may interact in unpredictable ways. Concurrency patterns help ensure that threads or processes collaborate effectively, avoiding common issues like data races, deadlocks, and resource contention. They provide structured approaches to synchronization, communication, and coordination, leading to more efficient and reliable concurrent software.

One key pattern is the **Active Object Pattern**, which decouples method invocation from execution, allowing objects to communicate asynchronously. This pattern involves a central scheduler, known as the "active object," which manages and queues method calls. This setup enables objects to interact without directly waiting for methods to execute, enhancing both concurrency and responsiveness.

Another important pattern is the **Barrier Pattern**, which synchronizes multiple threads at a specific point in the program. Threads pause at the barrier until all participating threads arrive, and then continue executing together. This pattern is useful in scenarios where parallel tasks need to coordinate their progress, such as different stages of parallel computation.

Finally, the **Double-Checked Locking Pattern** is a synchronization technique designed to optimize the performance of acquiring locks. It involves initially checking a condition without acquiring a lock, and only if the condition is met, acquiring the lock for further processing. This approach reduces the overhead associated with locking, improving concurrency and efficiency.

Active Object Pattern

The Active Object Pattern is a concurrency design pattern that decouples method invocation from execution. It allows objects to handle method calls asynchronously, enabling them to run in separate threads. This is particularly useful in systems where multiple requests need to be handled concurrently without blocking the main program's execution.

Problem: In a concurrent system, objects may interact and perform time-consuming operations. Traditional synchronous method calls can lead to performance bottlenecks, thread blocking, and potential issues like race conditions. If a method invocation blocks until execution completes, it can significantly reduce system responsiveness and scalability.

Solution: The Active Object Pattern solves this problem by introducing a central component—the active object—that manages and queues method requests. The client submits requests to this active object, which processes them asynchronously in the background, allowing the client to continue without waiting for the request to complete. This improves overall system performance and responsiveness.

Key Components

1. **Client**: Initiates requests for services from the active object.

2. **Proxy**: An intermediary that the client uses to communicate with the active object. It forwards requests to the active object and returns the results.

3. **Active Object**: Receives requests and executes them asynchronously. It maintains a queue to manage these requests and processes them in the order they were received.

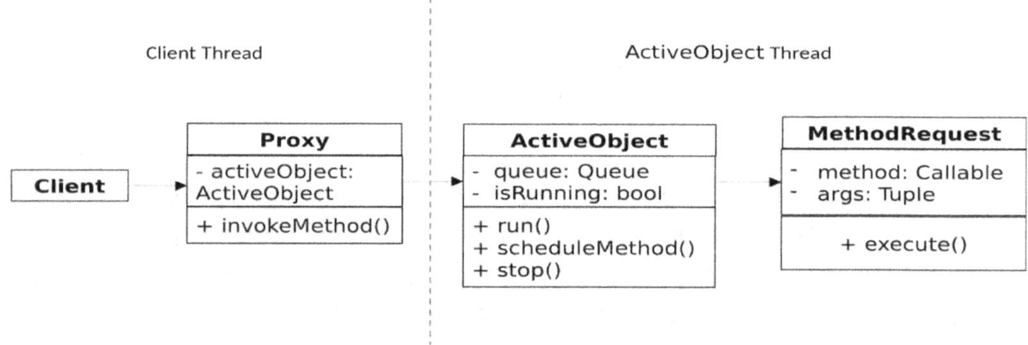

Example Implementation:

```go
package main

import (
    "fmt"
    "sync"
)

// MethodRequest encapsulates a method call along with its
arguments
```

```go
type MethodRequest struct {
    method func()
}

// Execute runs the method
func (mr *MethodRequest) Execute() {
    mr.method()
}

// ActiveObject encapsulates its own thread of control and
executes methods asynchronously
type ActiveObject struct {
    queue      chan *MethodRequest
    isRunning bool
    wg         sync.WaitGroup
}

// NewActiveObject creates a new ActiveObject
func NewActiveObject() *ActiveObject {
    return &ActiveObject{
        queue:     make(chan *MethodRequest),
        isRunning: true,
    }
}

// Run executes method requests
func (ao *ActiveObject) Run() {
    ao.wg.Add(1)
    defer ao.wg.Done()
    for ao.isRunning || len(ao.queue) > 0 {
        select {
        case methodRequest := <-ao.queue:
            methodRequest.Execute()
        }
    }
}

// ScheduleMethod schedules a method request
func (ao *ActiveObject) ScheduleMethod(method func()) {
    ao.queue <- &MethodRequest{method: method}
}

// StopThread stops the ActiveObject thread
func (ao *ActiveObject) StopThread() {
    ao.isRunning = false
    close(ao.queue)
```

```go
}

// Proxy acts as a wrapper around the ActiveObject and forwards
method calls to it
type Proxy struct {
    activeObject *ActiveObject
}

// NewProxy creates a new Proxy
func NewProxy(ao *ActiveObject) *Proxy {
    return &Proxy{ao: ao}
}

// InvokeMethod invokes a method request
func (p *Proxy) InvokeMethod(method func()) {
    p.activeObject.ScheduleMethod(method)
}

// Client Code
func main() {
    // Create an instance of ActiveObject and Proxy
    ao := NewActiveObject()
    proxy := NewProxy(ao)

    // Start the ActiveObject thread
    go ao.Run()

    // Invoke methods on the Proxy
    proxy.InvokeMethod(func() { fmt.Println("Hello") })
    proxy.InvokeMethod(func() { fmt.Println("World") })

    // Wait for the ActiveObject thread to complete
    ao.StopThread()
    ao.wg.Wait()
}
```

Output:

```
Hello
World
```

Explanation:

This code demonstrates the Active Object design pattern. Here's a breakdown of
how it works:

1. **MethodRequest Struct**: The **MethodRequest** struct encapsulates a method call, represented by a function (**func()**). The **Execute()** method runs the encapsulated function when called.

2. **ActiveObject Struct**: The **ActiveObject** struct manages its own thread of control by maintaining a channel (**queue**) for **MethodRequest** objects. The **Run()** method continuously checks the queue for method requests and executes them asynchronously. The **ScheduleMethod()** method allows new tasks to be added to the queue, while **Stop** signals the **ActiveObject** to stop processing.

3. **Proxy Struct**: The **Proxy** struct acts as a simple interface to the **ActiveObject**, allowing clients to schedule methods for asynchronous execution without directly interacting with the **ActiveObject**.

4. **Client Code (main function)**: The **main** function demonstrates the usage of these components. An **ActiveObject** and its **Proxy** are created, and the **ActiveObject** starts processing in a separate goroutine. Methods are invoked asynchronously through the **Proxy**, and the **ActiveObject** is gracefully stopped after all tasks are completed.

Consequences

The Active Object pattern provides several advantages:

1. **Asynchronous Invocation**: Clients can send method requests to Active Objects without having to wait for their completion, enhancing system responsiveness and concurrency.

2. **Thread Safety**: By handling method calls in a single-threaded manner, the Active Object pattern minimizes the risk of thread-related issues such as race conditions and deadlocks.

3. **Modularity**: Active Objects encapsulate the implementation details of the underlying object, promoting better separation of concerns and easier maintainability.

4. **Scalability**: Asynchronous method invocation and independent execution enable the system to scale more effectively to accommodate increased workloads.

However, the Active Object pattern also introduces certain trade-offs:

1. **Overhead**: The addition of a message queue and scheduling mechanism introduces some overhead to method invocations, potentially impacting performance for low-complexity or frequently called methods.

2. **Complexity**: Implementing the Active Object pattern can increase complexity, particularly in handling errors, synchronization, and ensuring proper communication between the Proxy, Scheduler, and Real Object.

3. **Latency**: Although the pattern improves client responsiveness, it can introduce latency since method calls are queued and processed in the background.

Barrier Pattern

The **Barrier Object design pattern** is a concurrent programming pattern that addresses synchronisation challenges in multithreaded or parallel processing systems. It is used to coordinate multiple threads or tasks to ensure that they reach a specific point in execution before proceeding further. The pattern provides a simple and efficient way to manage the flow of execution, helping to synchronise threads that depend on each other's completion.

Problem: Multiple threads or tasks need to work together to achieve a collective goal, it becomes essential to ensure proper synchronisation among them. Some tasks might rely on the completion of others before they can proceed, leading to the risk of race conditions, data inconsistency, or deadlock situations. Without proper coordination, the program's behaviour becomes unpredictable and could result in errors and unexpected outcomes.

Solution: The Barrier Object pattern introduces a synchronisation construct called a "barrier." A barrier acts as a rendezvous point for multiple threads or tasks, requiring them to wait until all participants have reached the barrier before allowing any of them to proceed. It enables the threads to synchronise and coordinate their progress efficiently.

The typical usage involves the following steps:

1. Initialise the barrier with the number of threads or tasks that need to synchronise.

2. Each thread or task performs its work independently until it reaches the barrier.

3. Upon reaching the barrier, the thread/task waits for all other participants to arrive at the same barrier.

4. Once all participants have reached the barrier, they are released simultaneously to proceed with their next steps.

The Barrier Pattern involves the following components:

1. **Barrier**: A synchronisation primitive that blocks threads until all threads have reached the barrier point. Once all threads have reached the barrier, the barrier is released and all threads can proceed.

2. **Threads**: A set of threads that need to wait for each other to reach a certain point of execution before proceeding.

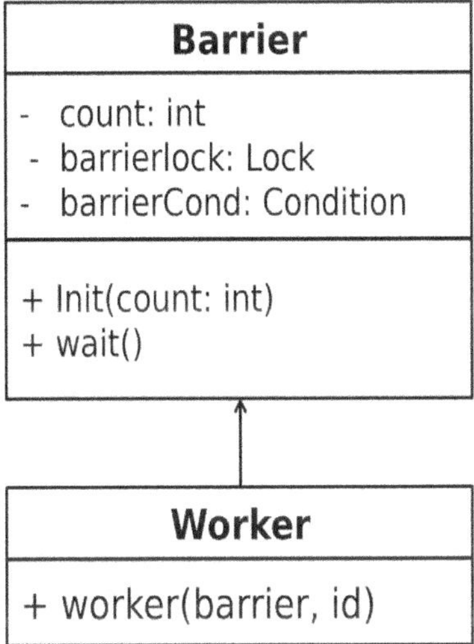

Example Implementation:

```go
package main

import (
    "fmt"
    "sync"
    "time"
)

// Barrier represents a synchronization barrier
type Barrier struct {
    count int
    lock  sync.Mutex
```

```go
    cond  *sync.Cond
}

// NewBarrier creates a new Barrier with the given count
func NewBarrier(count int) *Barrier {
    b := &Barrier{count: count}
    b.cond = sync.NewCond(&b.lock)
    return b
}

// Wait waits until all goroutines have called Wait on the
barrier
func (b *Barrier) Wait() {
    b.lock.Lock()
    defer b.lock.Unlock()

    b.count--
    if b.count > 0 {
        b.cond.Wait()
    } else {
        b.cond.Broadcast()
    }
}

// Worker represents a worker goroutine
type Worker struct {
    id      int
    barrier *Barrier
}

// NewWorker creates a new Worker with the given id and barrier
func NewWorker(id int, barrier *Barrier) *Worker {
    return &Worker{id: id, barrier: barrier}
}

// Work simulates work for the worker
func (w *Worker) Work() {
    fmt.Printf("Worker %d started\n", w.id)
    for i := 0; i < 3; i++ {
        fmt.Printf("Worker %d working...\n", w.id)
        time.Sleep(time.Second)
    }
    fmt.Printf("Worker %d finished\n", w.id)
    w.barrier.Wait()
}
```

```go
// Client Code
func main() {
    numWorkers := 3
    barrier := NewBarrier(numWorkers)
    var wg sync.WaitGroup

    for i := 0; i < numWorkers; i++ {
        wg.Add(1)
        worker := NewWorker(i, barrier)
        go func() {
            defer wg.Done()
            worker.Work()
        }()
    }

    wg.Wait()
    fmt.Println("All workers finished.")
}
```

Output:

```
Worker 0 started
Worker 0 working...
Worker 2 started
Worker 1 started
Worker 1 working...
Worker 2 working...
Worker 0 working...
Worker 1 working...
Worker 2 working...
Worker 0 working...
Worker 1 working...
Worker 2 working...
Worker 1 finished
Worker 0 finished
Worker 2 finished
All workers finished. Proceeding to the next step.
```

Explanation:

This code demonstrates the usage of the Barrier pattern to coordinate multiple workers using threads. Let's go through it step by step:

1. **Barrier Class:**

   - **Barrier** class is defined with an integer variable **count** representing the number of threads that need to reach the barrier before they can proceed.

- It uses a **ReentrantLock** named **barrierLock** to provide mutual exclusion while updating the count and checking conditions.

- It also utilizes a **Condition** named **barrierCondition** associated with the lock, which allows threads to wait until a certain condition is met.

- The constructor initializes the count.

- **waitBarrier**() method is responsible for decrementing the count and waiting until all threads have reached the barrier.

2. Worker Class:

- **Worker** class implements the **Runnable** interface, meaning instances of this class can be executed by a thread.

- Each worker has an associated barrier (**Barrier** instance) and an ID.

- The **run()** method simulates some work (printing messages and sleeping for 1 second) and then waits at the barrier by invoking **barrier.waitBarrier().**

3. BarrierPattern Class (Main):

- The **main()** method initializes the number of workers (**numWorkers**) and creates a **Barrier** instance.

- It creates an array of **Thread** objects to run the worker tasks concurrently.

- Each worker is associated with the barrier and a unique ID.

- Threads are started for each worker.

- The main thread (in **main()**) waits for all worker threads to complete (**join()** method is used).

- Once all workers have finished, it prints a message indicating that all workers have finished, and the program proceeds to the next step.

Consequences

List of advantages for using the Barrier Object pattern:

- **Simplifies Synchronization**: The pattern provides a straightforward way to synchronize multiple threads or tasks, ensuring they all reach a specific execution point before proceeding.

- **Prevents Race Conditions**: By requiring all threads to wait at the barrier, it prevents race conditions where threads may access shared resources in an unsynchronized manner.

- **Ensures Data Consistency**: Helps maintain data consistency by coordinating thread execution, ensuring that operations dependent on the completion of others are properly ordered.

- **Predictable Execution Flow**: Enforces a predictable sequence of execution, which makes it easier to reason about program behavior and debugging.

- **Reduces Complexity in Parallel Algorithms**: Facilitates the implementation of parallel algorithms that require phases of synchronized work, such as iterative calculations where each step depends on the previous one.

List of trade-offs for using the Barrier Object pattern:

- **Not Suitable for All Scenarios**: The pattern may not be appropriate for every synchronization challenge. Other synchronization mechanisms like semaphores, mutexes, or condition variables might be more effective depending on the application's needs.

- **Risk of Deadlocks**: If not implemented carefully, there is a risk of deadlocks, where threads wait indefinitely for others to reach the barrier, causing the program to freeze.

- **Potential Performance Bottlenecks**: The barrier can become a performance bottleneck if threads reach it at significantly different times, causing some threads to idle while waiting for others.

- **Requires Careful Coordination**: All participating threads must be well-coordinated to reach the barrier. If any thread fails to reach the barrier, it can cause the entire system to halt.

- **Increased Overhead**: Synchronization introduces additional overhead, especially in systems with a high number of threads or tasks, potentially reducing overall performance.

Double-Checked Locking Pattern

The **Double-Checked Locking (DCL) pattern** is a software design pattern that enables efficient, thread-safe lazy initialization of a singleton object. It is useful in situations where creating an object is expensive, and the object is only needed under specific conditions.

Problem: In early implementations of the Singleton pattern, such as basic lazy initialization, there could be performance issues in a multi-threaded environment. If multiple threads concurrently request the singleton instance, more than one instance might be created, violating the singleton principle and leading to inconsistent behavior and wasted resources.

Solution: The Double-Checked Locking (DCL) pattern optimizes the Singleton pattern to address the multi-threading issue and enhance performance. This technique uses a combination of synchronized blocks and conditional checks to ensure that only one instance of the singleton is created, even when multiple threads are involved.

Example implementation :

```go
package main

import (
    "fmt"
    "sync"
)

// Database represents a dummy database
type Database struct{}

// NewDatabase creates a new Database instance
func NewDatabase() *Database {
    fmt.Println("Database created")
    return &Database{}
}

// AddData adds data to the database
func (d *Database) AddData(data string) {
    fmt.Println(data)
}
```

```go
// Singleton represents a singleton object
type Singleton struct {
    db *Database
}

var (
    instance *Singleton
    once      sync.Once
    mu        sync.Mutex // Mutex for synchronization
)

// GetInstance returns the singleton instance
func GetInstance() *Singleton {
    if instance == nil { // Check without acquiring lock to
improve performance
        mu.Lock()
        defer mu.Unlock()
        if instance == nil {
            instance = &Singleton{db: NewDatabase()}
        }
    }

    return instance
}

// AddData adds data to the database via the singleton instance
func (s *Singleton) AddData(data string) {
    s.db.AddData(data)
}

// Client Code
func main() {
    s1 := GetInstance()
    s2 := GetInstance()

    fmt.Println(s1)
    fmt.Println(s2)

    s2.AddData("Hello, world!")
}
```

Output:

```
Database created
&{0x5500b8}
```

```
&{0x5500b8}
Hello, world!
```

Explanation:

1. **Database Class:**

   - The **Database** class represents a simple database and has a method **AddData()** to add data to it.

   - It is a basic utility class that the **Singleton** class utilizes.

2. **Singleton Class:**

   - The **Singleton** class is designed to ensure that only one instance exists throughout the application's lifetime.

   - It contains a private constructor to prevent direct instantiation from outside the class.

   - A static volatile instance of the class (**instance**) ensures changes are immediately visible to other threads.

   - It also has a static instance of the **Database** class (**db**).

   - The class includes a static final object (**lock**) for synchronization purposes.

   - The **GetInstance()** method provides access to the singleton instance using double-checked locking to ensure thread safety and efficient lazy initialization.

   - Inside **GetInstance()**, an initial check for instance being nil is performed. If nil, it enters a synchronized block to ensure only one thread can create the instance. Inside the synchronized block, it checks again for nil before creating the instance, ensuring that unnecessary synchronization is avoided once the instance is initialized.

   - The **AddData()** method adds data to the database through the db instance.

3. **Client Code:**

   - The **main()** function demonstrates the usage of the **Singleton** class.

   - It obtains two instances (**s1** and **s2**) of the **Singleton** class using the **GetInstance()** method.

- It prints the references of **s1** and **s2** to verify they reference the same instance.

- It then adds data to the database through **s2**.

Consequences

Advantages of the DCL:

- **Thread-Safe Initialization**: The DCL pattern ensures that only one instance of the singleton is created, even in a multi-threaded environment, avoiding the risks of multiple instances.

- **Performance Optimization**: The initial check outside the synchronized block reduces the overhead of synchronization after the instance is initialized, improving performance in scenarios where the singleton is accessed frequently.

- **Efficient Resource Utilization**: Only initializes the singleton object when needed, conserving resources.

Trade-Offs of the DCL:

- **Complex Implementation**: Implementing DCL correctly can be tricky due to the nuances of language/compiler optimizations or different memory models across platforms, potentially leading to subtle bugs.

- **Compatibility Issues**: Some programming languages and runtime environments may not fully support DCL due to how they handle memory and synchronization, requiring careful attention to language specifics.

- **Alternative Approaches**: In modern programming languages and frameworks, other methods, such as built-in lazy initialization constructs, can offer simpler and more reliable ways to implement thread-safe singletons.

Summary

In this chapter, we explored Concurrency Patterns, which help manage the execution of multiple threads or processes, improving efficiency and reliability in concurrent systems. Key patterns include:

1. **Active Object**: Decouples method requests from execution, allowing asynchronous processing and improving responsiveness.

2. **Barrier**: Synchronizes threads at a specific point, ensuring all threads reach the same execution stage before continuing.

3. **Double-Checked Locking**: Optimizes locking performance by checking conditions before acquiring a lock, reducing synchronization overhead.

These patterns provide effective strategies for handling concurrent programming challenges and enhancing system performance.

Exercises

1. **Thread Pool with Active Object Pattern Problem**: Implement a thread pool using the Active Object pattern to manage task execution with worker threads.

   Instructions:

   - Create an **ActiveObject** class to manage a queue of tasks.

   - Implement a thread pool that uses a fixed number of worker threads to execute tasks from the queue.

   - Enable dynamic addition of tasks to the queue.

   - Ensure the system shuts down gracefully, processing all tasks before stopping.

2. **Barrier Pattern in Pipeline Problem**: Develop a data processing pipeline with three stages: fetching, processing, and saving. Utilize the Barrier pattern to synchronize stages and manage multiple concurrent pipelines.

   Instructions:

   - Design a pipeline with three distinct stages: fetching data, processing data, and saving data.

   - Use a **Barrier** to synchronize the completion of each stage across multiple pipelines.

   - Execute each stage in a separate goroutine to allow concurrency.

   - Implement logging to visualize the progress and synchronization of the stages.

3. **Singleton with Double-Checked Locking Problem**: Create a thread-safe singleton logger using the double-checked locking pattern.

    Instructions:

    ○   Implement a singleton **Logger** class that ensures only one instance is created, even in a multithreaded environment.

    ○   Use double-checked locking with lazy initialization to ensure thread safety and efficient resource use.

    ○   Ensure the **Logger** class provides a method to log messages safely, managing concurrent access, such as with a file access mutex.

Solution of Exercises

Solution 1. Thread Pool with Active Object Pattern

```go
type Task func()

type ActiveObject struct {
    tasks chan Task
    wg    sync.WaitGroup
}

func NewActiveObject(workerCount int) *ActiveObject {
    ao := &ActiveObject{tasks: make(chan Task)}
    for i := 0; i < workerCount; i++ {
        go func() {
            for task := range ao.tasks {
                task()
                ao.wg.Done()
            }
        }()
    }
    return ao
}

func (ao *ActiveObject) Submit(task Task) {
    ao.wg.Add(1)
    ao.tasks <- task
}

func (ao *ActiveObject) Shutdown() {
    close(ao.tasks)
    ao.wg.Wait()
```

```go
}

func main() {
    ao := NewActiveObject(3)
    for i := 0; i < 10; i++ {
        i := i
        ao.Submit(func() { fmt.Printf("Task %d is being
processed\n", i) })
    }
    ao.Shutdown()
}
```

Solution 2. Barrier Pattern in Pipeline

```go
func stageWorker(id int, inCh, outCh chan int, wg
*sync.WaitGroup, barrier *sync.WaitGroup) {
    defer wg.Done()
    for data := range inCh {
        outCh <- data + id
        time.Sleep(100 * time.Millisecond)
    }
    if outCh != nil {
        close(outCh)
    }
    barrier.Done()
}

func main() {
    var wg sync.WaitGroup
    barrier := &sync.WaitGroup{}
    barrier.Add(1)

    fetchCh, processCh := make(chan int), make(chan int)
    wg.Add(3)
    go stageWorker(0, nil, fetchCh, &wg, barrier)
    go stageWorker(1, fetchCh, processCh, &wg, barrier)
    go stageWorker(2, processCh, nil, &wg, barrier)

    for i := 0; i < 3; i++ {
        fetchCh <- i
        time.Sleep(100 * time.Millisecond)
    }
    close(fetchCh)

    wg.Wait()
```

```
        barrier.Wait()
}
```

Solution 3. Singleton with Double-Checked Locking

```
type Logger struct {
      mu sync.Mutex
}

var instance *Logger
var once       sync.Once

func GetInstance() *Logger {
      once.Do(func() { instance = &Logger{} })
      return instance
}

func (l *Logger) Log(message string) {
      l.mu.Lock()
      defer l.mu.Unlock()
      fmt.Println(message)
}

func main() {
      GetInstance().Log("This is a log message.")
}
```

ARCHITECTURAL PATTERNS

Architectural patterns provide foundational structures for designing software systems, guiding developers in organizing their code and defining clear roles and responsibilities for different components. These patterns, such as Model-View-Controller (MVC), Model-View-Presenter (MVP), and Model-View-ViewModel (MVVM), Layered pattern and Pipe and Filter pattern, help in achieving modularity, scalability, and maintainability by promoting a separation of concerns. By following these patterns, developers can create systems that are easier to develop, test, and adapt to changing requirements.

Model-View-Controller Pattern

The **Model-View-Controller (MVC) pattern** is a widely used design pattern in software development that divides an application into three interconnected components: the Model, the View, and the Controller. This separation of concerns enhances code reusability, maintainability, and clarity.

Here's an overview of the three components in the MVC pattern:

1. **Model**: The Model represents the application's data and business logic. It encapsulates the data and provides methods for accessing and manipulating it. The Model defines the structure and behavior of the application's data, including validation, calculations, and interactions with databases or external services. It also notifies the View of any data changes, ensuring synchronization between the Model and the View.

2. **View**: The View is responsible for the presentation and visualization of data to the user. It defines the user interface and displays data from the Model. The View observes the Model for any changes and updates its presentation accordingly. The View should not contain any business logic or directly modify the data; its primary purpose is to present the data and handle user interactions, which are then forwarded to the Controller.

3. **Controller**: The Controller acts as an intermediary between the Model and the View. It receives and processes user input from the View and interacts with the Model to update the data. The Controller contains the application's logic and orchestrates the flow of data and events between the Model and the View. It separates user interactions from the underlying data, delegating responsibilities to the appropriate components.

The MVC pattern promotes loose coupling between components, allowing them to be developed and maintained independently. This modularity enhances code reusability and testability, as each component has a specific responsibility. Changes in one component can be made without affecting the others, facilitating application maintenance and evolution.

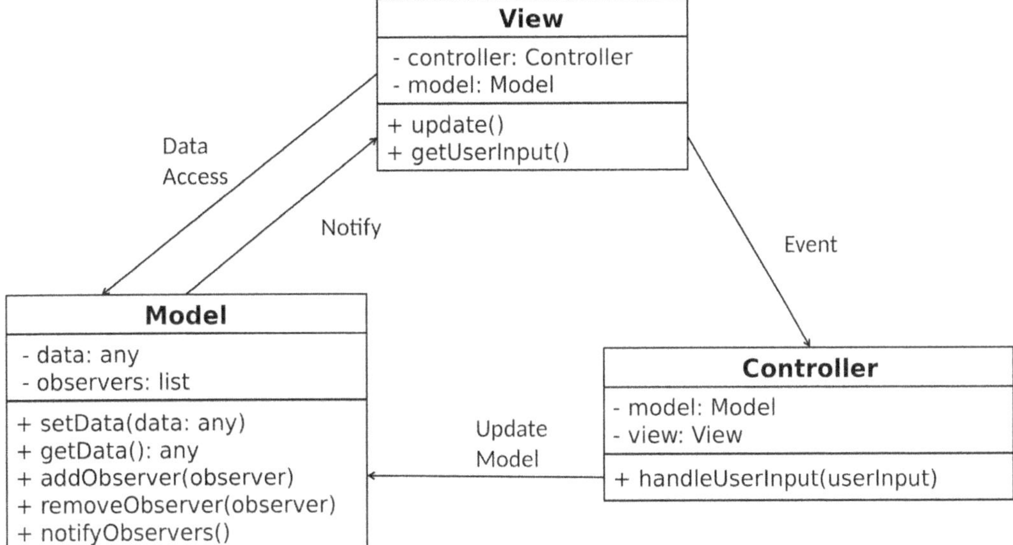

The interactions among the components in the MVC pattern are as follows:

1. The user interacts with the View, such as by entering data or triggering actions.

2. The View forwards the user input to the Controller.

3. The Controller processes the input, performs the necessary operations, and updates the Model accordingly.

4. The Model notifies the View of any changes in the data, maintaining synchronization. The Model maintains a list of observers (the View) and notifies them when the data changes. The Observer pattern is employed here.

5. The View retrieves the updated data from the Model and refreshes its presentation.

6. The user sees the updated View and can continue interacting with the application.

Example Implementation of the MVC Pattern :

```go
package main

import (
    "fmt"
    "bufio"
    "os"
)

// Model struct
type Model struct {
    data      string
    observers []*View
}

// NewModel constructor
func NewModel() *Model {
    return &Model{
        observers: make([]*View, 0),
    }
}

// SetData method
func (m *Model) SetData(data string) {
    fmt.Println("Model : Set data.")
    m.data = data
    m.NotifyObservers()
}

// GetData method
func (m *Model) GetData() string {
    fmt.Println("Model : Get data.")
    return m.data
}

// AddObserver method
func (m *Model) AddObserver(observer *View) {
    m.observers = append(m.observers, observer)
}

// RemoveObserver method
func (m *Model) RemoveObserver(observer *View) {
    for i, obs := range m.observers {
        if obs == observer {
```

```go
            m.observers = append(m.observers[:i],
m.observers[i+1:]...)
            break
        }
    }
}

// NotifyObservers method
func (m *Model) NotifyObservers() {
    fmt.Println("Model : Notify observers.")
    for _, observer := range m.observers {
        observer.Update()
    }
}

// View struct
type View struct {
    controller *Controller
    model      *Model
}

// NewView constructor
func NewView(model *Model, controller *Controller) *View {
    view := &View{
        model:      model,
        controller: controller,
    }
    model.AddObserver(view)
    return view
}

// Update method
func (v *View) Update() {
    fmt.Println("View : Update.")
    data := v.model.GetData()
    fmt.Println("Data:", data)
}

// GetUserInput method
func (v *View) GetUserInput() {
    fmt.Print("View : Enter user input: ")
    scanner := bufio.NewScanner(os.Stdin)
    scanner.Scan()
    userInput := scanner.Text()
    v.controller.HandleUserInput(userInput)
}
```

```go
// Controller struct
type Controller struct {
    model *Model
}

// NewController constructor
func NewController(model *Model) *Controller {
    return &Controller{
        model: model,
    }
}

// HandleUserInput method
func (c *Controller) HandleUserInput(userInput string) {
    fmt.Println("Controller : Handle user input.")
    c.model.SetData(userInput)
}

// Client Code
func main() {
    model := NewModel()
    controller := NewController(model)
    view := NewView(model, controller)
    view.GetUserInput()
}
```

Output:

```
View : Enter user input: hello, world!
Controller : Handle user input.
Model : Set data.
Model : Notify observers.
View : Update.
Model : Get data.
Data: hello, world!
```

Explanation: This program follows these steps:

1. The **View** receives user input and passes it to the **Controller**.

2. The **Controller** processes the user input and updates the **Model**.

3. The **Model** updates its data and notifies all registered observers (in this case, the **View**).

4. The **View**, upon being notified of the change, updates its display with the new data from the **Model**.

Variations and Adaptations of the MVC Pattern

It's important to note that there are variations of the MVC pattern, such as **Model-View-Presenter (MVP)** and **Model-View-ViewModel (MVVM)**, which introduce slight differences in the responsibilities and interactions of the components. However, the core principle of separating concerns remains consistent across these variations.

Drawbacks of MVC and Advantages of MVP

Drawbacks of MVC:

1. **Massive View Controllers**: In MVC, the Controller can become bloated with responsibilities, leading to what is commonly referred to as "Massive View Controllers." As the application grows in complexity, the Controller can become difficult to maintain and understand.

2. **Tightly Coupled Views and Controllers**: In MVC, the View and the Controller are often tightly coupled. The Controller must know details about the View and vice versa, making it challenging to replace or modify one without affecting the other.

3. **Testing Challenges**: Proper unit testing of MVC applications can be difficult, mainly due to the tight coupling between Views and Controllers. It can be challenging to test the interactions between the View and Controller independently.

Advantages of MVP:

1. **Better Separation of Concerns**: MVP improves the separation of concerns compared to MVC. In MVP, the Presenter acts as a mediator between the View and the Model, reducing direct interactions between them and promoting better isolation of responsibilities.

2. **Clearer Roles**: In MVP, each component (Model, View, Presenter) has a distinct role, making the codebase easier to understand and maintain. The Presenter handles user interactions and updates the Model, while the View focuses on rendering and handling user input.

3. **Easier Testing**: MVP makes unit testing more straightforward. The Presenter can be easily tested with mock implementations of the View and Model, allowing for more independent and focused testing.

4. **Enhanced Reusability**: Because the Presenter acts as an intermediary between the View and Model, the View can be implemented with minimal logic, making it easier to reuse across different platforms or UI frameworks.

5. **Support for Interfaces and Dependency Injection**: MVP encourages the use of interfaces and dependency injection, which enhances flexibility and decouples components. This enables easier swapping of implementations and improves overall maintainability.

6. **Flexibility for UI Frameworks**: MVP is considered more flexible for working with various UI frameworks, as the Presenter can abstract the business logic from the specifics of the UI implementation.

Model-View-Presenter Pattern

The **Model-View-Presenter (MVP) pattern** is a software architectural approach that separates concerns in an application, specifically targeting data presentation, user interaction, and business logic. This separation enhances the application's maintainability, testability, and reusability.

Components of MVP

1. **Model**:

- Represents the data and business logic of the application.

- Manages data structures, algorithms, and operations related to the application's functionality.

- Operates independently of both the View and Presenter.

2. **View**:

- Handles the presentation of data and captures user interactions.

- Remains passive, without containing any business logic.

- Implemented using GUI elements like forms, dialogs, or web pages.

- Communicates with the Presenter through interfaces or callbacks.

3. **Presenter**:

- Acts as an intermediary between the Model and the View.

- Retrieves and processes data from the Model for display in the View.

- Manages user interactions from the View, processes them, and updates the Model accordingly.

- Decouples the View from the Model by abstracting their interactions through interfaces.

- Does not directly know the implementation details of the View and Model.

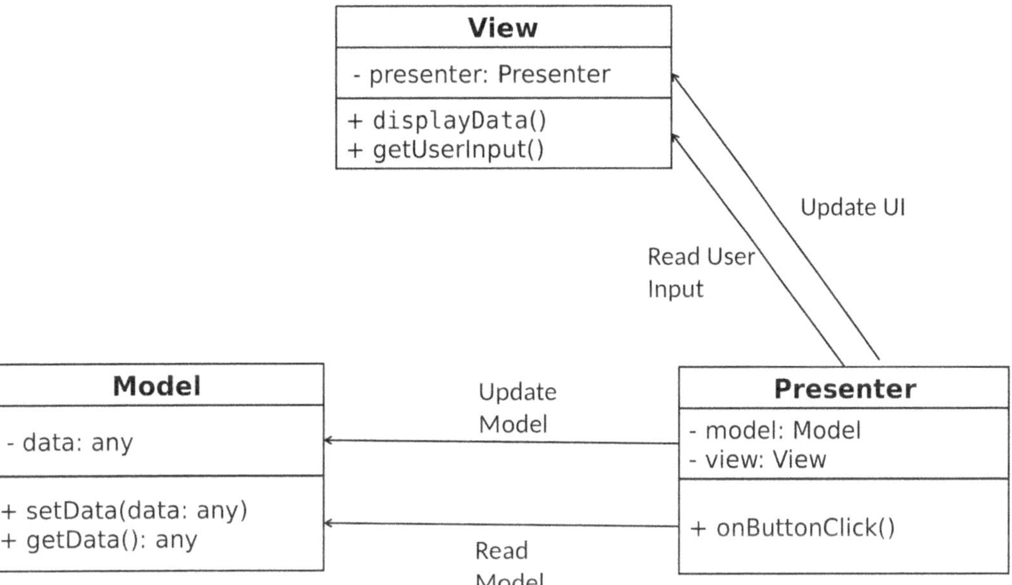

Interaction Flow in MVP

1. The user interacts with the View, triggering an event.

2. The View notifies the Presenter of the user interaction.

3. The Presenter reads the user data from the View and processes it.

4. The Presenter updates the Model.

5. The Presenter reads the data from the Model and updates the View.

6. The View displays the updated data to the user.

Benefits of MVP:

- **Separation of Concerns**: Clearly defines roles for each component, improving code organization.

- **Testability**: The Model can be tested independently; the Presenter can be unit tested by mocking the View and Model.

- **Maintainability**: Changes to the View or Model do not impact the other component, facilitating easier updates.

Example Implementation:

```go
package main

import (
    "fmt"
    "bufio"
    "os"
)

// Model struct
type Model struct {
    data string
}

// NewModel constructor
func NewModel() *Model {
    return &Model{
        data: "Hello",
    }
}

// SetData method
func (m *Model) SetData(data string) {
    fmt.Println("Model: Set data:", data)
    m.data = data
}

// GetData method
func (m *Model) GetData() string {
    fmt.Println("Model: Get data:", m.data)
    return m.data
}
```

```go
// View struct
type View struct{}

// GetUserInput method
func (v *View) GetUserInput() string {
    fmt.Println("View: getUserInput")
    //fmt.Println("View: Enter user input: Hello, World!")
    //return "Hello, World!"
    fmt.Print("View: Enter user input: ")
    scanner := bufio.NewScanner(os.Stdin)
    scanner.Scan()
    userInput := scanner.Text()
    return userInput
}

// DisplayData method
func (v *View) DisplayData(data string) {
    fmt.Println("View: Display Result:", data)
}

// Presenter struct
type Presenter struct {
    model *Model
    view  *View
}

// NewPresenter constructor
func NewPresenter(model *Model, view *View) *Presenter {
    return &Presenter{
        model: model,
        view:  view,
    }
}

// OnButtonClick method
func (p *Presenter) OnButtonClick() {
    fmt.Println("Presenter: onButtonClick.")
    data := p.view.GetUserInput()
    p.model.SetData(data)
    data = p.model.GetData()
    p.view.DisplayData(data)
}

// Client Code
func main() {
    model := NewModel()
```

```
    view := &View{}

    presenter := NewPresenter(model, view)
    presenter.OnButtonClick()
}
```

Output:

```
Presenter: onButtonClick.
View: getUserInput
View: Enter user input: Hello, World!
Model: Set data: Hello, World!
Model: Get data: Hello, World!
View: Display Result: Hello, World!
```

Explanation: Here's a step-by-step explanation of what the code does:

1. **Model Class**: Represents the data layer and contains methods to set and retrieve the data.
2. **View Class**: Manages user interaction by capturing input and displaying output using methods for input and display operations.
3. **Presenter Class**: Serves as an intermediary between the Model and the View. It handles user input from the View, updates the Model with the new data, retrieves updated data from the Model, and instructs the View to display the updated data.
4. **Client Code**: Initializes instances of the Model, View, and Presenter classes, setting up the application.
5. **Presenter's Role in User Actions**: The Presenter's **onButtonClick()** method simulates a user action, handling the logic when a button is clicked, which is central to the MVP pattern.
6. **Process Flow in MVP**: The Presenter receives user input from the View, updates the Model with this input, retrieves the modified data from the Model, and finally instructs the View to present the updated data to the user.

Drawbacks of MVP and Advantages of MVVM

Drawbacks of MVP:

1. **Boilerplate Code**: The MVP pattern often requires a considerable amount of boilerplate code due to the need for explicit interfaces between the View, Presenter, and Model. This can lead to a larger and more complex codebase.
2. **Manual View-Update Synchronization**: In MVP, the Presenter is responsible for manually updating the View whenever there are changes in

the Model. This manual synchronization can introduce potential bugs if not implemented carefully.

3. **Presenter Overhead**: The Presenter in MVP serves as a mediator between the View and the Model, which can result in an increased number of classes and methods. This additional layer can make the architecture more complex and harder to maintain.

Reasons for MVVM:

1. **Data Binding**: A key advantage of MVVM over MVP is the use of data binding. In MVVM, the ViewModel exposes properties that the View can bind to directly. When data changes in the ViewModel, the View is automatically updated, reducing the need for manual synchronization and minimizing errors.

2. **Simplified View**: MVVM simplifies the View by making it primarily responsible for rendering UI elements and binding to properties from the ViewModel. This results in cleaner, more maintainable code within the View, as it focuses solely on presentation logic.

3. **Enhanced Testability**: MVVM enhances testability by allowing the ViewModel to be unit tested independently of the View. This separation makes it easier to write focused and comprehensive tests, improving code quality.

4. **Loose Coupling**: MVVM promotes loose coupling between the View and ViewModel, as the ViewModel does not need to know about the specific implementation details of the View. This separation of concerns allows for greater flexibility in designing and maintaining the UI.

5. **Platform Independence**: MVVM is widely supported in various frameworks that offer data binding capabilities, such as WPF in .NET, Android Data Binding, and Knockout.js in JavaScript. This makes MVVM a popular choice for cross-platform development, as the same ViewModel can be reused with different platform-specific Views.

6. **Efficient State Management**: MVVM often utilizes observable properties within the ViewModel, which streamlines state management and simplifies handling user interactions. This approach allows the View to react automatically to changes in the ViewModel, improving responsiveness and reducing complexity.

Model-View-ViewModel Pattern

The **Model-View-ViewModel (MVVM) pattern** is a software architecture pattern primarily used for designing user interfaces (UIs). It separates the concerns of the UI from the business logic and data models of an application. Introduced by Microsoft in 2005 as a variation of the Model-View-Controller (MVC) pattern, MVVM helps in organizing code to enhance maintainability and testability.

Components of MVVM:

1. **Model**: Represents the data and business logic of the application. This could involve any data source, such as a database, a web service, or any other backend system. The Model handles data retrieval, storage, and manipulation.

2. **View**: Represents the UI of the application. It includes all the visual elements that the user interacts with, such as buttons, text boxes, and images. The View is responsible for defining the structure, layout, and appearance of what the user sees on the screen.

3. **ViewModel**: Serves as a mediator between the View and the Model. The ViewModel contains the presentation logic, such as data formatting, validation, and commands that the View can bind to. It communicates with the Model to retrieve or update data and exposes data and commands that the View binds to, ensuring a clear separation of concerns.

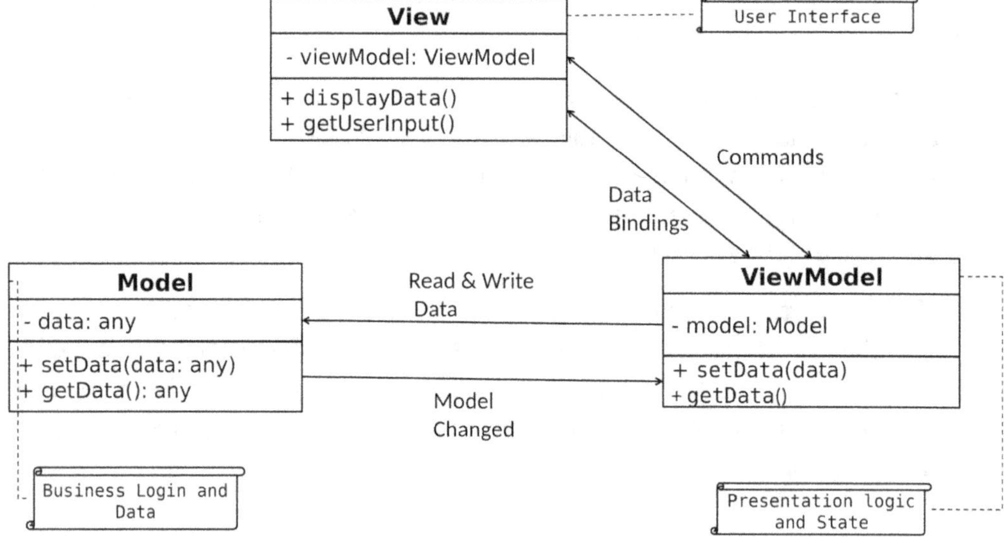

The primary advantage of using the MVVM pattern is that it promotes a clear separation of concerns, which simplifies maintenance and testing of the application. Additionally, the ViewModel can be reused across multiple Views, enhancing code reusability.

Simplified Implementation of the MVVM Pattern:

```go
package main

import (
    "fmt"
    "bufio"
    "os"
)

// Model struct
type Model struct {
    data string
}

// SetData method
func (m *Model) SetData(data string) {
    fmt.Println("Model: Set data.")
    m.data = data
}

// GetData method
func (m *Model) GetData() string {
    fmt.Println("Model: Get data.")
    return m.data
}

// View struct
type View struct {
    viewModel *ViewModel
}

// NewView constructor
func NewView(viewModel *ViewModel) *View {
    return &View{
        viewModel: viewModel,
    }
}
```

```go
// DisplayData method
func (v *View) DisplayData() {
    fmt.Println("Display Data:", v.viewModel.GetData())
}

// GetUserInput method
func (v *View) GetUserInput() {
    fmt.Print("View: Enter user input: ")
    scanner := bufio.NewScanner(os.Stdin)
    scanner.Scan()
    userInput := scanner.Text()
    v.viewModel.SetData(userInput)
}

// ViewModel struct
type ViewModel struct {
    model *Model
}

// NewViewModel constructor
func NewViewModel(model *Model) *ViewModel {
    return &ViewModel{
        model: model,
    }
}

// SetData method
func (vm *ViewModel) SetData(data string) {
    fmt.Println("ViewModel: Set data.")
    vm.model.SetData(data)
}

// GetData method
func (vm *ViewModel) GetData() string {
    fmt.Println("ViewModel: Get data.")
    return vm.model.GetData()
}

// Client Code
func main() {
    model := &Model{data: "Default."}
    viewModel := NewViewModel(model)
    view := NewView(viewModel)

    // Display initial data
    view.DisplayData()
```

```
    // Get user input and update data
    view.GetUserInput()

    // Display updated data
    view.DisplayData()
}
```

Output:

```
ViewModel: Get data.
Model: Get data.
Display Data: Default.
View: Enter user input: hello, world!
ViewModel: Set data.
Model: Set data.
ViewModel: Get data.
Model: Get data.
Display Data: hello, world!
```

Explanation:

1. **Model Class**: Represents the data layer, with methods to set and retrieve the data.

2. **View Class**: Interacts with the user, capturing input and displaying data using methods that call the ViewModel.

3. **ViewModel Class**: Acts as the intermediary between the Model and the View. It updates the Model with user input and retrieves data from the Model to provide it to the View.

4. **Client Code**: Initializes the Model, ViewModel, and View, setting up the application flow.

5. **User Interaction Flow:**

   ○ The View prompts the user for input and then calls the ViewModel to update the Model with this new data.

   ○ The ViewModel updates the Model accordingly.

   ○ Finally, the View retrieves the updated data from the ViewModel and displays it to the user.

Layered Pattern

The **Layered Pattern** is a software design pattern that structures an application into layers or groups of related functionality, with each layer providing services to the layer above it. Each layer typically interacts only with the layer directly above or below it, communicating through a well-defined interface. This pattern improves modularity, maintainability, and scalability by isolating functionality into distinct layers.

A common implementation of the Layered Pattern is the n-tier architecture, which divides an application into three primary layers:

1. **Presentation Layer**: Handles the user interface and manages user input and output. It interacts with the user and displays information.

2. **Business Layer**: Contains the business logic and rules that dictate the application's functionality. It processes data and makes decisions based on business rules.

3. **Data Layer**: Manages data access components and handles interactions with the data store, such as a database or file system.

Simplified Example of n-Tier Architecture:

```go
package main

import "fmt"

// DataAccessLayer struct
type DataAccessLayer struct {
    products []string
}

// NewDataAccessLayer constructor
func NewDataAccessLayer() *DataAccessLayer {
    return &DataAccessLayer{
        products: make([]string, 0),
    }
}

// GetData method
func (dal *DataAccessLayer) GetData() []string {
    return dal.products
}
```

```go
// AddData method
func (dal *DataAccessLayer) AddData(product string) {
    dal.products = append(dal.products, product)
}

// BusinessLogicLayer struct
type BusinessLogicLayer struct {
    dataAccess *DataAccessLayer
}

// NewBusinessLogicLayer constructor
func NewBusinessLogicLayer(dataAccess *DataAccessLayer)
*BusinessLogicLayer {
    return &BusinessLogicLayer{
        dataAccess: dataAccess,
    }
}

// GetAllProducts method
func (bll *BusinessLogicLayer) GetAllProducts() []string {
    return bll.dataAccess.GetData()
}

// AddProduct method
func (bll *BusinessLogicLayer) AddProduct(product string) {
    bll.dataAccess.AddData(product)
}

// PresentationLayer struct
type PresentationLayer struct {
    businessLogic *BusinessLogicLayer
}

// NewPresentationLayer constructor
func NewPresentationLayer(businessLogic *BusinessLogicLayer)
*PresentationLayer {
    return &PresentationLayer{
        businessLogic: businessLogic,
    }
}

// DisplayProducts method
func (pl *PresentationLayer) DisplayProducts() {
    products := pl.businessLogic.GetAllProducts()
    for i, product := range products {
```

```go
        fmt.Printf("%d. %s\n", i+1, product)
    }
}

// AddProduct method
func (pl *PresentationLayer) AddProduct(product string) {
    pl.businessLogic.AddProduct(product)
}

// Client Code
func main() {
    dataAccess := NewDataAccessLayer()
    businessLogic := NewBusinessLogicLayer(dataAccess)
    presentationLayer := NewPresentationLayer(businessLogic)
    presentationLayer.AddProduct("Apple")
    presentationLayer.AddProduct("Banana")
    presentationLayer.AddProduct("Mango")
    presentationLayer.DisplayProducts()
}
```

Output:

```
1. Apple
2. Banana
3. Mango
```

Explanation:

1. **Data Access Layer (DAL)**: The **DataAccessLayer** manages the list of products and provides methods to retrieve (**GetData()**) and add data (**AddData()**). It interacts directly with the data source, handling all data-related operations.

2. **Business Logic Layer (BLL)**: The **BusinessLogicLayer** interacts with the **DataAccessLayer** to enforce business rules. It provides methods to get all products (**GetAllProducts**) and add a product (**AddProduct**), encapsulating the logic needed to manipulate the data.

3. **Presentation Layer (PL)**: The **PresentationLayer** manages user interactions and utilizes the **BusinessLogicLayer** to perform operations. It provides methods to display products (**DisplayProducts**) and add a product (**AddProduct**), thereby serving as the interface for the user.

4. **Client Code**: In the **main** function, instances of the three layers are created. The client code demonstrates adding products and displaying them, showcasing the interaction between layers according to the n-tier architecture.

Pipe and Filter Pattern

The **Pipe and Filter Pattern** is a software design pattern that divides an application into a series of independent processing stages, known as filters, connected by channels, called pipes, that transmit data between them. Each filter is responsible for performing a specific task or transformation on the data and then passing the result to the next filter through the pipe. This design pattern enhances modularity, maintainability, and scalability by allowing individual processing stages to be added, removed, or modified without affecting the entire system.

Simplified Example of the Pipe and Filter Pattern:

```go
package main

import (
    "fmt"
    "strings"
)

// Filter interface
type Filter interface {
    Process(data string) string
}

// CapitalizeFilter struct
type CapitalizeFilter struct{}

// Process method for CapitalizeFilter
func (c *CapitalizeFilter) Process(data string) string {
    return strings.ToUpper(data)
}

// ReplaceSpaceFilter struct
type ReplaceSpaceFilter struct{}

// Process method for ReplaceSpaceFilter
func (r *ReplaceSpaceFilter) Process(data string) string {
    return strings.ReplaceAll(data, " ", "_")
}

// RemoveSpecialCharactersFilter struct
type RemoveSpecialCharactersFilter struct{}
```

```go
// Process method for RemoveSpecialCharactersFilter
func (r *RemoveSpecialCharactersFilter) Process(data string)
string {
    var specialCharacters = ",@!"
    var result strings.Builder
    for _, c := range data {
        if !strings.ContainsRune(specialCharacters, c) {
            result.WriteRune(c)
        }
    }
    return result.String()
}

// DataProcessingPipeline struct
type DataProcessingPipeline struct {
    filters []Filter
}

// NewDataProcessingPipeline constructor
func NewDataProcessingPipeline() *DataProcessingPipeline {
    return &DataProcessingPipeline{
        filters: make([]Filter, 0),
    }
}

// AddFilter method for DataProcessingPipeline
func (d *DataProcessingPipeline) AddFilter(filter Filter) {
    d.filters = append(d.filters, filter)
}

// ProcessData method for DataProcessingPipeline
func (d *DataProcessingPipeline) ProcessData(data string) string
{
    for _, filter := range d.filters {
        data = filter.Process(data)
    }
    return data
}

// Client Code
func main() {
    pipeline := NewDataProcessingPipeline()
    pipeline.AddFilter(&CapitalizeFilter{})
    pipeline.AddFilter(&ReplaceSpaceFilter{})
    pipeline.AddFilter(&RemoveSpecialCharactersFilter{})
```

```
    data := "Hello, World!"
    result := pipeline.ProcessData(data)
    fmt.Println("Result:", result)
}
```

Output:

```
Result: HELLO_WORLD
```

Explanation:

1. **Filter Interface and Implementations:**

   ○ **Filter Interface**: Defines a single method, **Process**, for transforming data.

   ○ **CapitalizeFilter**: Converts all text to uppercase.

   ○ **ReplaceSpaceFilter**: Replaces all spaces with underscores.

   ○ **RemoveSpecialCharactersFilter**:   Removes   specific   special characters (,, @, !).

2. **DataProcessingPipeline Class:**

   ○ **Purpose**: Manages a sequence of filters and processes data through them sequentially.

   ○ **Methods**:

      ▪ **AddFilter()**: Adds a new filter to the pipeline.

      ▪ **ProcessData()**: Processes input data through each filter in the order they were added.

3. **Client Code:**

   ○ **Setup**: Creates an instance of **DataProcessingPipeline** and adds the desired filters.

   ○ **Data Processing**: The input string "Hello, World!" is processed through the pipeline, resulting in "HELLO_WORLD".

Summary

In this chapter, we examined Architectural Patterns, which provide structured approaches for organizing software systems to enhance modularity and maintainability. Key patterns include:

1. **Model-View-Controller (MVC)**: Separates application logic, user interface, and input control, making systems easier to manage and scale.

2. **Model-View-Presenter (MVP)**: Splits responsibilities between the model, view, and presenter to improve testability and maintain separation of concerns.

3. **Model-View-ViewModel (MVVM)**: Facilitates a clear separation between UI design and business logic, enabling more manageable and testable codebases.

4. **Layered Pattern**: Organizes software into layers with specific roles, allowing easier maintenance and flexibility.

5. **Pipe and Filter Pattern**: Breaks down data processing tasks into sequential stages, enhancing reusability and scalability.

These patterns guide developers in building robust, scalable, and adaptable software systems.

Exercises

1. Exercise: Implementing an application in MVC, MVP, and MVVM: Create a simple to-do list application using the Model-View-Controller (MVC), Model-View-Presenter (MVP), and Model-View-ViewModel (MVVM) patterns. This exercise will help you understand how to separate concerns among different components and how each architectural pattern organizes these concerns differently.

   Tasks

   MVC Pattern:

   - Model: Implement a Task struct with properties such as ID, Description, Completed, and methods to get and set these properties.

   - View: Create a simple console-based UI that displays the list of tasks and allows the user to add, delete, and mark tasks as completed.

   - Controller: Implement the logic to handle user inputs, update the model accordingly, and notify the view to refresh.

   MVP Pattern:

   - Model: Reuse the Task struct and methods from the MVC implementation.

- ○ View: Modify the console-based UI to delegate user input handling to a Presenter.

- ○ Presenter: Implement a Presenter that interacts with the Model to perform actions based on user input and then updates the View.

MVVM Pattern:

- ○ Model: Reuse the Task struct and methods from the MVC implementation.

- ○ View: Create a console-based UI that is bound to a ViewModel. The View should reactively update whenever the ViewModel changes.

- ○ ViewModel: Implement a ViewModel that exposes properties and commands for the UI to bind to. It should handle user actions, update the Model, and notify the View of changes.

2. Designing a Pipe and Filter System: Design a simple data processing pipeline using the Pipe and Filter pattern.

   Tasks:

   - ○ Create a program that processes a list of integers. The pipeline should:

   - ○ Filter 1: Remove all negative numbers.

   - ○ Filter 2: Multiply each number by 2.

   - ○ Filter 3: Output only the numbers that are greater than 10.

   - ○ Implement each step as a separate function or class (depending on your language) that takes an input and produces an output.

   - ○ Chain the functions together to form a pipeline.

   Hints:

   - ○ Think of each filter as a step that takes an input, processes it, and passes the output to the next step.

   - ○ Use function composition or chaining to connect the steps.

3. Applying the Layered Pattern: Objective: Implement a simple web service using the Layered pattern to understand the separation of concerns.

   Tasks:

- Presentation Layer: Create a simple HTTP server that handles requests and responses.

- Business Logic Layer: Implement the core logic for processing requests, such as handling CRUD operations for a basic entity (e.g., User or Product).

- Data Access Layer: Implement data storage and retrieval using in-memory storage or a simple file-based approach.

Hints:

- Ensure each layer interacts only with the layers directly above or below it.

- The Presentation Layer should not directly interact with the Data Access Layer.

Solution of Exercises

Solution 1: To-Do Application in MVC, MVP, and MVVM

MVC Pattern

```go
type Task struct {
    ID          int
    Description string
    Completed   bool
}

var tasks = []Task{}

func displayTasks() {
    for _, t := range tasks {
        fmt.Printf("%d: %s - %v\n", t.ID, t.Description,
t.Completed)
    }
}

func addTask(desc string) {
    tasks = append(tasks, Task{ID: len(tasks) + 1, Description:
desc})
    displayTasks()
}

func markCompleted(id int) {
    for i := range tasks {
```

```go
        if tasks[i].ID == id {
            tasks[i].Completed = true
            break
        }
    }
    displayTasks()
}

func main() {
    addTask("Learn MVC")
    markCompleted(1)
}
```

MVP Pattern

```go
type Task struct {
    ID          int
    Description string
    Completed   bool
}

var tasks = []Task{}

type View interface {
    Display([]Task)
}

type Presenter struct {
    model []Task
    view  View
}

func (p *Presenter) AddTask(desc string) {
    t := Task{ID: len(p.model) + 1, Description: desc}
    p.model = append(p.model, t)
    p.view.Display(p.model)
}

func (p *Presenter) MarkCompleted(id int) {
    for i := range p.model {
        if p.model[i].ID == id {
            p.model[i].Completed = true
            break
        }
    }
    p.view.Display(p.model)
```

```go
}

type ConsoleView struct{}

func (v *ConsoleView) Display(ts []Task) {
    for _, t := range ts {
        fmt.Printf("%d: %s - %v\n", t.ID, t.Description,
t.Completed)
    }
}

func main() {
    view := &ConsoleView{}
    presenter := &Presenter{view: view}
    presenter.AddTask("Learn MVP")
    presenter.MarkCompleted(1)
}
```

MVVM Pattern

```go
type Task struct {
    ID          int
    Description string
    Completed   bool
}

var tasks = []Task{}

type ViewModel struct {
    Tasks []Task
}

func (vm *ViewModel) AddTask(desc string) {
    t := Task{ID: len(tasks) + 1, Description: desc}
    tasks = append(tasks, t)
    vm.Tasks = tasks
}

func (vm *ViewModel) MarkCompleted(id int) {
    for i := range tasks {
        if tasks[i].ID == id {
            tasks[i].Completed = true
            break
        }
    }
    vm.Tasks = tasks
```

```go
}

type View interface {
    Display([]Task)
}

type ConsoleView struct{}

func (v *ConsoleView) Display(ts []Task) {
    for _, t := range ts {
        fmt.Printf("%d: %s - %v\n", t.ID, t.Description,
t.Completed)
    }
}

func main() {
    vm := &ViewModel{}
    view := &ConsoleView{}
    vm.AddTask("Learn MVVM")
    vm.MarkCompleted(1)
    view.Display(vm.Tasks)
}
```

Solution 3: Pipe and Filter System

```go
func filterNegative(nums []int) []int {
    var result []int
    for _, n := range nums {
        if n >= 0 {
            result = append(result, n)
        }
    }
    return result
}

func multiplyByTwo(nums []int) []int {
    var result []int
    for _, n := range nums {
        result = append(result, n*2)
    }
    return result
}

func filterGreaterThanTen(nums []int) []int {
    var result []int
    for _, n := range nums {
```

```go
        if n > 10 {
            result = append(result, n)
        }
    }
    return result
}

func main() {
    nums := filterNegative([]int{-1, 5, 7, 10, 12})
    nums = multiplyByTwo(nums)
    nums = filterGreaterThanTen(nums)
    fmt.Println(nums) // Output: [12 14 20]
}
```

Solution 4: Layered Pattern

```go
// Data Access Layer
var users = make(map[int]string)

func getUser(id int) string {
    return users[id]
}

func saveUser(id int, name string) {
    users[id] = name
}

// Business Logic Layer
func createUser(id int, name string) {
    saveUser(id, name)
}

func getUserName(id int) string {
    return getUser(id)
}

// Presentation Layer
func main() {
    createUser(1, "Alice")
    fmt.Println("User 1:", getUserName(1))
}
```

ANTI-PATTERNS

Anti-patterns are common but counterproductive solutions to recurring problems in software design. Unlike design patterns, which provide structured and effective solutions, anti-patterns can lead to software that is difficult to maintain, understand, and extend. Recognizing these anti-patterns is crucial for developers to improve code quality and adhere to best practices. Some well-known anti-patterns include:

1. **Blob anti-pattern**: This anti-pattern occurs when a single class accumulates excessive responsibilities, handling various unrelated tasks, leading to a monolithic and unmanageable codebase. It violates the Single Responsibility Principle (SRP) and makes the code hard to test, maintain, and modify.

2. **Spaghetti Code**: Characterized by a disorganized and tangled structure, spaghetti code lacks clear organization or modularization. This results in code that is hard to read, understand, and debug, as control flow and logic are spread haphazardly throughout the application.

3. **Swiss Army Knife**: This anti-pattern emerges when a single class or module tries to handle too many different functionalities. While it may seem convenient to have all functionalities in one place, this approach often leads to a lack of cohesion and difficulties in understanding and maintaining the code.

4. **God Object**: Similar to the Blob anti-pattern, a God Object tries to control or know too much about the system, often holding numerous methods and properties. This creates a single point of failure and results in code that is overly complex and tightly coupled, making modifications risky and testing challenging.

The Blob Anti-Pattern

The **Blob Anti-Pattern** is a software design anti-pattern that occurs when a class becomes excessively large and takes on too many responsibilities. This class becomes a "blob" of various functionalities, handling numerous tasks such as data processing, validation, storage, and more, all within a single unit. This lack of separation of concerns leads to a codebase that is tightly coupled, hard to maintain, and challenging to test.

The Blob Anti-Pattern often arises due to the following reasons:

- **Lack of Adherence to Separation of Concerns**: Developers fail to distribute responsibilities among various classes, leading to a single class handling multiple unrelated functions.

- **Violation of the Single Responsibility Principle (SRP)**: A class should only have one reason to change, but a blob class has multiple reasons, making it a maintenance nightmare.

- **Insufficient Use of Abstraction**: Not utilizing interfaces, abstract classes, or inheritance can lead to large, monolithic classes that attempt to manage everything themselves.

The presence of a Blob Anti-Pattern can lead to several issues:

- **Poor Modularity**: The class is hard to understand and modify because it lacks a clear purpose.

- **Difficult Maintenance**: Changes in one part of the class can have unintended consequences elsewhere, leading to fragile code.

- **Testing Challenges**: Testing a large class with multiple responsibilities is cumbersome and often requires extensive setup, reducing test reliability and effectiveness.

Example Implementation of the Blob Anti-Pattern :

```go
package main

// Blob struct
type Blob struct {
    data string
}

// NewBlob constructor
func NewBlob(data string) *Blob {
    return &Blob{data: data}
}

// ProcessData method
func (b *Blob) ProcessData() {
    // Process data
}
```

```go
// ValidateData method
func (b *Blob) ValidateData() {
    // Validate data
}

// SaveData method
func (b *Blob) SaveData() {
    // Save data to database
}

// SendNotification method
func (b *Blob) SendNotification() {
    // Send notification
}

// GenerateReport method
func (b *Blob) GenerateReport() {
    // Generate report
}

// BackupData method
func (b *Blob) BackupData() {
    // Backup data
}

// ArchiveData method
func (b *Blob) ArchiveData() {
    // Archive data
}

// PurgeData method
func (b *Blob) PurgeData() {
    // Purge data
}

// Client Code
func main() {
    // Create an instance of Blob
    blob := NewBlob("example data")

    // Call methods on Blob instance
    blob.ProcessData()
    blob.ValidateData()
    blob.SaveData()
    blob.SendNotification()
```

```
    blob.GenerateReport()
    blob.BackupData()
    blob.ArchiveData()
    blob.PurgeData()
}
```

Analysis:

In this example, the Blob class handles numerous unrelated tasks, such as data processing, validation, storage, notification sending, report generation, data backup, archiving, and purging. This makes the class a single point of complexity, violating the Single Responsibility Principle and leading to a tightly coupled codebase.

To prevent the Blob Anti-Pattern, developers should:

1. **Adhere to Separation of Concerns**: Ensure each class has a clear, single responsibility.

2. **Use Abstraction**: Implement interfaces and abstract classes to distribute responsibilities across multiple classes.

3. **Refactor Regularly**: Continuously review and refactor code to break down large classes into smaller, manageable components.

4. **Apply Design Patterns**: Use appropriate design patterns to address specific problems and improve code maintainability.

The God Object Anti-Pattern

The **God Object Anti-Pattern** is a software design flaw where a single class or module becomes overly responsible for many parts of an application. This leads to code that is tightly coupled, hard to maintain, and challenging to test.

This anti-pattern typically emerges when developers fail to apply the principles of separation of concerns and the Single Responsibility Principle (SRP). Instead of dividing functionality into smaller, manageable components, they implement everything in a single class or module. The result is code that is hard to understand, modify, and is prone to errors.

To prevent the God Object Anti-Pattern, follow these best practices for software design:

- **Separation of Concerns**: Ensure that each class has a clear, single responsibility, with well-defined interfaces between components.

- **Loose Coupling**: Components should interact through well-defined interfaces rather than relying on global state or direct method calls.

- **Abstraction**: Utilize interfaces, abstract classes, and inheritance to decompose large classes into smaller, manageable components.

- **Refactoring**: Regularly review and refactor code to identify and eliminate code smells, such as overly complex or monolithic classes.

- **Design Patterns**: Apply appropriate design patterns to address specific design issues and improve overall code maintainability.

Example Implementation of the God Object Anti-Pattern:

```go
// GodObject struct
type GodObject struct {
    data   []interface{}
    user   User
    db     Database
    mailer Mailer
}

// NewGodObject constructor
func NewGodObject() *GodObject {
    return &GodObject{
        data:   make([]interface{}, 0),
        user:   NewUser(),
        db:     NewDatabase(),
        mailer: NewMailer(),
    }
}

// ProcessData method
func (g *GodObject) ProcessData() {
    // Process data
    g.db.Connect()
    g.user.Authenticate()
    g.data = g.db.Query()
    g.db.Disconnect()
}

// ValidateData method
func (g *GodObject) ValidateData() {
    // Validate data
    g.user.Authorize()
```

```go
    g.db.Connect()
    g.db.Validate()
    g.db.Disconnect()
}

// SendNotification method
func (g *GodObject) SendNotification() {
    // Send notification
    g.user.Authorize()
    g.db.Connect()
    data := g.db.Query()
    g.mailer.SendEmail(data)
    g.db.Disconnect()
}

func main() {
    // Create an instance of GodObject
    godObject := NewGodObject()

    // Call methods on GodObject instance
    godObject.ProcessData()
    godObject.ValidateData()
    godObject.SendNotification()

    fmt.Println("GodObject methods called successfully.")
}
```

Analysis:

In this example, the GodObject class handles all aspects of the application, including data processing, validation, database connectivity, user authentication, and email notifications. This design is tightly coupled, difficult to understand, and hard to maintain. To avoid this anti-pattern, functionality should be divided into smaller, focused components, each responsible for a single task. This approach will result in a more maintainable, testable, and adaptable codebase.

The Spaghetti Code Anti-Pattern

The **Spaghetti Code Anti-Pattern** occurs when code lacks structure or organization, becoming overly complex and difficult to understand. The term "spaghetti code" describes the tangled flow of control in such code, similar to a plate of spaghetti noodles.

Spaghetti code often results from inadequate planning, poor coding practices, or evolving requirements that lead to a tangled and complicated codebase. This type of code is difficult to read, modify, and maintain, leading to several problems:

1. **Reduced Productivity**: Spaghetti code is hard to understand and takes longer to modify, reducing developer productivity.

2. **Bugs and Errors**: The tangled logic makes it hard to track down and fix bugs.

3. **Reduced Reusability**: Such code is often not reusable because it's challenging to extract useful parts from the mess.

4. **Increased Costs**: Maintaining spaghetti code can be expensive due to the effort required to modify, test, and fix it.

Best Practices to Avoid Spaghetti Code:

1. **Planning**: Thoroughly plan your code structure based on requirements, use cases, and architecture.

2. **Separation of Concerns**: Divide code into smaller, manageable components that handle specific tasks, such as input validation or database access.

3. **Modularity**: Ensure your code is modular, with clear interfaces between components.

4. **Code Reviews**: Regularly review code to identify potential issues and ensure it is well-structured and organized.

5. **Refactoring**: Be prepared to refactor code to improve structure and organization.

Example Implementation of Spaghetti Code Anti-Pattern:

```go
func processData(data string) (*sql.Rows, error) {
    // Validate input
    if data == "" {
        fmt.Println("Invalid data")
        return nil, nil
    }

    // Define connection parameters
    connStr := "user=user dbname=mydb password=password sslmode=disable"

    // Connect to the database
    db, err := sql.Open("postgres", connStr)
```

```
    if err != nil {
        log.Fatal(err)
    }
    defer db.Close()

    // Process data
    query := "SELECT * FROM mytable WHERE data = $1"
    rows, err := db.Query(query, data)
    if err != nil {
        log.Fatal(err)
    }

    return rows, nil
}
```

Explanation:

This function mixes input validation, database connectivity, and processing logic into a single method, making it difficult to understand and maintain. A better approach would separate these concerns into distinct functions or classes, improving modularity and making the code easier to maintain and modify over time.

The Swiss Army Knife Anti-Pattern

The **Swiss Army Knife Anti-Pattern** occurs when a single component or class tries to perform too many unrelated tasks, leading to excessive complexity, tight coupling, and low cohesion. This is analogous to a Swiss Army Knife, which can perform many functions but is often not ideal for any single task.

This anti-pattern emerges when developers add too many features to a single component instead of breaking down functionality into specialized, simpler components. This results in code that is hard to understand, maintain, and modify and is prone to errors.

Common Issues with the Swiss Army Knife Anti-Pattern:

1. **Complexity**: The code becomes overly complex due to the numerous functions combined into a single component.

2. **Tight Coupling**: The component becomes tightly coupled with others, making it difficult to change without affecting other parts of the system.

3. **Low Cohesion**: Functions within the component are not closely related and would be better implemented separately.

4. **Code Bloat**: The component becomes bloated with unnecessary features, increasing memory usage and reducing performance.

Best Practices to Avoid the Swiss Army Knife Anti-Pattern:

1. **Separation of Concerns**: Design components to handle specific tasks and avoid bundling unrelated functionalities together.

2. **Modularity**: Ensure components are modular, with well-defined interfaces.

3. Cohesion: Keep functions that are closely related together within a component.

4. **Single Responsibility Principle**: Ensure each component has a single responsibility.

5. **Code Reviews**: Regularly review code to ensure it is well-structured and follows best practices.

Example Implementation of the Swiss Army Knife Anti-Pattern:

```go
package main

import "fmt"

// DataProcessor struct
type DataProcessor struct {
    data string
}

// NewDataProcessor constructor
func NewDataProcessor(data string) *DataProcessor {
    return &DataProcessor{data: data}
}

// ProcessData method
func (dp *DataProcessor) ProcessData() {
    dp.validateData()
    dp.cleanData()
    dp.filterData()
    dp.sortData()
    dp.groupData()
    dp.calculateStatistics()
```

```go
    dp.formatOutput()
}

// validateData method
func (dp *DataProcessor) validateData() {
    // Validation logic
}

// cleanData method
func (dp *DataProcessor) cleanData() {
    // Data cleaning logic
}

// filterData method
func (dp *DataProcessor) filterData() {
    // Data filtering logic
}

// sortData method
func (dp *DataProcessor) sortData() {
    // Data sorting logic
}

// groupData method
func (dp *DataProcessor) groupData() {
    // Data grouping logic
}

// calculateStatistics method
func (dp *DataProcessor) calculateStatistics() {
    // Statistics calculation logic
}

// formatOutput method
func (dp *DataProcessor) formatOutput() {
    // Output formatting logic
}

// Client Code
func main() {
    data := "exampleData"
    processor := NewDataProcessor(data)
    processor.ProcessData()
    fmt.Println("Data processing completed.")
}
```

Analysis:

The **DataProcessor** class attempts to handle multiple unrelated tasks such as data validation, cleaning, filtering, sorting, grouping, and formatting. This design leads to high complexity and low cohesion. A better approach would divide these responsibilities into separate, specialized components, each focusing on a single task. This will result in more modular, understandable, and maintainable code.

Summary

In this chapter, we explored Anti-Patterns, which are common but ineffective solutions that can negatively impact software design and development. Recognizing these patterns helps developers avoid pitfalls that lead to complex and unmanageable code. Key anti-patterns discussed include:

1. **Blob Anti-Pattern**: Occurs when a single class takes on too many responsibilities, leading to code that is difficult to maintain and violates the Single Responsibility Principle (SRP).

2. **Spaghetti Code Anti-Pattern**: Describes code with a tangled and disorganized structure, making it hard to read, debug, and maintain due to its lack of modularity and clear control flow.

3. **Swiss Army Knife Anti-Pattern**: Involves a class or module trying to handle multiple unrelated functionalities, resulting in low cohesion and difficulties in understanding and maintaining the code.

4. **God Object Anti-Pattern**: Similar to the Blob anti-pattern, this involves an object that knows too much or does too much, creating a tightly coupled system that is complex and difficult to modify or test.

By identifying and avoiding these anti-patterns, developers can improve code quality and adhere to best practices in software design.

REAL-WORLD EXAMPLES OF DESIGN PATTERNS

This chapter illustrates the practical application of design patterns to solve specific problems through detailed case studies. The following examples demonstrate how various design patterns can be effectively utilized in real-world scenarios.

Case Study 1: E-commerce System

Description: This case study explores the design and implementation of an e-commerce system that enables users to browse and purchase products online. Key features include product catalog management, shopping cart functionality, order processing, and payment integration.

Design Patterns Used:

Several design patterns can be applied in the design and development of an e-commerce system:

1. **Model-View-Controller (MVC)**: The MVC pattern is employed to separate the user interface (View), application logic (Controller), and data representation (Model). This separation enhances modularity, reusability, and maintainability of the system.

2. **Singleton Pattern**: The Singleton pattern ensures that only one instance of the shopping cart exists throughout a user's session, providing a centralized and consistent shopping experience.

3. **Factory Method Pattern**: This pattern is used to create different types of products. It allows the system to define a common interface for product creation, while enabling specific subclasses to implement their unique creation logic.

4. **Strategy Pattern**: The Strategy pattern is ideal for managing various payment methods. It allows the system to define a family of interchangeable payment strategies (e.g., credit card, PayPal, bank transfer) and dynamically select the appropriate strategy based on user preferences or system configurations.

5. **Observer Pattern**: The Observer pattern is applied to notify users about order status updates. When an order's status changes, the system alerts

interested parties (observers), such as customers or administrators, ensuring timely and relevant communication.

Case Study 2: Social Networking Platform

Description: This case study examines the design and development of a social networking platform where users can create profiles, connect with friends, post updates, and interact with each other. The platform aims to deliver a user-friendly and engaging experience.

Design Patterns Used:

Several design patterns can be applied in the design and development of a social networking platform:

1. **Decorator Pattern**: The Decorator pattern is used to add additional features or functionalities to user profiles. It enables dynamic and flexible customization by attaching new responsibilities to the base profile object.

2. **Composite Pattern**: This pattern represents hierarchical relationships between users and their connections. It provides a unified interface that treats both individual users and groups as interchangeable entities, facilitating efficient management of social connections.

3. **Observer Pattern**: The Observer pattern is used to notify users about new posts, friend requests, or other relevant updates. Users can subscribe to specific events or profiles, and the system notifies them whenever new activities occur, enhancing real-time interaction.

4. **Template Method Pattern**: This pattern defines a common structure for different types of posts. It allows variations in content and presentation while maintaining a consistent overall structure, ensuring uniformity across the platform.

Case Study 3: Financial Trading System

Description: This case study focuses on the architecture of a financial trading system that allows users to buy and sell various financial instruments such as stocks, bonds, and derivatives.

Design Patterns Used

Design Patterns Applied:

1. **Observer Pattern**: Widely used in financial systems, the Observer pattern handles real-time updates and notifications. It is used to alert users about changes in stock prices, market movements, or specific events affecting their financial instruments.

2. **Strategy Pattern**: The Strategy pattern manages different trading algorithms and strategies, allowing the system to easily switch between approaches like algorithmic trading, high-frequency trading, or manual trading without altering the core logic.

3. **Factory Method Pattern**: This pattern helps create different types of financial instruments (e.g., stocks, bonds, derivatives) while adhering to a common interface, promoting decoupling and enhancing code maintainability.

4. **Composite Pattern**: The Composite pattern is useful for handling hierarchical structures, such as portfolios containing multiple financial instruments. It allows individual instruments and portfolios to be treated uniformly, simplifying portfolio management.

5. **Command Pattern**: The Command pattern encapsulates trade orders as objects, enabling the parametrization of clients with different requests. It is used to implement undo/redo functionality for trade orders, enhancing flexibility.

6. **Singleton Pattern**: This pattern ensures a single instance of critical components, such as a connection manager for interacting with external trading platforms or data providers, maintaining consistency and control.

7. **Template Method Pattern**: The Template Method pattern defines the skeleton of a trading algorithm, allowing subclasses to override specific steps without altering the overall structure. It enables customization for different types of financial instruments.

8. **Facade Pattern**: The Facade pattern simplifies the trading system's complexity by providing a unified interface that abstracts underlying subsystems. It offers a streamlined interface for placing trades, handling order execution, and managing positions, hiding the complexities of various trading platforms and exchanges.

Case Study 4: Mobile Application Development

Description: Mobile application development involves creating software applications designed to run on mobile devices like smartphones and tablets. These applications serve various purposes, including entertainment, productivity, communication, and more. The development process typically includes designing the user interface, implementing the application's functionalities, and ensuring compatibility across different mobile platforms (e.g., Android, iOS).

Design Patterns Used

In mobile application development, several design patterns can enhance code organization, maintainability, and scalability:

1. **Model-View-Controller (MVC) Pattern**: MVC is a foundational architectural pattern that divides the application into three interconnected components: Model (data and business logic), View (user interface), and Controller (user input and application updates). This separation promotes code modularity, making it easier to update and maintain the application.

2. **Model-View-Presenter (MVP) Pattern**: MVP is a variation of MVC where the Presenter acts as an intermediary between the Model and the View. The Presenter handles user interactions, updates the Model, and ensures that the View reflects these changes. This pattern enhances the independence and testability of the View by centralizing UI logic within the Presenter.

3. **Model-View-ViewModel (MVVM) Pattern**: Commonly used with data-binding frameworks, MVVM extends MVC by introducing the ViewModel, which bridges the Model and View. The ViewModel exposes data and commands to the View, facilitating maintainability and simplifying UI testing.

4. **Singleton Pattern**: The Singleton pattern ensures that a class has only one instance and provides global access to that instance. In mobile app development, it can manage global application state, create shared resources (e.g., network managers, database helpers), or handle configurations.

5. **Factory Pattern**: The Factory pattern abstracts object creation without specifying the exact class. This pattern is useful for creating platform-

specific implementations in mobile apps, such as different camera interfaces for Android and iOS.

6. **Observer Pattern**: The Observer pattern enables communication between app components by allowing objects (observers) to subscribe to changes in other objects (subjects). It is particularly useful for event handling, notifying UI components about data changes, and responding to user interactions.

7. **Decorator Pattern**: The Decorator pattern allows dynamic addition of behavior to individual objects without modifying their class. In mobile development, this pattern is useful for extending the functionality of UI components or adding optional features without altering core implementation.

8. **Command Pattern**: The Command pattern encapsulates requests as objects, enabling the parametrization of clients with different requests. It can be employed to manage user actions, such as implementing undo/redo functionality or handling gestures.

9. **Adapter Pattern**: The Adapter pattern reconciles incompatible interfaces to work together. This pattern is valuable in mobile app development for integrating external libraries, services, or APIs that have different interfaces than those required by the app.

Case Study 5: Web Development

Description: Web development involves creating and maintaining websites or web applications for the Internet, combining frontend (client-side) and backend (server-side) development to deliver a seamless user experience. Web development tasks include presenting content, handling user interactions, processing data, and communicating with databases and external services.

Design Patterns Used

Design patterns are crucial in web development for solving common problems and enhancing code organization, reusability, and maintainability:

1. **Model-View-Controller (MVC) Pattern**: The MVC pattern separates the application logic into three components:

   - **Model**: Represents data and business logic.

- ○ **View**: Manages presentation and user interface.

- ○ **Controller**: Handles user input and orchestrates communication between the Model and View.

2. **Singleton Pattern**: The Singleton pattern ensures that a class has only one instance, providing a global access point. It is often used for components that need to be instantiated once and shared across different parts of the web application.

3. **Factory Pattern**: The Factory pattern abstracts object creation, allowing for different object types, such as various database connections, based on configuration or runtime conditions.

4. **Observer Pattern**: The Observer pattern manages one-to-many dependencies between objects, where multiple observers are automatically notified of changes in a subject. It is ideal for real-time updates, notifications, and event-driven interactions in web development.

5. **Decorator Pattern**: The Decorator pattern dynamically adds behavior to individual objects without affecting others of the same class. It is useful for extending the functionality of web components, such as adding features or modifying rendering behavior.

6. **Adapter Pattern**: The Adapter pattern converts one class's interface into another expected by clients, facilitating the integration of third-party libraries or APIs into a web application.

7. **Strategy Pattern**: The Strategy pattern allows dynamic selection of algorithms or behavior at runtime, useful for switching between different implementations based on varying requirements.

8. **Facade Pattern**: The Facade pattern simplifies complex systems by providing a unified interface, making it easier to use. It can be applied to create a single interface for interacting with various backend services or APIs, hiding their complexities from the frontend.

9. **Template Method Pattern**: The Template Method pattern defines the overall structure of an algorithm while allowing subclasses to override specific steps. It is useful in web development for defining the basic structure of a page or component, with customization achieved through subclassing or template engines.

Case Study 6: Internet of Things (IoT) Systems

Description: Internet of Things (IoT) systems are networks of interconnected physical devices, vehicles, appliances, and other objects embedded with sensors, software, and network connectivity. These devices collect and exchange data, interact with each other, and central systems to perform tasks, make intelligent decisions, and provide valuable insights. IoT systems have applications in smart homes, industrial automation, healthcare monitoring, smart cities, and more.

Design Patterns Used

Design patterns enhance the design and functionality of IoT systems:

1. **Publish/Subscribe Pattern**: This pattern enables efficient communication and data sharing among devices and services in IoT systems. Devices publish data to specific topics, and other devices or services subscribe to those topics, facilitating scalable and asynchronous communication.

2. **Command Pattern**: The Command pattern controls and manages remote devices from a central location, sending commands to IoT devices to trigger specific actions. It is essential for smart home automation and industrial control systems.

3. **Observer Pattern**: This pattern implements real-time monitoring and event handling in IoT systems. Observers subscribe to sensors or data streams, receiving notifications whenever there are changes or events of interest, crucial for real-time data updates like environmental monitoring or security systems.

4. **State Pattern**: The State pattern manages devices with different states and behaviors based on their current conditions. For instance, a smart thermostat may have states like "heating," "cooling," and "standby," each with specific rules and actions.

5. **Proxy Pattern**: The Proxy pattern represents and controls access to remote devices or resources, acting as intermediaries for communication, authentication, and security between the central system and IoT devices.

6. **Chain of Responsibility Pattern**: This pattern processes data streams or events through a series of handlers or filters. Each handler processes

the data and passes it to the next, allowing flexible data processing
pipelines.

7. **Adapter Pattern**: The Adapter pattern integrates existing or legacy IoT
   devices into new systems by converting one device's or protocol's
   interface to match the new system's requirements, enabling seamless
   integration of diverse devices.

Case Study 7: Game Development

Description: Game development involves creating interactive experiences,
typically in the form of video games, for platforms like PCs, consoles, mobile
devices, and web browsers. Successful game development requires attention to
graphics, audio, user input, physics, game mechanics, and other elements that
contribute to an engaging and enjoyable player experience.

Design Patterns Used

Various design patterns enhance game development by improving code
organization, efficiency, and flexibility:

1. **State Pattern**: This pattern is crucial for managing the different states of
   game objects, characters, or scenes (e.g., idle, running, jumping,
   attacking). It efficiently handles transitions between these states.

2. **Observer Pattern**: Commonly used for event-driven systems, this
   pattern allows various game elements (such as AI controllers, UI
   components, or audio systems) to respond to events like collisions, input
   changes, or character actions.

3. **Factory Method Pattern**: Useful for dynamically creating objects based
   on specific conditions or configurations, this pattern can generate game
   levels, enemy waves, or various game assets.

4. **Singleton Pattern**: This pattern is ideal for creating unique, globally
   accessible instances of key game components, such as game managers,
   audio managers, or resource managers.

5. **Flyweight Pattern**: Employed to optimize memory usage, the Flyweight
   Pattern is effective when managing a large number of similar objects
   (e.g., particles, trees, bullets) by reusing shared data to minimize
   memory overhead.

6. **Command Pattern**: This pattern is valuable for implementing flexible input handling and game controls. User inputs (from keyboards, mice, or gamepads) are encapsulated as commands that can be executed or undone.

7. **Strategy Pattern**: Useful for implementing varied AI behaviors or game mechanics, this pattern allows for the dynamic selection of algorithms or strategies, enhancing adaptability during runtime.

8. **Prototype Pattern**: The Prototype Pattern enables efficient cloning and instantiation of objects, which is particularly useful for spawning new game entities or generating procedural content.

Case Study 8: Data Processing and Analytics

Description: Data processing and analytics involve collecting, transforming, analyzing, and interpreting large datasets to extract insights and inform data-driven decisions. This field includes tasks such as data ingestion, storage, cleansing, transformation, mining, machine learning, and reporting.

Design Patterns Used

Design patterns are vital in building scalable, maintainable, and efficient data processing and analytics systems:

1. **Observer Pattern**: Useful for monitoring changes in data sources, databases, or streams, triggering data processing tasks when new data arrives.

2. **Adapter Pattern**: Integrates diverse data sources into a unified format, facilitating easier processing and analysis.

3. **Facade Pattern**: Simplifies interaction with complex data processing systems by providing a streamlined interface to access various data sources, storage systems, and processing components.

4. **Composite Pattern**: Aggregates data from different sources into a hierarchical structure, useful for managing complex data models and multi-entity aggregation.

Case Study 9: Enterprise Software Systems

Description: Enterprise Software Systems are large-scale, complex applications designed to meet the needs of large organizations. These systems often include multiple modules, integrate with various other systems, and manage vast amounts of data. They support critical business processes such as Customer Relationship Management (CRM), Enterprise Resource Planning (ERP), Supply Chain Management (SCM), and Human Resources Management (HRM).

Design Patterns Used

Design patterns are crucial for the development of scalable, maintainable, and efficient enterprise software systems:

1. **Layered Architecture Pattern**: Divides the system into distinct layers (e.g., presentation, business logic, and data layers) to ensure clear separation of concerns, enhancing maintainability and scalability.

2. **Service-Oriented Architecture (SOA)**: Design software components as independent, loosely coupled services that communicate using standard protocols, enabling flexibility, reusability, and seamless integration.

3. **Microservices Architecture**: Decomposes the application into small, independently deployable services, each focusing on a specific business capability, allowing for independent team development and scaling of services as needed.

4. **Singleton Pattern**: Useful for creating a single, global instance of a class, such as a centralized configuration manager or database connection pool.

5. **Factory Pattern**: Creates objects without specifying the exact class. In enterprise systems, it's often used to generate instances of database connectors, data access objects, or other essential components.

6. **Observer Pattern**: Facilitates communication between loosely coupled components, such as notifying various modules about changes in shared data or significant events.

7. **Command Pattern**: Encapsulates a request as an object, allowing for the parameterization of clients with different requests and supporting undo/redo functionality. In enterprise systems, it's used for queuing and processing asynchronous tasks.

8. **Adapter Pattern**: Enables seamless integration of legacy systems or third-party components by converting their interfaces to match those of the enterprise system, allowing interaction without modifying existing code.

9. **Composite Pattern**: Manages hierarchical structures, such as organizational hierarchies, product categories, or workflow processes, by representing them as composite objects.

Case Study 10: Machine Learning and Artificial Intelligence

Description: Machine Learning (ML) and Artificial Intelligence (AI) are closely related fields focused on creating algorithms and systems that can learn from data and make intelligent decisions. AI encompasses a wide range of techniques that exhibit human-like intelligence, while ML is a subset of AI that specifically deals with algorithms that learn patterns and make predictions from data without explicit programming.

In ML, models are trained on large datasets using statistical techniques to identify patterns and relationships. These models are then used to make predictions or decisions on new, unseen data. AI includes not only ML but also other techniques such as rule-based systems, natural language processing (NLP), computer vision, robotics, and more.

Design Patterns Used

Various Design Patterns Used in Machine Learning and Artificial Intelligence:

1. **Model-View-Controller (MVC) Pattern:** The MVC pattern is applicable in AI systems where a clear separation is needed between the model (data processing and ML model), the view (user interface), and the controller (business logic). This pattern ensures a modular and scalable design for AI applications.

2. **Factory Pattern for Model Creation:** The Factory Pattern is useful for creating ML models based on various parameters or configurations. It encapsulates the object creation logic, making it easier to switch between different model architectures or hyperparameters.

3. **Observer Pattern for Real-Time Updates:** The Observer Pattern is beneficial in AI systems that require real-time updates or notifications. For example, in a real-time anomaly detection system, observers can be notified immediately when anomalies are detected.

4. **Strategy Pattern for Algorithm Selection:** The Strategy Pattern is ideal for selecting the appropriate algorithm when multiple ML algorithms or techniques can be used for a task, such as classification or regression, based on the problem context or data characteristics.

5. **Singleton Pattern for Resource Management:** The Singleton Pattern is applied to manage shared resources, such as data pipelines, connection objects, or caching mechanisms, ensuring a single instance of these resources throughout the AI system.

6. **Template Method Pattern for Feature Engineering:** The Template Method Pattern is employed in feature engineering to define the overall feature extraction process, while subclasses can provide specific implementations for extracting particular features.

7. **Chain of Responsibility Pattern for AI Processing Pipelines:** The Chain of Responsibility Pattern is useful in AI systems with complex processing pipelines, such as natural language processing tasks, where each component in the chain handles a specific task, and the output of one becomes the input for the next.

8. **Adapter Pattern for Data Integration:** The Adapter Pattern is used to integrate data from various sources or formats into a unified format that ML models can consume, allowing different data sources to be converted into a common interface for model training and prediction.

9. **Proxy Pattern for Lazy Loading:** The Proxy Pattern is employed for lazy loading of AI models or expensive computations, deferring their instantiation until they are actually needed.

Case Study 11: Internet Applications and Services

Description: Internet applications and services refer to software systems accessible over the internet, allowing users to perform tasks, access information, and communicate with others. These applications run on remote servers and are accessed through web browsers or specialized client software, covering functionalities such as social media platforms, email services, online shopping, search engines, and cloud storage.

Design Patterns Used

Various Design Patterns used in Internet Applications and Services:

1. **Model-View-Controller (MVC) Pattern**: The MVC pattern is widely used in internet applications to separate the user interface (View) from the business logic and data processing (Model) and the control of interactions (Controller). This separation improves code maintainability, reusability, and testability.

2. **Singleton Pattern**: The Singleton pattern ensures that certain critical components, such as database connections, configuration managers, or authentication modules, have only one instance throughout the application's lifetime, avoiding unnecessary overhead and ensuring consistency.

3. **Observer Pattern**: The Observer pattern is used to handle real-time updates and notifications in internet applications. For example, in social media platforms, users can follow or subscribe to other users or topics, and the Observer pattern can notify them about new posts or updates.

4. **Factory Method Pattern**: The Factory Method pattern abstracts the object instantiation process from client code, allowing for the flexible creation of objects like user accounts, product instances, or API clients.

5. **Decorator Pattern**: The Decorator pattern adds behavior to individual objects dynamically. In internet applications, decorators can add features to services or components without modifying their core implementation, such as adding spam filtering or encryption in email services.

6. **Strategy Pattern**: The Strategy pattern is used to handle multiple algorithms or behavior variations for specific tasks. For instance, in search engines, different ranking algorithms can be implemented using the Strategy pattern, and the engine can switch between them based on user preferences.

7. **Adapter Pattern**: The Adapter pattern enables collaboration between incompatible interfaces, which is helpful when integrating with external APIs or services that have different data formats or communication protocols.

8. **Facade Pattern**: The Facade pattern simplifies complex interactions in internet applications by providing a unified interface that hides underlying subsystems. For example, in cloud storage services, the Facade pattern abstracts away the complexities of interacting with various storage providers.

9. **Command Pattern**: The Command pattern encapsulates requests as objects, allowing for parametrization and decoupling of the sender and receiver. In internet applications, this pattern can be used to implement undo/redo functionality or handle user commands in a command-line interface.

Case Study 12: Embedded Systems and Firmware Development

Description: Embedded systems are computing systems designed to perform specific functions within a larger system, often with real-time constraints and limited resources. These systems are found in applications such as consumer electronics, automotive, industrial automation, and medical devices. Firmware development involves creating software that runs directly on the hardware of embedded systems, controlling their behavior and functionality.

Design Patterns Used

Design Patterns used in Embedded Systems and Firmware Development:

1. **State Pattern**: The State Pattern manages the different states of an embedded system and controls its behavior accordingly. For example, in a state machine representing a communication protocol, the system's behavior may change based on the current state, such as initializing, waiting for data, or processing data.

2. **Singleton Pattern**: The Singleton Pattern ensures that certain hardware access or configuration objects have only one instance, avoiding resource conflicts and promoting efficient resource management.

3. **Observer Pattern**: The Observer Pattern is valuable for implementing event-driven communication between different parts of an embedded system, such as sensors acting as subjects and various components reacting to changes in sensor data.

4. **Factory Method Pattern**: The Factory Method Pattern abstracts the creation of different components in an embedded system, such as creating appropriate sensor or actuator instances based on specific requirements.

5. **Command Pattern**: The Command Pattern encapsulates requests or operations as objects, which is useful in embedded systems for implementing command objects representing specific actions or tasks to be executed.

6. **Template Method Pattern**: The Template Method Pattern defines a high-level algorithm in a firmware module while allowing subclasses or configuration settings to implement specific steps or behaviors.

7. **Adapter Pattern**: The Adapter Pattern integrates existing software libraries or drivers with new firmware or hardware interfaces, allowing the firmware to work with different components seamlessly, even if their interfaces differ.

8. **Composite Pattern**: The Composite Pattern is useful for managing hierarchical structures of embedded components, such as handling multiple sensors and actuators as a unified entity.

9. **Memento Pattern**: The Memento Pattern captures the internal state of an embedded system or firmware component, allowing it to be restored later if needed, which is useful for state transitions and error recovery.

10. **Proxy Pattern**: The Proxy Pattern controls access to hardware resources or provides an interface for interacting with remote components efficiently.

Case Study 13: Robotics and Automation Systems

Description: Robotics and Automation Systems involve the design, development, and implementation of machines, robots, and software to automate tasks and processes. These systems range from simple automated machines in manufacturing to complex robotic systems utilized across various industries, including healthcare, logistics, and exploration. The primary objectives are to enhance efficiency, precision, and safety while minimizing human intervention.

Design Patterns Used

Various Design Patterns Used in Robotics and Automation Systems:

1. **State Pattern**: Robots often operate in different states, such as idle, moving, executing a task, or in an error state. The State Pattern models and manages these states efficiently, with each state represented as an object. The robot's behavior changes according to its current state, and transitions between states are well-defined, making the system more manageable and scalable.

2. **Command Pattern**: The Command Pattern is valuable for encapsulating commands as objects. Robots receive various commands, such as moving to a specific location, picking up an object, or performing a particular action. By encapsulating these commands, the system can manage and execute them flexibly, decoupling the sender (e.g., control system) from the receiver (e.g., the robot).

3. **Strategy Pattern**: The Strategy Pattern handles different algorithms or strategies for robot behavior. For example, robots may use various algorithms for navigating obstacles, picking up objects, or planning trajectories. The Strategy Pattern enables easy switching between algorithms without altering the robot's core functionality.

4. **Observer Pattern**: The Observer Pattern facilitates communication between various components and sensors. Robots often rely on sensors (e.g., cameras, proximity sensors) to observe their environment. The Observer Pattern allows other components to be notified of changes in sensor data, enabling appropriate responses and actions.

5. **Decorator Pattern**: The Decorator Pattern extends the functionality of robotic components dynamically. Robots may need different tools or sensors for specific tasks. The Decorator Pattern enables adding these functionalities at runtime without affecting the robot's core behavior.

6. **Factory Method Pattern**: The Factory Method Pattern is used to create different types of robots or automation modules while adhering to a common interface. This pattern decouples the creation of robot instances from their usage, simplifying the introduction of new robot types.

7. **Composite Pattern**: In systems requiring the coordination of multiple robots or robot modules as a single entity, the Composite Pattern allows individual robots and robot groups to be treated uniformly, simplifying management and coordination.

8. **Template Method Pattern**: The Template Method Pattern defines the overall structure of robot behavior, allowing subclasses (specific robot types) to implement specific actions or algorithms. This pattern promotes code reuse and standardization across different robot implementations.

Case Study 14: Natural Language Processing and Text Processing

Description: Natural Language Processing (NLP) is a field of artificial intelligence focused on enabling computers to understand, interpret, and process human language in a meaningful and useful way. NLP encompasses tasks such as text processing, language translation, sentiment analysis, speech recognition, and information retrieval. The goal is to bridge the gap between human language and machine understanding, allowing computers to interact with humans more naturally and intuitively.

Text processing, a subset of NLP, involves the manipulation, analysis, and transformation of textual data. This includes operations such as tokenization, stemming, lemmatization, part-of-speech tagging, named entity recognition, text classification, sentiment analysis, and text generation. Text processing is fundamental to many NLP applications, as it helps extract meaningful information from unstructured text data.

Design Patterns Used

Design Patterns Used in NLP and Text Processing:

1. **Pipeline Pattern**: The Pipeline Pattern is commonly used in NLP workflows. It involves chaining together multiple processing steps in a sequence to transform raw text into a structured, processed format. Each step performs a specific NLP task (e.g., tokenization, POS tagging, sentiment analysis), with the output of one step becoming the input for the next.

2. **Decorator Pattern**: The Decorator Pattern adds additional functionalities to text processing components without modifying their core behavior. For example, in sentiment analysis, decorators can include sentiment intensifiers or negation handling, enhancing the analysis's accuracy and context.

3. **Factory Method Pattern**: The Factory Method Pattern is used to create different NLP models or text processing algorithms while adhering to a common interface. This pattern decouples the creation of NLP components from their usage, making it easier to switch between different implementations.

4. **Observer Pattern**: The Observer Pattern handles real-time updates and notifications. For instance, in a chatbot application, the Observer Pattern can notify the bot of user inputs, triggering appropriate responses.

5. **Interpreter Pattern**: The Interpreter Pattern is used to design domain-specific languages or grammars. In NLP, this pattern is valuable for creating custom rule-based language processing systems or query languages for information retrieval.

6. **Adapter Pattern**: The Adapter Pattern integrates different NLP libraries or APIs that might have incompatible interfaces. Adapters enable seamless interaction with multiple NLP tools.

7. **Singleton Pattern**: The Singleton Pattern ensures that only one instance of resource-intensive components exists in the system, avoiding redundant processing and resource wastage.

8. **Strategy Pattern**: The Strategy Pattern is useful for handling multiple algorithms or models for specific NLP tasks (e.g., sentiment analysis). The pattern allows dynamic switching between strategies based on the context or requirements.

Case Study 15: User Interface Design

Description: User Interface Design (UI Design) involves crafting interfaces that enable users to interact seamlessly with digital products or systems. It focuses on the visual layout, user interactions, and overall user experience. The primary objective of UI design is to create an interface that is intuitive, user-friendly, and aesthetically pleasing, ensuring that users can efficiently achieve their tasks and goals.

Design Patterns Used

Various Design Patterns Used in User Interface Design:

1. **Model-View-Controller (MVC)**: The MVC pattern is an architectural framework that separates an application into three components: Model, View, and Controller. In UI design, MVC helps divide the user interface into distinct layers. The Model represents the data and business logic, the View handles the visual presentation, and the Controller manages user interactions, updating both the Model and View accordingly.

2. **Observer Pattern**: The Observer Pattern establishes a one-to-many relationship between objects. In UI design, this pattern allows UI elements to subscribe to changes in underlying data or state. When the data changes, the UI elements are automatically notified and updated, ensuring that the interface remains synchronized with the application's data.

3. **Decorator Pattern**: The Decorator Pattern enables dynamic addition of new features or behaviors to objects. In UI design, this pattern is useful for enhancing UI elements without modifying their original class. For example, decorators can add borders, shadows, or animations to buttons or other visual components.

4. **Adapter Pattern**: The Adapter Pattern allows incompatible interfaces to work together. In UI design, this pattern is often used to integrate external components or libraries with different interfaces into an application. The adapter acts as a bridge, ensuring seamless integration.

5. **Singleton Pattern**: The Singleton Pattern ensures that a class has only one instance, providing a global access point to that instance. In UI design, this pattern is useful when only one instance of a particular UI component, such as a global configuration manager or theme manager, should exist.

6. **Factory Method Pattern**: The Factory Method Pattern provides an interface for creating objects, allowing subclasses to decide which class to instantiate. In UI design, this pattern is employed to create various UI components (e.g., buttons, text fields, dropdowns) while adhering to a common interface, facilitating flexible component creation and customization.

7. **State Pattern**: The State Pattern enables an object to alter its behavior when its internal state changes. In UI design, this pattern is used to manage different states of UI elements based on user interactions or system events. For example, a button may exhibit different behaviors depending on whether it is enabled, disabled, or in a loading state.

8. **Command Pattern**: The Command Pattern encapsulates a request as an object, allowing clients to be parametrized with different requests. In UI design, this pattern is useful for handling user actions as commands, enabling features like undo/redo functionality or queuing user interactions.

Case Study 16: Internet Security and Cryptography

Description: Internet security and cryptography are critical components of modern computing, ensuring the confidentiality, integrity, and authenticity of data transmitted and stored over the internet. Internet security encompasses a broad range of measures and protocols aimed at protecting information and systems from unauthorized access, data breaches, and cyberattacks. Cryptography, a fundamental aspect of internet security, involves using mathematical algorithms and techniques to encode data, making it unintelligible to unauthorized parties.

Design Patterns Used

Several design patterns are integral to the implementation of internet security and cryptography:

1. **Singleton Pattern**: The Singleton Pattern is used to create a single, globally accessible instance of cryptographic services or security configurations. For example, a singleton encryption manager or cryptographic key store can ensure consistent and secure access to encryption and decryption services across the application.

2. **Factory Method Pattern**: The Factory Method Pattern is applied to create cryptographic objects, such as encryption algorithms or hash functions, while abstracting specific implementations from the client code. This pattern promotes code flexibility and simplifies switching between different cryptographic algorithms.

3. **Chain of Responsibility Pattern**: The Chain of Responsibility Pattern is employed to create a chain of cryptographic handlers, each responsible for a specific security task, such as signature verification, encryption, or decryption. Incoming data passes through this chain to undergo various security checks and transformations before processing.

4. **Decorator Pattern**: The Decorator Pattern adds additional layers of security to data or network communications. For instance, encryption can

be wrapped with a decorator to incorporate authentication and data integrity verification alongside confidentiality.

5. **Observer Pattern**: The Observer Pattern is utilized for implementing logging and auditing mechanisms in security-related components. Observers monitor security events, logging them for auditing and forensic purposes.

6. **Proxy Pattern**: The Proxy Pattern creates proxy objects that act as intermediaries between clients and actual cryptographic or security services. Proxies provide additional security measures, such as access control, logging, and rate limiting.

7. **Template Method Pattern**: The Template Method Pattern defines a common structure for security protocols or cryptographic operations while allowing specific steps to be implemented by subclasses. This pattern ensures consistency in implementing security procedures across the application.

8. **Adapter Pattern**: The Adapter Pattern converts between different cryptographic interfaces or formats, facilitating the seamless integration of existing cryptographic libraries or algorithms into the application.

9. **Command Pattern**: The Command Pattern encapsulates cryptographic operations as commands, enabling better management of security tasks, such as queuing and undo/redo functionalities.

Index

9 789334 024876